The Lone Brit on 13

THE LONE BRIT ON 13

A Prisoner's Hell in Spain's Toughest Jail

Christopher Chance

MAINSTREAM
PUBLISHING

EDINBURGH AND LONDON

First published in Great Britain in 2005 by
MAINSTREAM PUBLISHING COMPANY (EDINBURGH) LTD
7 Albany Street
Edinburgh EH1 3UG

ISBN 1 84018 957 6

A catalogue record for this book is available
from the British Library

Typeset in Futura and Galliard

Printed and bound in Great Britain by William Clowes Ltd, Beccles, Suffolk

This book contains language and attitudes that some readers may find offensive or upsetting.

ACKNOWLEDGEMENTS

I wrote this book partly in my cell but mostly in the bedlam of the *sala* on *modulo* 13. The process of writing provided me with an imaginary carpet that whisked me away from the underclass, junkies and corrupt, conniving prison officers that surrounded me as I wrote. I could not have finished this work without the drive and support of my brave wife Susan, who shared the anguish and suffering of that daunting period in our life together. So heartfelt thanks go to her with all my love.

I am also deeply indebted to Bill Campbell and his team for editing and accepting my work for publication. So a giant thank you to all at Mainstream.

A donation from the proceeds of this book will go to the charity Prisoners Abroad.

CONTENTS

ONE

The transsexual lifted his shirt and showed us a perfect set of tits. As good as any I've seen on a woman. The Moroccans cackled with laughter, which was feigned, because there was nothing funny about these tits. They were genuine boobs. A screw looked over at the sudden outburst so the shirt dropped quickly down again. Vanessa, who is a 32-year-old heroin-addicted poof, trying hard to be a woman, cackled through a mouthful of green frosted tombstones. The very last place one would put one's cock. But Vanessa is a champion cocksucker. Should all the cocks that Vanessa sucked be placed end to end there would be sufficient to make a handrail around Gibraltar.

The cry '*Metadona*' rang out across the patio so all the junkies ran to form a queue outside the screws' office for their daily ration of methadone, the heroin substitute. The pushing and pulling died down as Don Juan, the poison dwarf, called for silence. Don Juan is the cruel, sadistic little screw who was boss of the wing on this day. He scrutinised each prisoner as they knocked back the tiny beaker full of liquid methadone, then he made them talk to ensure it had been swallowed.

There is a brisk trade in the lavatories with puked-up methadone. The lowest of the low lurk in these stinking shitholes. They buy with sex or cigarettes the methadone that has been swallowed. The normal means of delivery is by the thrusting of a grimy finger down the throat of the seller to induce vomiting so the methadone and phlegm can be ejected into a plastic cup, then frantically swallowed by the creature who offered his arse for it. When Don Juan isn't on duty, the methadone is simply spat out of the mouth into a plastic cup in the lavatories, which are a hundred metres' walk away from the screws' office. So by the time the methadone is spat into the cup, there's a lot of saliva mixed with it. Ugh! These creatures always have runny noses and rattling chests, so God knows what's being passed around in these plastic cups.

Violence is a daily occurrence here and the enforced surrender of heroin substitute is commonplace. Vanessa, the transsexual, had taken his dose of methadone and sat next to me to prevent intimidation from the pack of degenerates who were now unsettled because of their cravings. They were like hyenas suddenly excited by the stink of blood. Two greasy gypsies were edging nearer to Vanessa to bully him to the stinking shithouse to regurgitate his methadone. The gypsies had arrived here the day before from another wing so they didn't yet know the score on *modulo* 13. They thought the transsexual, Vanessa, and the lone Englishman were an item, so we were easy meat. They couldn't have been more wrong.

The tall gypsy cruelly grabbed one of Vanessa's tits and yanked him to his feet; the other gypsy grabbed an arm. Vanessa looked at me with a mixture of fear and hope in his big blue eyes. I moved in quickly for the kill, thrusting my right hand up the inside leg of the tall one's shorts, taking a handful of dick and bollocks whilst simultaneously grabbing his Adam's apple and windpipe with my left hand. I gave him his first Glasgow kiss, with my forehead impacting with a tremendous crunch into the bridge of his nose. I was choking him with my left hand whilst crushing his testicles and savagely yanking his genitalia by the roots with my right hand. I shredded his left eyebrow with another head-butt, then tore into his left nipple with my teeth. I released the grip on throat and bollocks, then, taking his right hand in both of mine, I gave him *kotegaeshi*, a bone-crunching, two-handed wrist throw which landed him violently on the back

12

of his head, rendering him unconscious. His pal was wildly punching Vanessa when I simply punched into his carotid artery so hard he fell as though poleaxed.

I sat on my chair watching Vanessa stomp the faces of his attackers, squealing with delight as the screws arrived to restrain him. He explained the assault on his person and was escorted to the office to write his statement. The two scumsuckers were removed to the *enfermería* for treatment, then rehoused on another wing. I went to the showers to wash my hands and clean my mouth.

* * *

A typical day in Malaga prison, back in May 2001 when I was first banged up here. I'm on *modulo* 13, the toughest wing in the prison, specially reserved for troublemakers. Most of the Brits are on *modulo* 5, and there are a few on *modulo* 9. But I am the lone Brit on 13. I prefer to be alone because the few Brits who were here were petty thieves and junkies, so I can do without that sort of company. One of them was that creature who smashed a bottle into an air hostess's face. That pathetic prick put a huge crucifix around his neck and called himself 'Stevie Jesus'. I couldn't answer him when he spoke to me. Apart from to say, 'Fuck off, arsehole.' His case was famous in England and on the Costa del Sol, but he only did two of a four-year sentence. Probably something to do with his Jesus act. Thank Christ he's gone. He left in November 2001. He was on my wing for only one week. It's now Christmas 2001 and I am alone again so I spend my time reminiscing. My thoughts take me through the cobwebs of time, back to my boyhood.

As a boy, I was a bit of a handful and I learned to defend myself early in life. As a youngster, I used to play rugby – not good rugby, just schoolboy rugby. There was no soccer when I was a boy. That was for Nancy-boys. During summers, I played cricket and when I wasn't playing cricket I was generally a nuisance and pain in the arse. School years are fading memories of harsh discipline, split lips and walking everywhere. Winters were cold and summers hot. I remember wintry evenings spent carol singing and freezing my arse off for pennies, then running to the Penguin Café to buy steaming hot OXO in a big mug to thaw out. Thawing out was difficult in the Penguin. It was that cold the condensation was on the outside! I wonder why they called it the Penguin?

In the summers, we used to walk for miles in the then lovely countryside to swim naked in various isolated ponds with newts and sticklebacks and the occasional nesting coot or waterfowl. We would take their eggs home and fry them. Mmm, lovely!

Young life was a haze – either a heat haze or a chill haze. Nevertheless, a haze and quite meaningless. Everybody was working class. There was the occasional rebel neighbour who dared to put a Tory candidate poster in his front window. But whilst he was at work driving his bus or whatever, his missus would be constantly wiping the spit and snot from her window.

I remember my mother finding our next-door neighbour lying dead with his head resting in a full piss pot. The chamber pot was the usual ornate type, with a blue willow pattern design around it, full to the brim with stinking piss.

The new neighbours who moved in were very different. The man of the house was an army sergeant and his wife was from India. Being the first foreign or coloured lady I ever saw, she looked very exotic to my young eyes. She was always swathed in silk scarves and had some kind of red splotch on her forehead. She was always aloof and serene until her husband came home at the weekend and used her as his punch-bag. He seemed to be a nice man. He used to give us kids a few pence and then in he would go and give the old punch-bag the good news.

They stayed there for a few years, providing various weekend entertainment. They were replaced by a posh lady who was very glamorous. I was coming up to 16 years old by then and Tennessee Ernie Ford was singing 'Sixteen Tons' and Frankie Laine was belting out 'Cool Water'.

It was about this time I noticed one of my schoolteachers – a married man – furtively entering my new neighbour's house. I will never forget the expression on his face as he clocked me. Don't worry, Sir, I won't disclose your name in this book. But everybody in our street knew all about you and, of course, so did everybody at Fisher-More Secondary Modern.

Another little incident springs to mind. My brother John and I nicked a big truck tyre for our gang's bonfire. The night watchman, a right nasty bastard, must have been tipped off because he came banging on our front door. My grandma answered the door and the man was growling about me being a little bastard so she rendered him unconscious with the milk bottle that was sat on the doorstep and shut the door. She was great, my gran.

Anyway, life rolled by and rock'n'roll happened and I thought I was grown up. I lost my cherry to a lovely girl and I fathered my first daughter at the ripe old age of 16. Unfortunately, my brains were in my cock. Maybe they still are, who knows?

My life rolled aimlessly along through the '50s and '60s until I joined the army in 1964. By this time in my life, I was well into the martial arts with boxing and judo training, which until I joined the army was quite erratic because I was a steel-erector and travelled the country with my work.

I had met a new girl and married her by the time I enlisted in the army. I was still adjusting to married life when off I went to Germany, where eventually our first daughter was born. Then followed a tour of duty in the Far East from where I returned to Germany where our second daughter was born.

It was in Singapore during 1965 that I joined a small karate class in the YMCA building. Karate was in its infancy then in Europe and nobody knew how popular it would become. The Singapore Karate Club was a painful experience but a most beneficial insight into self-protection, which I truly value. My mentor was a Chinese bloke called Han Lee (no relation to Bruce), who liked to be called Noel. Noel Lee taught a style which he called '*T'ang shou*', which means Chinese hands. I consider myself very fortunate and honoured to have met this man. I assume he has gone to a better place now because he was much older than me.

I enjoyed 12 years in the army and I left as a senior non-commissioned officer with an Exemplary Discharge Report. I went into the pub and restaurant business in which I held a

Justices Licence for 18 years. During the 18 years of business, I trained with a professor of the martial arts who is possibly the highest-graded martial artist in the United Kingdom.

The pressures of the restaurant trade and my dedication to the martial arts took its toll on my marriage. When the marriage broke down, I moved to Spain to set up a martial-arts business on the Costa del Sol. Shortly after my move to Spain, I was joined by a fellow black belt, Susan, whom I married in Gibraltar shortly after my divorce came through.

We worked hard, Susan and I, trying to make a living teaching karate and ju-jitsu. We found ourselves working from dawn till dusk and life was truly a struggle. I rented premises, which we transformed into a *dojo* and we also rented an apartment from a new friend who ran a gymnasium and aerobics business nearby. I'll call this 'friend' Steve, although we later came to refer to him as Shithead. Steve eventually offered us a *finca* (farmhouse), complete with swimming pool, in a little town called Coín. We became indebted to him because we were really struggling to pay our way as the lousy bastard who rented us the *dojo* was demanding more and more rent. We did not know at the time that he was Steve's partner and we were being set up like lambs for the slaughter.

Susan and I were worn out with work. We worked all day till ten o'clock in the evening, seven days a week, then we'd go home to sleep and start all over again, day in, day out. All we had to show for the hard work were pennies.

Eventually, we found out through various means that Steve was a dope smuggler, and because I was 55 years old and had never broken the law in my life, I was perfect to become a mule (courier) for Steve. I was offered the farmhouse rent free, along with enough money to pay off all my considerable debts and have loadsadough left over. All this for doing the occasional mule job taking a few kilos of happy herb to Steve's regular customers in Liverpool – all mature, consenting adults who'd been smoking quality hashish for years, no youngsters involved.

In desperation, I volunteered my services. I realised later how Steve and his partner had conned me into the smuggling game but by then I was as guilty as they were and I was enjoying the adrenalin. I had become a fully-fledged hashish smuggler, and a chain of events had been set in motion which would rob me of my freedom and Susan of her husband. All the powers in the universe cannot unspill this milk, so my stupidity and guilt will remain on my conscience for ever.

TWO

The first Spanish prison I ever had the misfortune of inhabiting was Madrid's notorious Carabanchel. I was detained there awaiting trial from May 1998 until it was closed down that October and I had to be moved. The mere mention of this name still evokes fear in Spanish minds, as it scarred the lives of so many people. I have heard there are plans to bulldoze it to the ground and to build a massive shopping precinct over the site in an effort to seal in the remains of the dead and missing persons who mysteriously disappeared when the dark hand of Franco controlled things around here. Carabanchel was a hellhole well after Franco's death, too. Spain's latest authorities no doubt wish to obliterate the memory of an atrocious establishment which looms large on the nation's conscience in their attempt to become European, or at least in their attempt to make the rest of Europe *think* they have a conscience; you will never convince me. I was blissfully ignorant of all of this, though, as the police van brought me there from the holding pens of a downtown police station.

I had been arrested several days beforehand. It all started with a telephone call from a Spanish friend of mine (I no longer have Spanish friends) who had major problems with a Spanish drugs gang. He pleaded with me to help him because his family were threatened by this gang. His name is Paco and he had an estate agency business in the town square of Los Boliches near Fuengirola on the Costa del Sol. Paco had a part to play with these gangsters but he couldn't make his end of the deal because his transport pals got cold feet. So now there were guns to his head threatening to do him and his family if he did not deliver. So in desperation he called me because he knew I had a minibus which was capable of transporting 500 kilos of puff to Burgos, north of Madrid, where it would be transferred to a lorry en route for Amsterdam.

Like a fool, I listened to Paco's tale of woe, as did the secret police, who were eavesdropping the conversation because Paco was bugged. Unbeknown to all concerned, the police had been piping him for two years (this information was revealed at the trial). In the mean time, I made arrangements to meet him to discuss the problem.

'*Hola*, Chancer,' a distraught Paco greeted me at Mustang Sally's bar on the *paseo* (seafront) at Los Boliches. The noisy jukebox sheltered our conversation as he told me about the threat to his wife and kids. He slurped his whisky and glanced furtively from side to side to make sure nobody was in earshot, then told me that two members of the gang were from Galicia in the north of Spain where they were faces with a reputation for killing.

The crazy thing was that he had to move the shit tomorrow, because that was when the lorry passed through Burgos and if the puff was not at the rendezvous, the lorry would travel on to Amsterdam minus 500 kilos of cannabis nine-bars (the name given to quarter kilos of low-grade hashish normally sent to the UK). Should that happen, *adios* Paco and family.

We discussed the loading and transfer arrangements and everything seemed to be uncomplicated, so because I am a soft touch I agreed to prevent the execution of the family Paco, thereby making the most cataclysmic moment-of-weakness decision of my life.

The following morning, I met Paco at his house in Los Boliches. I had prepared my Volkswagen Caravelle for a long journey and I was champing at the bit because I wanted to get there and back quickly because I was sailing from Fuengirola to Tenerife in two days' time.

My instructions were to drive to a BP gas station in Torremolinos to pick up Angel, the spick who lives with the puff at his *finca* near Cártama. I pulled into the gas station and a scruffy tramp shuffled in front of me with his dirty hands waving me down to stop. He poked his finger into his chest and mouthed 'Angel' (pronounced 'Ankhel'). I studied him, momentarily wishing I had a mobile sheep dipper. I imagined the cockroaches at his farmhouse to be as big as Volkswagens. He clambered into the passenger seat and pointed ahead with a finger resembling a charred barbecued sausage, which promptly disappeared up his right nostril. He pulled out of his head something looking like a snail minus its shell. He buried this into his crotch then sent the snail-catching sausage up his other nostril. I made a mental note never to accept food or drink at this spick's farmhouse.

The *finca* was well off the beaten track and I had to drive carefully along a rutted pathway to get there. I drove into the farmyard where two men with pistols appeared with Paco, who was tremendously relieved to see me. They put their pistols on a nearby wall and started loading the bales of hashish into the minibus. I carefully arranged the bales under and between the seats and hid them from view with travel rugs and towels. The load was evenly distributed across the minibus floor and hidden from prying eyes.

Paco explained that the three of them would be ten minutes ahead of me to warn me of police roadblocks, so now we had to add each other's numbers to our mobile phones to save time dialling should an emergency arise.

I ran through with him again the transfer details to ensure it was the same hotel car park where I would pick up a guide by the name of Momo, an Algerian who would take me to the warehouse in Burgos where I would meet the lorry. There was no change of plan so I set off on the long drive to Burgos realising that I was the patsy should things go to ratshit.

I didn't clock anybody on my tail but I did get the wind up when I thought I saw the same van pass me twice. I couldn't be sure of this but there was something about it that registered in my brain. I was now alert and on my guard so I wasn't going to enjoy this ride across Spain's sunbaked boring landscape.

I needed a comfort break because I was bursting for a piss so I pulled into a gas station at La Carolina on the N1V, the main *carretera* from Jaén to Madrid. I relieved myself, then tanked up. I also had a drink and a sandwich from my cooler box. I set off again feeling much better and tried to enjoy the ride but I couldn't get my mind off that van.

I jumped out of my skin when my mobile phone rang. It was Paco telling me to pull off the *carretera* at exit 13 near Madrid where there is a gas station and restaurant where we could tank up and have something to eat. I agreed but I could smell a rat. Why stop at exit 13 unless there was a change of plan? Paco knew I had food and drink on board, so apart from filling my tank when I needed to, there was no reason for me to stop. So I called him back telling him the stop he just spoke about was not necessary. He then told me that exit 13 was the meeting place for other members involved in the deal so please could I pull into exit 13 where everything would be explained.

There was possibly another hour or more to drive to exit 13 so the Old Bill had plenty of time to set their trap. Paco had been gobbing off to other members without using any kind of code or disguised manner of speaking. This fact was revealed to us when we received copies of the telephone transcripts before the trial. Paco had actually used my name in plain language during discussions with others. The spick twats whom he spoke to couldn't be bothered either to make some kind of effort at security. They just had a lazy cavalier attitude to everything; so lazy, they shat in the bed and kicked it to the bottom. The police knew everything they wanted to know.

I was nearing exit 13 so I was preparing to enter the filter lane when a car came alongside me and stayed level with me for the few hundred metres it took to enter the filter lane. I know now that it was a covert police car positioned there in case I didn't turn into the filter lane where 11 police cars awaited me.

Paco and his gang were already in the bag so I had no warning. As I cleared the *carretera* and was entering the area of the gas station, the ambush was sprung. Three cars came at me from the front against the flow of traffic, two more came diagonally from my left and two more cars came up behind me riding abreast of each other in the filter lane, blocking any following traffic. All of the cars were unmarked and there wasn't a uniform to be seen.

Men in civilian clothes came running at me pointing pistols to my head. A wild-eyed, long-haired lout was screaming at me and nervously shaking his pistol at me when I slammed the minibus door into him as I exited the minibus to dash amongst the spectator cars. I cleared the bonnet of one car, then ran up the bonnet and onto the roof of the car behind. My momentum took me over the hedge at the side of the road but I winded myself when I landed badly on the other side. I got up and ran towards a hotel on the other side of a service road where I could see cars parked to the rear, which meant I had to get through the hotel to reach them. I burst through a side door of the hotel to find myself in a reception area with a choice of four doors in a deserted hall of marble tiles and mirrors. I tried each of the four doors but they were all locked. I turned to exit the place when five men entered with handguns pointed at my head.

'*Tranquilo*,' I said as I raised my hands above my head. The muzzles of two 9 mm Brownings pressed against my temples as I was viciously spun around and my face was slammed into the tiled wall. My left hand was pulled down behind my back and a handcuff was quickly fitted to my wrist, then my right arm received the same treatment. When the handcuffs were in place, they were fastened so tight they were crushing the radial and ulnas bones together. My face suddenly slammed into the tiled wall again but this time my nose broke. I could see the tip of my nose under my left eye. My kidneys received the good news with several blows from hard objects, not fists. I could hear the working parts of handguns rattling, so I guess that's what they used. The starbursts of pain told me I would have problems pissing for a while. My legs were then pulled from under me so I landed on my face breaking several teeth. My legs were prised apart, then my testicles exploded in my head. It was as though my head was filled with Catherine wheels and Roman candles, all exploding together. I was being pistol-whipped about the head but I felt detached from it now because everything seemed to be going numb; it all seemed to be happening in the distance.

I could no longer see because the blood from the head wounds poured into my eyes and I couldn't wipe them. I don't know how long I lay there but when they lifted me from the floor, I could not see because the blood had congealed on my eyelashes, binding them shut. My body seemed to be thudding with a rhythmical beat of pain, especially between my legs where my testicles were suffering the throes of compression by toecaps.

I felt momentarily embarrassed as I noticed a warm runny sensation in my underpants. I thought I'd shat myself but thank God I hadn't; it was only blood oozing out of my arse where the toecaps had ruptured the exit hole.

The valiant spick coppers were booed by a crowd of spectators, but who gives a fuck? They do whatever they want with impunity: this is Spain, a member of the EU. I was violently pushed into a covert car, which brought another peal of derisory heckling. I used the moment to wipe my eyes across the back of the seat in front. At last, I could see vaguely and was no longer totally blind. The car raced away at great speed to their HQ somewhere in Madrid.

There were no uniformed policemen in this secure area. It resembled a military camp with chain-link fences everywhere. I was shoved into a corridor with several offices on either side of it. Further down the corridor, I could see Paco and his gang sitting on the floor with their backs against the wall, all wearing handcuffs. A short-legged man came towards me and in good English asked if I was well. I replied, 'Loosen my handcuffs, please, wipe my eyes for me and take me to hospital.' I raised my right leg so the blood could drop from my shoe onto his nice clean floor. 'But first, I would like to see the British consul so I can show him the good work of your brave men.' I glared at him with my one opened eye. 'Medals and commendations all round for this one, Guv'nor, especially for the five brave cunts who worked me over *after* they got the handcuffs on.'

'You shouldn't have put up a fight with them, we know all about you. You have a martial-arts business in Fuengirola so my men responded aggressively because you became aggressive towards them, especially in the hotel.'

'Can you get one of your brave lads to loosen the handcuffs, please, I promise not to be violent.'

'Do not take the piss, Mr Chance, or I will put you in leg irons.'

'You didn't throw all the *Generalísimo*'s shite out then when he pegged out.' He turned his head and shouted up the corridor for somebody to bring a key. Another shortarse came out of a room further up the corridor and scurried towards us jangling a bunch of keys on a silver chain attached to his belt. He quickly moved behind me to undo the manacles and started tut-tutting when he saw how swollen my hands had become. The heat in my hands rose rapidly when he undid the handcuffs. I was trying to rub my hands and wrists when he grabbed them again to put the cuffs back on with my hands to the front. '*Espera*,' I said as I tried to wipe my eyes. Shortarse got all nasty and excited so I put both my hands together to make things easy for me and for him. The English-speaking dwarf said, 'We'll clean you up in a minute, Mr Chance, in readiness for the television cameras waiting for you down at the hospital. Somebody leaked out to the press that this is the biggest drugs haul the Madrid police have encountered. Rest assured, your family in England will see you on television tonight. Mr Whitcombe, your precious British consul, will be informed the moment we put you in the Carabanchel, our finest hotel. However, he will probably see you on television tonight.'

I was escorted to the lavatories where there was a shower and wash-hand basin. The cuffs were removed to enable me to wash. I cleaned the blood from my eyes and was shocked to see how unrecognisable I was. I stood with my hands in the bloody water and started to breathe deeply through my mouth as I concentrated on my blocked broken nose. I quickly grabbed my nose with both hands, and using my forefingers and thumbs I crunched it back into line. I knew I only had one chance at getting this right because I realised I wouldn't have the nerve to inflict this pain on myself a second time. Blood spurted out of my nostrils as the cartilage squeaked and grated back into some semblance of order in the middle of my face. The area around my eyes immediately started to swell as my eyes took on the appearance of two giant puffed-wheat kernels. My eyes were now practically shut tight because of the swelling. One of my brave escorts dashed into a nearby bog to puke his innards out. I couldn't resist the urge to laugh mockingly.

I turned to the white-faced dwarf with my hands held out so he could cuff me. He shook his head and shouted for the head dwarf to come here. He came scurrying in shouting angrily at his minions, then turned to me shouting, 'Get in the shower, Mr Chance, or I will be forced to use a fire hose on you.'

'Get on with it then because I'm not cleaning your dirty work for the cameras.'

'You need to clean yourself up, then you must give me a statement regarding your Volkswagen full of hashish.'

'There will be no fucking statements from me until I have had my head stitched and my bollocks treated. My kidneys and my arse need to be checked out and I need a dentist.'

The handcuffs were put back on and I was shoved back out into the corridor where Paco and his gang were sat at the far end feeling all sorry for themselves. 'Have you given a statement, Chancer?' shouted Paco.

'No, have I fuck!' I said.

'OK, nobody gives a statement until we see the magistrates tomorrow.'

'OK, that's fine by me. I'm going to hospital soon so I don't know if I'll see you until tomorrow anyway.'

Paco peered at me, focusing on my face from 30 metres away. His expression turned to shock as he made out my injuries. Nudging his neighbour with his elbow they all looked at me incredulously and immediately started shouting and got to their feet stamping and remonstrating about my injuries. The heavy gang came along to quieten them. As I was being led away, I heard a dwarf say that I was only a *giri* (an offensive word meaning foreigner).

I was shoved into an unmarked police car and driven at high speed with escort vehicles using sirens to clear the way to hospital. Television crews and spectators were crowding the entrance to the hospital. The uniformed national police seemed to be in charge at the hospital and there was some doubt or problem as to who was responsible for me whilst in the confines of the hospital. A senior officer caught my elbow and ushered me through the main entrance of the hospital, steering me into a small office. He looked at me, shocked at my injuries, and asked one of the secret police who was responsible for my appalling condition. I was delighted as this incident grew rapidly into a full-blown row.

The uniformed officer gently parted my blood-matted hair. '*Pistola*,' he announced as all the uniformed men gave withering looks to the secret police. The senior policeman asked if I would like coffee and brandy to which I replied, '*Si, muchas gracias.*' A uniform left the room to get my coffee.

Aggressive chatter between secret and national police ensued and I detected the words '*Karate*' and '*artes marciales*'. The senior uniformed officer looked at me with a concerned look. '*Cinturón negro?*' he asked.

'*Si*,' I said. 'Yes, I am a black belt.'

'*Yo también,*' he said proudly, letting me know that he too was a black belt. Thank God for the brotherhood of the martial arts. He asked me my grade so I told him I was a fourth-dan ju-jitsu but I also had dan grades in other martial-art styles such as Aikido and *Buguei Espanol* ju-jitsu, the latter being a Spanish branch of the Japanese *Buguei*, in which I had graded *shodan* (first degree) a few years ago.

Things changed rapidly. My handcuffs were instantly removed, the protesting secret police disregarded. I was given a chair but I couldn't sit on it because of my torn arsehole. The uniforms understood when they saw the sopping bloodstains on the hardwood seat as I gingerly got off it.

The medical team came to see me and I was asked to strip '*por favor*'. I stripped naked as every jaw hung open. My back and legs were yellow and purple, interlaced with weals and livid bruises. My testicles were monstrous and fresh blood flowed from my arse. Suddenly, my nose started to bleed again as I sucked and pulled with my tongue at one of the loose teeth. The tooth clicked out of my gum so I spat it at the feet of the secret policeman standing nearest to me. That moment will remain precious for the rest of my days, as every eye looked first at the tooth, then at me, then at the secret police. Rivalry is always evident between police departments; the look on the uniforms' faces was pure hatred.

The medical team took me to a treatment room and started their work. The police stayed with me so I had quite an audience. I had numbing injections around my arse so I didn't feel too uncomfortable down there while they sorted out the problem. I don't know what they did to my bollocks but I hope I never experience that freezing sensation ever again.

They were finished apart from my head so I waited for a 'head' person to see me. In came Irma Grese, the commandant of the female section of Belsen. This large woman was the dead spit of that infamous murderess. She had in her hands a stainless-steel tray with a big curved stitching implement and a green surgical wrap to place over my head with a hole in it to facilitate the stitching.

She produced a pair of scissors and a razor. 'I will first shave your head,' she said in fair English.

'No, you won't.'

'Your hair will get caught up in the stitches.'

'No haircut.'

'Very well. Your fault if there's an infection later,' she said, throwing the scissors and razor into the nearby sink.

The room was silent as I sat on a pillow on a chair with the surgical wrap on my head. She made a big deal about adjusting it and pulling the first wound open. In my heart, I knew she had already decided to hurt me as I readied myself for the unforgettable experience about to take place. I started my deep breathing and concentrated on my skull. She dug her needle into the flesh so hard and deep she noisily scraped the bone, creating a sickening scratching sound. I couldn't see her evil face but I knew she was enjoying her attempt at getting me to cry out. Several times, she scraped my skull but I didn't make a sound.

Only the senior officer and one secret policeman were in the treatment room when she was stitching the final wound. The others didn't have the stomach to watch all of it. The senior officer asked her several times about the necessity of scratching my skull with the needle. I know I ruined her orgasm by remaining silent.

During my ordeal with Irma, I concentrated on my skull, but I had abstract thoughts about being an Englishman and showing them why an Englishman always wins wars. I also wondered how old was the Cyprus mule that shagged Irma.

I was told a dentist would see me in the Carabanchel prison and the prison doctors would examine my kidney problem. I was now nice and clean and feeling slightly better. All was well until I asked for a copy of the medical report. The secret police went apeshit; the senior officer wanted to give me a copy and keep one for himself. I didn't get a copy and ten months later at my trial there was no evidence of me being treated at that hospital. Surprise, surprise . . .

I was taken from the hospital to holding cells somewhere in Madrid. The place was packed with lunatics. The guards were 100 metres away down a long stinking corridor. Every time somebody needed the lavatory there were several minutes of shouting and screaming to get their attention.

The guard in charge was a tiny, ugly, noisy, aggressive piece of shit, typical of small, uneducated spick tosspots, whose world was at the end of this stinking corridor. The whole of his working life had been spent supervising the ablutions and screaming at the rats in what he perceived to be his own special domain. May you live forever in your own glorious shithole, you gormless twat.

The food was unbelievably bad, some kind of animal shit shovelled into a plastic bag served with a stale bread roll and washed down with tap water. Sleeping, eating and shitting were difficult in this rathole. Pissing wasn't so bad; there was an open drain just outside my cell so I could piss directly into it through the bars, so I didn't need to plead with the shortarsed cockroach who was in charge. It was painful to piss for several days but I still managed to hit the drain.

Half an hour after each mealtime, a bloke with a wheelbarrow came down the corridor to collect the waste food. The plastic food containers were tossed through the bars onto the wheelbarrow as it trundled by. The cell opposite mine housed a Chinese bloke and, like most wayward chinks, he could speak Ingrish.

'Hey Limey, glub shit aeeha,' were the first words he spoke to me, letting me know that the food was lousy.

'What you in here for, Chinky?' I asked.

'Heloin, smack. Chinee only deal with smack or lestaulant, so me smack dealer, you know: heloin. What you do, Limey?'

'Oh, hashish. Somebody stole my vehicle and put hashish in it. Police blame me.'

'Oh, fuck your ruck, Limey.' I wondered how he could say 'Limey' but couldn't say 'luck'. Fucking weird.

When the food came to the cells, I watched him eat some, then he shit into the plastic container. He called across to me, 'Shit in prastic, Limey, then chuck prastic into barrow. Much better not use shithouse.'

I was kept in this rathole overnight, then taken to a magistrates' court the next morning where I met the rest of the gang. There wasn't much time to speak to each other before we were bundled in front of the beak: another shortarse dressed in black flowing robes with a woven badge resembling that of the Order of the Garter stitched onto the right breast of the robe, but this one had gravy on it. He probably wore it across the street in the *tapas* bar. I thought about a miniature Winston Churchill sporting a Joe Stalin moustache. I didn't understand a fraction of what happened but he waved us all away with that sinister word, 'Carabanchel'.

We were handcuffed to each other, then bundled into a meatwagon for the journey across Madrid to the Carabanchel prison. I lapsed into silence during my journey to the evil place. The cigarette smoke inside the van was making me gag. The chattering spicks were a nuisance to me so I filled my mind with thoughts of my dearest wife Susan, who by now must have been out of her mind wondering where I was.

The consequences of my stupidity had been turning my brains to mush since my arrest, but now there was the absolute realisation of being locked up for God knew how long. This was my punishment for being so bloody cavalier about life. Now the punishment really began. The crushing, excruciating panic, hidden from the others in the police van, attacked my conscience as I imagined the feelings of loss and uncertainty swirling around my beloved Susan. Then came a vision of my mother and other family members; the enormity of the wider implications of my stupidity was dawning inside my mind: my brain was being bludgeoned by a guilt-driven steak hammer.

I closed my mind to external distractions and said my first Act of Contrition since I was a child. I wondered at how the words came tumbling out of the ether of my mind from a nebulous nothing into a coherent prayer. By the time I had finished, I was inside the Carabanchel. I was so engrossed in begging my God for forgiveness, I hadn't noticed the entrance to hell.

The rear doors of the meatwagon flew open and the screaming screws invaded my ears, marking the end of my prayers and the beginning of my retribution, because I told God I would treat my future as a penance until I was given peace of mind or mental respite. How could I repair the damage to my wife and family, though? God was easy. I put my heart and soul into my prayers, and I hoped and believed that He would truly know that. But how could I make amends to my nearest and dearest?

'*Fuera, fuera,*' screamed the screw as we tumbled from the van to stand facing a high concrete wall. For the hundredth time, we were patted down and frisked before the Guardia-Civil officers removed the handcuffs. The handcuffs belonged to them and they were leaving.

'*Todos desnudar.*' Everybody started to strip, so I painfully undressed, leaving my bloodstained clothes at my feet. Everybody stood to attention as several screws fingered the seams of our clothes. A piece of wood about 2 ft long and 6 in. wide with a mirror attached to it was shoved between Paco's feet. '*Abajo en cuclillas rapido,*' screamed the screw. Paco immediately squatted over the mirror so the screw could look up his arse. We each in turn had to do this, so when I squatted a puzzled group of expert ring-spotters were angling their heads and wondering which species of brown speckled ringneck was nesting up my arse. I told Paco to tell them I tried to get a hacksaw up there, but Paco's face remained pokered. The chief screw told Paco to tell me I would go to the *enfermería* later, after I had been processed in.

We were herded into a windowless room where everybody immediately lit up their fags. In less than a minute, the room was full of stinking tobacco smoke which reminded me of my Uncle Joe telling me about the Battle of the Somme and how clouds of gas came drifting over the trenches. When the gas cleared, off would come the gas mask and he'd light up a Woodbine to clear his throat. The poor bugger died with a Woodbine in his gob, blaming Jerry mustard gas for his bad chest.

The screaming screw extracted us one at a time for fingerprinting, photographing and issuing of an ablution kit consisting of toothbrush and paste, soap, shaving cream, razor, bog roll, plastic knife, fork and spoon, all in a plastic bag. I was also given a hand towel and a pair of pyjama bottoms. I was then escorted by a screw to a shower stall where I had a cold shower. The impatient bastard kept shouting, '*Rapido, rapido, giri.*' I towelled myself quickly and dressed whilst being hassled by the annoying screw.

I bundled my bits into the plastic bag and stepped out of the shower stall to be taken away by another screw. Tall and willowy, he reminded me of Popeye's missus, Olive Oyl. He led me along corridors and up and down stairs until we arrived at a raised control room, which looked enormous to me. I can best describe this as an atrium, possibly six floors high with a massive domed skylight. The control room was at the centre of the domed circle with several prison wings branching off from the perimeter of the circle. The thought occurred to me that this could have been a bullring before it was a prison.

The prison wings here are called *galerías*. As Olive Oyl passed the control room, a head popped out and shouted, '*Galería cinco*, Antonio.'

'*Si, venga,*' replied Olive, their voices echoing around the atrium.

I was going to wing number 5. Our footsteps echoed as we reached the iron gate which had 'No. 5' in metre-high letters painted in black above the heavy iron stanchions surrounding the massive barred gate. Another screw opened the gate from his side. Olive prodded me through with his big stick as I stepped into the charge of Ignasius el Horrible. Olive departed to whence he came without a word, his receding footsteps echoing, adding to my forlorn feelings.

Don Ignasius pointed the way with a 30 in.-long black truncheon. His boozy breath, rheumy eyes and heavy breathing told me he was pissed, or at least half-pissed.

'*Venga, giri,*' he slurred as he pointed his nightstick along the murky corridor. I could see flickers of light from a television shining on the walls further along the corridor. This was the screws' office, in darkness except for the television. I could see the silhouettes of four screws captivated by transvestites on screen, normal for peak viewing time in Spain. I was made to stand outside the office while my escort had a drink with his workmates. Ten minutes later, when the adverts interrupted the transvestites, he came out from the smoke-filled office to take me to a cell.

He opened a heavy iron gate and nodded me through into the *galería*. It looked enormous with three floors of cells. I looked up at the ceiling, which looked to be 100 ft high, and I could see that everybody was locked up, the galleries on each floor were empty of human life but the rats scampered freely. Safety netting was strung between the galleries on each floor, which, as I found out, was fortunate for the inmates who were often thrown over the handrails for thieving.

Ignasius escorted me to the top gallery, tapping his stick on the handrail. He stopped at cell no. 98, inserted a big key, then slammed back an iron bolt the size of his truncheon. The door swung open and I was nodded in. The cell was occupied by two Arabs, who immediately jumped from their beds and stood to attention as the screw entered behind me.

'*Otro giri,*' he snarled.

'*Si, señor, muy bien, señor.*'

I thought it was the Everly Brothers, the way they both sang it out in unison. The snarling screw backed out of the cell pointing his nightstick at us threateningly. The cell door clanged shut and the massive sliding bolt clattered home. We listened as the creep's footsteps diminished to silence, then the Arabs enthusiastically grabbed my hands to welcome me to *Hotel Chivato* (pronounced chibato, meaning grass or informer).

They introduced themselves as Hassan and Tribak, but beyond that I couldn't understand a word they were saying. They spoke in Arabic, French, Spanish and then German. Thanks to Lingo, the god of languages, I'd learnt German during my army years. '*Hurra, ich verstehe,*' I said. The three of us spoke kraut, so feeling much better I listened to their litany of complaints and their loathing of all things Spanish. Being North African, they were treated like shit in Spain, in my experience the most racist country on the planet. Their kraut lingo was really good so I wasn't surprised to hear they had kraut wives and homes in Düsseldorf.

The cell was quite small with a tiny barred window through

which I could see the neighbourhood rooftops just showing above the high prison walls. Further away, I could see the tenements, beyond which I could see the heartbreaking sight of aircraft flying around Barajas airport, Madrid's busy international airport, the Cocaine Gate.

The cell was clinically clean and smelled strongly of bleach and soap. To my new Algerian friends, I must have looked terrible because my clothes were bloodstained and dirty. Everything in this cell was spick and span except me. Only the fact that I was an Englishman prevented these two Arabs from turning their noses up; had I been a spick, they would not have tolerated my presence. They quickly made up the third bed in the cell with fresh clean sheets and a pillowcase. They gave me a pair of flip-flops to wear only in the cell. Their cell etiquette was quite good really, because they did not enter the cell with their shoes on. Their shoes were removed at the door and placed into a cardboard box under the wash-hand basin, their flip-flops were kept by the door. Though they bleached the floor every day, they did not like bare feet on it so I complied with their sensible rules. It is a habit I stayed with during my years in spick ratholes. Even now in Malaga prison I abide by those rules learned long ago from my Arab pals. I have never had a problem with my feet but I know a lot of blokes who have.

When I removed my shirt, the Arabs fell into momentary silence as they gazed at the kaleidoscope of colours revealed by my undressing. Hassan asked, '*Polizei?*'

'*Ja,*' I said, feeling slightly awkward because they seemed shocked at my condition and sheepish after their tirade against all things spick. They sat on the edge of the bed momentarily speechless as I removed my trousers.

'*Mensh! Es heisst, dass sich der Mensch durch die Sprache vom Tier unterscheidet,*' roughly meaning that the only thing that distinguishes humans from animals is language. '*Diese Scheisskerl,*' (bastards) murmured Tribak. Hassan gave me a clean T-shirt. '*Nur für schlafen,*' he said, telling me I could have one of his shirts to sleep in. Tribak gave me a lumberjack shirt to wear during the day. I was banged up with two decent fellows whose small acts of kindness will never be forgotten. Wherever you are today, I hope the both of you are free and happy. *Inshallah.*

We all settled down to sleep but thoughts of Susan kept me from my much needed oblivion. My heart was torn apart as I visualised her alone in our home on a Spanish hillside. The realisation that I had thrust an ordeal of loneliness upon my most precious wife, my best friend, my mate, was crushing. Nowadays, I owe her a greater debt than ever before, as this loving, industrious, artistic, truly sensitive woman has become my support, my backbone, the drive behind my survival in Spain's penal ratholes. But for her constant support, I could well have sought solace in drugs like nearly everybody I know. I have only ever met two men during my years in Spanish jails that did not use drugs: Captain Peter Smith (Royal Marines, ret'd) and Ali Safave, whom I will tell you about later.

I eventually managed a fitful sleep, but at least I slept. The day started with *recuento*, the body count. The dramatic clang of sliding bolts being slammed open accompanied by the abusive shouting of the screws had me out of bed long before a wrathful retard opened no. 98. As the door swung open, I was not really surprised to see that all the threatening abuse emanated from another greasy dwarf. He stood in the doorway glaring at me, then at my cellmates. The beds were made, everything was neat and tidy and we were all standing looking at him with his Adolf Hitler haircut, plastered down with olive oil, which wasn't greasy enough to prevent the cowlick on his crown. He resembled a pouting schoolboy with his chin on his chest, showing the white underneath his eyeballs as he angled his eyes into the top of his head to see us, just like a crazy 'Just William' without his school cap. A grunt and he was gone.

Crash, bang, followed by screams of abuse as he found my next-door neighbours still in bed. I later learned that my next-door neighbours were Spanish gypsies, lowlifes by any other name.

My Arab friends told me that I might as well stay with them until I found my way around this pisshole. They took me down to breakfast, which was served in the *comedor*, a great hall filled with long tables and benches with possibly ten men at each table.

Hassan pointed to a table with just one man eating his breakfast of coffee, bread, margarine and jam. This breakfast has stayed the exact same the whole time I've been in Spanish prisons. Hassan told me that that was the English table, so I should join my countryman to take bread with him. I picked up my metal *bandeja* (tray) containing my breakfast and made my way to the English table.

In each of the four Spanish prisons that I've been detained in, there has been an English table. In fact, I had my bread and jam breakfast at the English table on *modulo* 13 in Malaga prison this morning. It's my table because I'm the only Englishman here. I was the only Englishman on *galería cinco* too, because I breakfasted with an American, not an Englishman, as suggested by Hassan.

As I sat on the long bench across the table from the man, I could see he was nervous and wary of everybody around him. 'Good morning,' I said, at which he started looking behind him to see whom I was talking to. This was the moment that I knew he was a nutter. He pushed a piece of bread into his mouth and slurped his coffee, averting his eyes. He had receding hair which still carried the vestiges of an Afro cut. His full beard was kind of matching but sparse looking, hiding a weak chin. I continued, 'Do you speak English, because this is the English table so I assume you're English?'

'Yank, I'm an American. Don't worry, I'll find another table at lunch-time. I didn't know the tables were reserved.'

'Fuck the tables,' I said. 'I'm only pleased to meet somebody who speaks English. I only hope you are not a nonce because if you are you can fuck off now.'

'What the fuck's a nonce when it's at home?'

'A child molester, a fucking pervert, a fucking paedophile.'

'Oh man, this place is solid with them. Every fucking wetback I know fucks kids.'

'I thought wetbacks were Mexicans,' I said as I tasted my coffee – weak and milky.

'Mexicans, South Americans, wetbacks, spicks, Colombianos, Spaniards, they're all the fucking same, they carry the same sick gene. Chicken shaggers, sheep shaggers, incest is the norm with them. Look around you, look at the fucking screws. If they are not the results of incest then I'm the fucking man in the moon.'

'OK, Buzz. Why're you in here?'

'I assaulted one of the clerks in the American embassy because they wouldn't take me back to the States. I'm broke, no dough, out on a limb, sleeping in the fucking park and the shits wouldn't help me. So now they have to help me because I'm here in fucking prison. How come you're here?'

'I got caught with a busload of cannabis on my way through Madrid,' I said, taking another swig of the coffee and a bite of bread and jam.

'I bet you was working with spicks.'

'Why do you say that?'

'Because only people who work with spicks end up in here. They are so fucking stupid they tell everybody what's going down and even their folks will snitch 'em. You didn't know that, huh? They're all fucking snitchers. It's the most virile Hispanic gene driving the strongest Spanish organ: the tongue.' I laughed at his remark but he shot back at me, 'Do not ever trust a spick under any circumstances; never befriend nor share a secret with a spick, never do a deal with one of them, you will regret it.' He stuffed more bread into his mouth as he glanced suspiciously from side to side.

Although my initial thoughts about this man being a nutter turned out to be correct, it didn't take me long to arrive at the same opinion. In my experience, he was bang on the money.

He finished his breakfast and, rising from the table, said, 'See ya around the *pateo*. D'ya play chess?'

'Yes, but not today, thanks,' as I thought of all my problems clouding any chance of concentration until I settled into some kind of routine.

I was sitting at the table in a world of my own when my thoughts were interrupted by a screw. '*Finito, fuera,*' he said, pointing to the yard with his big stick. I was the last person to finish breakfast and the screw wanted to close up. I got up and took my *bandeja* to the waste bins where they were all stacked. The flies practically snatched it from me as I put it down. Mangy pigeons were scrabbling around the waste bins and as I left the table, flocks of them descended from the rafters to shit and spread germs all across the dining tables as they pecked at the crumbs and leftovers thereon.

I went out into the prison yard to take in the depressing sight of the high walls surrounding me. Everywhere was heard the loud snorting of spicks drawing back the contents of their nasal passages to hawk and spit great green gobs of headshite across the *pateo* floor. Then there was the ritual blocking of one nostril with the knuckle whilst blasting out the contents of the other, stooping to avoid one's shoes. This ritual happens every morning throughout Spain and, I suspect, the whole of Africa.

I strolled around the yard for an hour or so, knowing I was being piped by screws and prisoners alike. I made sure my head was high and I wasn't slouching. A spick came alongside me and was rabbiting away about *café*. I could see by the look on his face that he'd been sent and he had an audience. '*Un cafelito, giri, sólo para mi*,' he kept repeating. It dawned on me that he wanted me to buy him a coffee from the prisoners' coffee shop which had just opened. I later learned the shop was called the *economato*. I said, 'No,' because I didn't know enough Spanish then to discuss my lack of funds.

I am an expert on eyes and body language; I need to be, I am a martial-arts teacher. Suddenly, I had five spicks moving near to me, but marching towards me were Hassan and Tribak with several more Arabs. Hassan shouted a warning, which was unnecessary because I had noticed the eyes change. I knew I had a problem. The begging spick lunged at my guts with a *pinchou* (spike, shank, chiv for stabbing).

Thanks to my training, I was much too experienced for a runt like this. His attack from the side was hesitant so I easily grabbed the thrusting wrist with my right hand whilst putting all my weight (240 lbs) behind my left-handed *shotei*, a palm-heel strike just beneath his right ear, breaking the jaw hinge, sending him to dreamland from where he would awaken with a crowd around him. I trod on the hand holding the *pinchou* whilst knocking unconscious another spick who was trying to pick it up. The shrill noise of whistles and running screws was getting nearer. I did not want a problem with the screws so I didn't resist as they grabbed my arms. I was about to be frog-marched away when Hassan screamed at the screws, '*Mira!*' He was pointing at the long metal spike in the runt's hand. '*Ustedes mas ciego que un topo.*' (You're as blind as a mole.) Reluctantly, the screws let go of my arms. I had six Arab witnesses jabbering at the screws explaining my innocence.

The screws tried to revive my attackers but slaps around the chops do not undo my work. They were now getting quite concerned so I revived both of them with an ancient kung fu method I'd learned many years ago. Hassan and his pals took me to the *economato*. I was no longer alone and everybody on the wing, including the screws, knew I was no pushover.

Hassan bought me a coffee and introduced me to his fellow Algerians. They didn't speak kraut so their French and Arabic were translated for me by Hassan and Tribak. Everything was fine as we all jabbered to each other, but then a big fat bloke started arguing with Tribak, poking his finger first at him then at me. Hassan told me the problem was that he was the brother of the spick whom I'd laid out, so I needed to be careful because I'd get the *pinchou* treatment when I went to the lavatory. The fat bloke became really aggressive and I could tell he was threatening me by the way he clenched his fist and jerked his thumb towards the toilets.

The Arabs were fidgety and concerned so I did what I do best. I shot my hand into Fatso's throat, taking a handful of Adam's apple and windpipe whilst at the same time delivering a savage leg-sweep, driving him backwards and downwards and ramming him violently into the concrete floor where he knew he would die in a minute. I quickly pulled him into a sitting position and moved behind him, supporting him with my right knee as I put on a *hadake-jime* choke with my left forearm crushing his windpipe. I rammed my head into the side of his head to increase the pressure on his carotid arteries and jugular vein, thereby causing rapid asphyxiation. I eased my grip to spare his life but kept it strong enough to keep control as I told Hassan to tell him that I would kill him or any other spick who came near me.

I pulled him to his feet and shoved him towards the lavatories, kicking his fat arse as he stumbled forwards. That kick hurt me more than him because my poor arse was still in a bad way. Fuck me, this was my first day in the Carabanchel and I was up to my arse in aggro. I was to find that every Spanish prison I stayed in gave me aggro on the first day. The spicks do not like the English; they think we are soft fruit, ripe for the picking (take note, Prime Minister).

I've had rucks in every wing that I've been put in but I always come first in every knockabout I've had, and believe me when I tell you I've had so many punch-ups I don't remember half of them. Admittedly, they were never long, drawn-out battles, they lasted only a few moments, but that's all I need.

In the time I spent in the Carabanchel, I didn't see another Englishman, but I did meet the Chinese bloke again. Chinky got a 12-stretch for the heroin job so he was well pissed off. He told me about all the various jobs he'd pulled; all successful, but his last job involved a spick, so here he was rotting his chink guts away in here. Some years before, he got a 20-year sentence in Australia but from what he said I think he was absent from the trial. Anyway, he'd been told that when he finished here he was going to Oz to do his 20. I believe he topped himself the day after I left the Carabanchel.

I am not easily shocked but on my second day in *galería cinco* I saw a very attractive young lady with an hourglass figure, huge tits and legs up to her arse. She marched across the yard in her tiny miniskirt and high heels and skipped into the showers followed by a pack of drooling spicks.

Chinky nudged me, saying, '*Maricón*,' meaning 'queer'. He gestured me to follow so we went into the shower to witness a pack of spicks ogling and wanking as the transsexual showered. The tranny's tits were real enough but his dick ruined the image. I watched a crowd of spicks pulling themselves off on one of their countrymen having a shower. The Yank was right, they're all fucking perverts. Personally, I blame the Spanish authorities for this. They issue an all-male environment with a monthly supply of condoms and administer hormone injections so the transsexuals don't lose their tits. Some people may think I'm a prude, but God made Adam and Eve, not Adam and Adam, and until the day I die nobody will persuade me to push my manhood into a tube of human shit. I will be staying celibate for the duration of my life in prison.

Transsexuals and corned-beef inspectors abound in Spanish

prisons so AIDS is rife, as is tuberculosis and other contagious infections. Everybody has a tuberculin scratch test to check for TB. The ablutions in the Carabanchel were the most unhygienic in the world. Phlegm, snot, shit, piss, sperm and perverts were all over the fucking show, so no wonder I worried about my health.

The screws relied on their grasses to know what was going on in the ablution block. Mind you, Malaga prison is just as bad, apart from the screws wearing surgical gloves when they visit the bogs on *modulo* 13. Things haven't changed much between then and now. The differences between Malaga prison and the now shut-down Carabanchel are mainly architectural. Malaga prison is a more modern structure, so the bricks and mortar are knocked up in a more linear style to house the same filth: subhuman screws, transsexuals, perverts, killers and the general flotsam and jetsam of the Costa del Sol, not forgetting, of course, the innocent who shouldn't be in here anyway.

I have seen innocent men locked in here for more than a year, then released without so much as a 'kiss my arse'. There is no compensation for illegal detention or innocent remand in this EU member's judicial system. Their response to a compensation claim is, 'We'll deduct it from your next sentence.'

THREE

The two things which kept me strong whilst in the care of the shambolic shitpile that was the Carabanchel were the support of my loving wife, Susan, and my martial-arts training. Over the years, I have practised and adhered to martial-arts philosophy and discipline, though I admit to going off the rails a tad in recent years. In life, we bring everything upon ourselves. We are our own accountants when we gamble the currency of life. Unfortunately, I didn't take into account the pain our loved ones suffer. Some of us have done this twice, or even more times because we thought we were fireproof and it's a victimless prank, an adventure. After all, the cannabis plant is naturally occurring and put down by God, the Creator, on the Third Day. And God saw that it was good (Genesis 1:11–13). So the fruits of the Earth delivered to us by God are denied us by law; not God's law, but rules devised by egomaniacs who are voted into office on the back of lies, deceit and shallow promises, who smoke the shit anyway. That, of course, is not martial-arts philosophy, but freedom of thought is. So now I have found the mental strength to dominate my own wayward spirit so I will never again subject my nearest and dearest to the anguish of my incarceration, because they love me and I stupidly, inconsiderately disregarded their feelings. However, regarding philosophy, I find it necessary to have two sets: one for life in here and one for life in liberty – two completely different worlds.

When you enter a Spanish prison, you become a citizen of the netherworld. Your outlook on life changes the moment that big iron gate clangs shut. The strength of your moral fibre will be tested daily until you re-enter the normal world at the end of your sentence. The onus of whether or not you learn by your mistakes is entirely on you; nobody in the prison system can claim any credit should you learn by your mistakes and become an upright citizen when you get out. If you re-offend, it is simply down to your attitude of 'Blessed is he who isn't caught'.

My martial-arts training helps me enormously, especially now, in the netherworld of prison. My time here seems false, a constant feeling of the unreal, a limbo existence, a dream-like suspended animation from which I hope to wake in a minute, a bit like standing at the bus stop for a couple of years. Martial arts requires training of the mind as well as the body, the ability to focus the mind and not be distracted by the environment; not the 'polish the mirror of my soul' philosophy portrayed by popular martial-artist film stars like Steven Seagal and Jackie Chan, bless 'em. No, I'm talking about Bushido, the Way of the Warrior: the ability to meditate on the skills of combat, remaining focused during the chaos of an attack on your person by lunatics who will kill you if they can; the constant readiness to defend yourself with deliberate violence, intentionally breaking bones and inflicting hideous facial wounds to effect a deterrent to other sociopaths who can't wait to hurt you. They are all here in this mad underworld in Spain. I sometimes wonder if I have a bit-part in *Judge Dredd*.

Years ago, I developed the will and commitment to continue practice despite distractions and adversity, but here in this dark place courage and stoicism are a survival necessity. Around every group of spick thugs, there hangs a testosterone vapour floating on hot air. If the ringleader of the group feels the need to bully or intimidate you, you must have the resolve, skills and courage to seriously destroy the strutting bullfighter's ego with an unstoppable battering or you will suffer the whims of every spick bully for each day of your sentence, especially if you are the lone Brit on the wing.

Considering that I am also the oldest prisoner on the wing, I thank Odin, the god of war, for giving me the skills and fitness that make my age irrelevant. Whenever I defend myself against an assailant, I make such a good job of it that I am inundated with blokes who want me to teach them. I refuse to teach Spanish prisoners, though, because there's always a possibility that they might be nonces. I wouldn't touch them, apart from giving them the good news. I'm never violent unless I am personally threatened and that's happened so often I've lost count.

I have no particular objections to training ETA terrorists, because they don't consider themselves to be Spanish. I befriended several of them in 1998, when I was the martial-arts instructor in the main gymnasium at the Carabanchel, but the screws didn't like it. I could befriend paedophiles, rapists, child killers, smack dealers, or any other type of scumsucker you can think of, but not ETA members: the screws don't like ETA blokes. I found that ETA members were quite well educated. Every one that I met had a profession and could speak at least three languages fluently, English being one of them. One day in the Carabanchel, I was teaching a group of ETA blokes techniques to defeat batons and knives. During the lesson, a large number of screws entered the gym and surrounded my class. The *jefe* (boss) called me off the *tatami* (judo mats) and escorted me to his office. I was told that if I taught anybody who was a member of ETA, I would be sacked and put in solitary. I returned to an empty gym.

To dissipate the stress of constant alertness, I daily adopt the *seiza* meditation posture in the privacy of my Malaga cell and allow myself the luxury of revisiting places of my past, hence the ability to recount episodes for this journal. I also focus on combat techniques, mentally rehearsing innumerable methods of blocking, striking, throwing, locking and choking, and mentally maintaining the arsenal of barehanded self-protection weapons buried in my psyche.

The self-imposed quest for many martial artists is to lead a meaningful life whilst trying to achieve a level of enlightenment. Many martial artists assume that there is a certain path to tread, which is not a religious path but a sort of political correctness path with shades of 'Grasshopper', the ethics involved in many kung fu films, especially the series starring David Carradine called *Kung Fu* on Western television during the Bruce Lee era. I won't go into the psychophysics of Shintoism and Buddhism here, or any other seemingly-ism which often gets stapled to the martial arts. The esoteric aspect will always exist simply because of jealousies between the various styles and also, of course, because of secret societies. The 'Brotherhood' is not only the domain of Holy Orders and Freemasonry; the rolling up of a trouser leg or a skullcap shave will not get you into a secret *Tong* or *Kwoon* or *Ronin* sect or even secret government and Presidential departments that laughably 'do not exist'. There are more 'Brotherhoods' than you can shake a stick at.

The 'knowledge' of the Way is bound by ethics and etiquette. However, when you are thrust into the daunting, appalling shitholes of Spain, the 'knowledge' is your lifeline and fuck ethics. During my meditations in my cell, especially here in Malaga prison, I have sought enlightenment with my own God. I have attempted to explore the relationship between mind and body, or soul and matter. Inevitably, transcendentalism enters the fray because without it your one-man debate will remain at the argumentative level. For me, the realisation that my soul, my spirit or my mind, which is not matter but essence, a non-specific, non-existing substance which enables me to think, is actually part and parcel of me just like my heart or bollocks. So I no longer pray for my everlasting soul whilst training its temporary home in an effort to keep it for as long as I can. I merely try to do what's right in life so that perfection of spirit hopefully happens before I peg out. Now, I simply go along my Way trying not to trespass on others. But until I join you in the free world, my Way is pure Bushido.

One of the artistic skills practised by Eastern martial artists, especially the Japanese, is flower arranging. Monstrous sumo wrestlers daintily setting blooms into a Hobart curve: a bit like Mike Tyson doing a bit of crocheting. I was pondering this when my Malaga cell door crashed open and a screw yelled, '*Fuera, abogado.*' In other words, get out, your lawyer's here.

This visit had been pre-arranged to coincide with a lawyer visiting a London face who wanted to see me. I put down my pen, put on my trainers and made my way down the stairs to the screws' office two floors below to await my escort to the *comunicación* block where visits were supervised. My escort arrived, a female screw, another skirted shortarse with stumpy little legs. She had the strangest hairdo, all piled up on top of her head in an effort to gain height, a bit like Homer Simpson's missus. Stick a banana in it and she'd be a dead ringer for Carmen Miranda. She had a list clipped to her millboard. 'Creestoffur,' she sang as she ticked my name, which was the only one on the A4 sheet, her little legs going twenty to my dozen along the corridors to the visitors' block.

The visitors' gallery is a row of glass-partitioned cubicles, possibly 200 metres long. The last six at the far end of the gallery are reserved for lawyers. Waiting to see their lawyer were five English blokes. I soon spotted the one I was meeting: Kerry Mayne, who used to be one of Kenny Noye's lieutenants working the Costa del Sol.

One of the lesser known faces, a gingernut called Darren, said to me, 'We need to get you in with us, Chancer, you'd soon sort out these fucking hayrabs on our wing. A right load of wankers, they are.'

Kerry Mayne gave him daggers. 'Shut up, Darren. Chancer is the banker on 13 and he runs the fucking show on that wing. He doesn't want to join us on *modulo* 9 just to clear the fucking Arabs off your arse. You bring it all on your fucking self anyway, you dopey cunt.' He tut-tutted as he held out his hand.

I said, 'How are you doing, mate?' as we shook hands, his 'Craft' handshake pressing between my second and third knuckle telling me he's a Master Mason.

I remembered Kenny Noye's 'Craft' handshake when I left him in Valdemoro prison just prior to his extradition to Blighty for the killing of Steven Cameron. It's a small world: here I am shaking hands with a man who worked for a man who is also locked up; we are all in fucking prison.

Kerry Mayne and I had deliberately coordinated our meetings with our lawyers so we could 'bump into' each other to discuss business. Inmates on different *modulos* often do this when they want to meet face to face; they send messages to each other to organise timings with their lawyers, then telephone their lawyers to arrange a legal visit at those times.

'I'll be out on bail shortly,' said Kerry.

'Yeah, me too. But I can't believe these lying bastards,' I said, nodding my head in the direction of the grabbing bastards disguised as lawyers.

'Yeah, I know what you mean, the bastards have taken a fortune off my lot and they've done fuck all. He reckons he needs more to sort the judge out,' said Kerry, pointing at his lawyer. 'Anyway, I'm gonna fuck off when I get bail. I don't need this fucking shithole of a country; I can go direct to a frog port and work from there. As soon as you get out, Chancer, call me on that number I gave you and the job's a good 'un.'

'Yeah, OK, mate, I'll do that. Listen, I don't want to come to *modulo* 9 so don't try to engineer a move for me.'

'Oh no, I won't do that, Chancer. Your influence is greater than mine around here. You're a fucking legend on 13. See ya soon. God bless, me old son.'

Carmen Miranda took me back to the wing where I was taken to my cell and locked up for the night. I had already decided I would never again see Kerry Mayne or any other maverick Freemason. I made my Act of Contrition with the Guv'nor and I meant it.

I get into my bed and wonder about Kenny Noye and the Kray twins being involved in Freemasonry. I come to the conclusion that Kenny Noye, like the Krays, will never leave prison alive because they fucked with the Establishment: the Krays with Lord Boothby and his cronies, and Mr Noye with policemen who proposed and seconded him into their West London Lodge.

I'm going to sleep now, pen, I've got a hard day in the gym tomorrow. My eyes start to close in sleep as my spirit embraces the laws of the universe telling me that all its powers cannot unspill the milk. My thoughts and experiences are woven and spliced into a thick rope, knotted at the end to beat myself with if I contemplate repeat performances of my past. If I start thinking, 'What if I do one more job?' the rope automatically uncoils in readiness to strike me. I need to be aware of the dangers of picking certain threads. However, my thoughts take me through these prison walls to happier times, to the sweet scent and sounds of my loving Susan who does not deserve the terrible unhappiness that I have thrust upon her. Her loyalty and strength of character I will cherish forever. Please, great Lord of the universe, keep her safe because when I finish this penance I will walk a straight road through the remainder of our life. Now I must escape into sleep.

FOUR

The dramatic wail of the block siren is the wake-up call for *modulo* 13, but for me it is merely an irritant as the decibels pierce my meditation and warn me of the impending *recuento*, the first body count of the day. So I perform my final breathing exercise before rolling up my exercise mat and tidying the cell.

I've been up since six o'clock so I've done one and a half hours of abdominal training, *chi gung* and *tai sabaki* routines in readiness for my hard training later in the gym. My *tai sabaki* and *kata* routines are practised in the confines of my cell, which is not big enough but I make do, because if I train in the yard somebody might take the piss and that spells trouble for the piss-taker.

I can hear the screw as he nears my cell, crashing open my neighbours' doors, so I do my shitting routine for when he opens my door. Some of these pedantic wankers expect you to stand to attention beside the bed facing the door, so that when he pulls the door open he finds you standing there like an obedient Boy Scout: so I have a shit.

They can't object to you having a shit, so I always make a raspberry noise with my lips during that moment of silence when he's opened the door wondering where I am. It never fails to give me a good start to the day. Fuck 'em.

Eventually, I made my way down to the *comedor* where I got my bread and jam with a cup of coffee. I headed for the English table as I said my 'good morning's to various international faces and sat alone to breakfast. The ETA table is opposite mine so Karlos 'Jackal' said his, 'Good morning, Mr Chance,' in an affected patrician piss-take.

I like Karlos. He's killed a few Guardia-Civil officers in his time and he keeps himself hard with military-style training routines. He watches me do my routines in the gym and it's nice to see him copy some of my exercises. He's a hard hitter and takes no shit from the spicks. The screws try to give him a hard time because he is graded FIES, which means *Fichero Interno Especial Seguimiento*, which is a category applied to dangerous buggers like Karlos. FIES is on every ETA prisoner, no matter which prison he's in.

Karlos does not talk to spicks so he usually talks to me or one of the clogs (Dutchmen). We've had some interesting conversations, Karlos and I. He told me about his training days in Algeria and Libya and how he spent a lot of time with the ALF (Algerian Liberation Front). His explosives training was done in the Algerian Police Academy. This is interesting because members of the IRA trained with him, both in Algeria and in Libya. The problem with Karlos is that he talks too much – he can talk a glass eye to sleep – but I like him.

He was talking to me across the aisle when this black bloke sat opposite me at my table.

'What do you want?' I said.

'I'm eating my bread, man.'

'Where're you from?'

'Nigeria, man.'

'Well, fuck off down there to the African table, this is the English table.'

'I don't know if I want to do that, man.'

'Have you just come in off the street?'

'No, I jus' come from *modulo* 5, man.'

'Did you sit at the English table on *modulo* 5?'

'No, they didn't let me, man.'

'What makes you want to sit at the English table?'

'Because I speaks English an' I don't like all dem niggers, man.'

'I don't like 'em either, so fuck off.'

A tear formed along the rim of his lower eyelash and his big bottom lip started to quiver.

'Finish your breakfast but don't come on this table again, sit with your own kind.'

A big black knuckle smeared the tear across his shiny cheek as his other big hand shoved half a loaf into his gob. 'Thanks, man. I'll find anudder table later.'

I chastised my inner self for being so unchristian with this man, but later, when I discovered he'd raped and killed a six-year-old boy, I wished I had cut his big shiny head off. There is always something wrong with a man when he doesn't join his countrymen in prison. The milk of human kindness does not flow across the tables of *modulo* 13, simply because nearly everybody in here has done something really bad.

I finished my scran and went for a stroll around the yard for an hour until the gym opened. One of the clogs, a big square-shouldered bloke by the name of Jan von Klapp, sidled next to me, adjusting his stride to mine. The clog was implicated in what was known here as the 'bin-bag murders'. Body parts were being found around Malaga and Jan got roped in because his apartment was used to kill one of the victims who happened to be a face from London. The victim was trussed above Jan's bath so his blood could be drained away to make him less heavy and messy.

Jan is an excitable man, prone to saying whatever comes into his head before considering the consequences: that is why I know so much about the case. Unfortunately for him, his co-defendants know how dangerous his mouth is. Any letters he receives from his co-ds come to me to be read out to him because though he speaks English he can't read it. His co-ds were trying to get him to join them in their *modulo* so they could put a lid on him. He became nervous and frightened because he thought the lid might be a wooden one.

Jan has a Spanish girlfriend who's a brass; she now runs the business from one of Jan's houses. She is also pregnant. The Spanish police used their usual cruel tactic of arresting innocent wives and girlfriends in an effort to extract more information or even a confession. In Jan's case, they arrested his heavily pregnant wife and two working girls, so the pressure was on and the boys in the neighbouring *modulo* knew it.

Jan suspects that I will be getting out of prison soon so he gave me details of a yacht he owns, which is moored in Essaouira on the west coast of Morocco. He told me this yacht would be put at my disposal for smuggling, just so long as he got a percentage of the profits I'd make. I went along with Jan just to perk him up and give him some peace of mind. We collared Mohamed El Ouassini, a good pal of mine, to contact his brother-in-law who is big in Marina Smir, one of the nicest ports on the North African coast. Mo's brother-in-law contacted the harbour-master in Essaouira, telling him to log the information that Mr Chance would be coming to take charge of *Lucky Lucy*, the ketch-rigged Jongert, whose papers were held in the safe in the harbour-master's office. Fine, says the harbour-master, but could somebody please pay the fucking mooring fees. All this was duly arranged and everybody settled down to dreaming about adventures at sea, especially Jan. He pestered me every day with plans for jobs running hashish out of Larache, then out of Safi and then everywhere as his head spilled over with a million tonnes of happy herb.

The gym opens at 10 a.m. so I left the clog to get my sports bag from Vanessa. In the main *sala*, which is the recreation room, I have my own table and chair at which I read and write when I am not training or strolling around the yard. The *sala* has a television set, which is permanently on full volume. There are rows of plastic chairs lined in front of it, all occupied by spicks. The cartoon channel is on all day and these gangsters are glued to the screen.

The *sala* is where most skirmishes and heated arguments happen, so the noise is similar to that of the monkey house at the zoo, drubbing into my head day in, day out. My table is in a position which enables me to see the screws' office, the entrance to the ablutions and the *economato*, while keeping my back to the wall.

Because I don't tolerate noisy spicks near me and everybody is aware that I like peace and quiet around my table, Vanessa and his boyfriend Jose put their table next to mine. In return for my bit of protection, they guard my kit and buy me treats like biscuits, cakes and coffee: just a little respect, if you know what I mean. Paradoxically, many bully victims try to sit near me for much the same reason. The bullies try to befriend me in an effort to neutralise my leanings. Fuck all of them, I just want to go home.

Placed in the middle of my table, I have a large placard with the word 'NO' written in thick black marker-pen ink. Keeping this sign on constant display saves me having to say the word a thousand times, especially to the spicks. They have a problem understanding every aspect of the word 'No' when they're asking for something. One time I was writing, engrossed in my work, when along came a spick who asked for my pen so he could keep the score of his domino game. I politely told him to fuck off time and again until eventually I become so irritated I booted the fucking domino table across the *sala*. Now I display my 'NO' placard for all to see.

Vanessa handed me my sports bag with my rolled-up exercise mat and a plastic bottle filled with cold water. Nobody will use my table and chair whilst I'm away from them; Vanessa doesn't get abused any more and when I return there will be a treat waiting for me. Symbiotic tolerance on my part, respect on theirs. You've got to earn it with your fists because violence is the single multi-lingual voice that is understood in the netherworld.

I dashed across to the gym because I wanted the bench-press this morning. I was doing chest and shoulders today with Geti and Daniel, two hard hitters from Romania. They beat me to it, but that's OK, we all know the score. They had garnered enough weights for what we were doing so we got on with our training.

We pumped iron till our chests and shoulders could take no more. I then went to a quiet corner in the gym to unroll my exercise mat and begin my abdominal and *chi gung* routine. I always begin with leg raises and other lower abdominal exercises before moving on to sit-ups and crunches for the upper abdomen, then I use a *chi gung* routine to warm down and end my session with a short form of *tai chi chuan*. I often use a form of *tai chi* that I learnt in Thailand, a much more flowing and slightly faster-moving form which involves more stretching. By finishing with *chi gung* and *tai chi* I am quite mentally relaxed so I am ready and eager to pick up my pen to release the happenings of the day into my journal. But first I have lunch.

The food-preparation areas and serveries here in Malaga prison are as unhygienic as they come. They are contaminated with cockroaches and are never cleaned properly. The men serving the food are not screened for tuberculosis or any other communicable disease. Men who serve food are smoking as they serve, coughing and sneezing all over it. I have seen blokes block one nostril and noisily discharge the contents of the other nostril, merely turning their heads so their snot doesn't hit their neighbours, who were busy ladling soup. European Community, my arse. These people will never reach European standards as long as their arses face downwards.

Salads are generally swimming in a mixture of engine oil and vinegar. I think the engine oil is supposed to be olive oil, but the colours of the rainbow can be seen shimmering around the black edges of the lettuce. It's a race between you and the maggots to see who eats the most.

Because Malaga is a fishing port, we get lots of fish, especially the fish the local population doesn't want. The sell-by date on the stuff we get is practically in Roman numerals. The chips that sometimes come with the fish are always cold and soggy and absolutely nothing is cooked properly. I have found cigarette ends and cockroach legs in my food but I don't shout about it because everybody else might want some.

One day, I had a whole pig's ear served onto my *bandeja* (metal tray). It was cooked but still had a big knob of wax in it and the lazy bastards hadn't even cut the hair. I didn't eat it; I used it to frighten the Arabs. Meat is always iffy in Spanish prisons; eating beef is like an endurance exercise for your jaw, a bit like eating Arnold Schwarzenegger's hamstring. Sausages and hamburgers are like compressed cotton waste, stuffed with duckshit and hair, with the texture of a carpetburger. My dogs would have a problem eating this shite.

Dinner is much the same as lunch apart from getting cold cuts of Spam and other compressed Spanish delicacies. The only meal that is sometimes enjoyable is served once a week. It is called *estofado*, similar to scouse or beef casserole. Sometimes, the meat is edible but often it stinks of putrefaction. I have promised myself never to put anything Spanish in my mouth ever again when I get out of here, and I'm going to piss in every Spanish reservoir. A British chip butty quite surpasses anything that has been produced in this shithole.

Fights often break out in the food queues, as with all other queues here, because spicks and North Africans don't follow the simple rules. They constantly try to barge in at the front: especially the Arabs, who simply don't understand the concept. Moroccans will stroll to the front of the queue and be bewildered by the abuse. If there is ever a queue on death row, a Moroccan will try to be first. (All Arabs hate Americans, pigs and queuing in that order. I was in my cell on 11 September 2001 when news came about the tragedy of the Twin Towers. All the Algerians and Moroccans were delighted, dancing and singing praises to Allah, showing their loathing of all things American.)

As I'd discovered early on in the Carabanchel, the queue is also the place where the bully lurks. He appears suddenly by your side urgently telling you to buy him cigarettes and coffee, his menacing sneer borrowed from *The Good, the Bad and the Ugly*. I was always the target for the new bully on the block. Being the only Englishman, I was bound to be a soft touch, or so they thought.

Anyway, lunch passed relatively without incident today so I duly dispatched my disgusting dish and got back to my writing and reminiscences.

Smuggling is the most exciting job I have ever done. The enemy of course is the Customs officer who competes with traffic wardens for the coveted title of 'Most Popular Person in the World'. Fancy having that job: a pariah in society, akin to being born with leprosy or syphilis. But I suppose somebody has to do it.

In January 1968 when I was a soldier, I came back to Blighty from Malaysia with my then wife and baby daughter. My mother and my in-laws had hired a minibus and come all the way down from Widnes to Heathrow to welcome us home and see their first grandchild. But before their very eyes we were stopped by a uniformed woman who was a dead ringer for Joyce Grenfell of 'jolly hockeysticks' fame. She emptied the flask of hot milk we had brought all the way from Kuala Lumpur because she thought there was contraband therein, and this was witnessed by many people waiting for passengers disembarking our flight. The stupid cow should have opened my kitbag; she would have found six thousand fags and six bottles of Scotch. But she won the popularity vote that day at Heathrow by emptying away my baby's hot milk. In the Customs officers' mess that night, they probably presented her with a thumbscrew or maybe a bear-trap. Wherever you are, Jolly Hockeysticks, just know that I visualise your stupid face whenever I cross a frontier. And I have crossed many frontiers.

I didn't become a professional smuggler until 1995 when I was conned into it by Steve, who knew I needed the money. I was busy trying to run my martial-arts business then in Fuengirola on the Costa del Sol. I thought me and Steve respected each other because we were alike in business and roots. He was from Liverpool and I come from Widnes, just 12 miles from the city.

At first, my smuggling exploits were really kamikaze because I went through various airports with five kilos of hashish wrapped around my body. Then I moved up in the world and started to use cars. But let me explain job number one first. I call it 'backpacking with a difference'.

I know a man who works with an oil- and heat-resistant rubber called neoprene. He made me a neoprene boob tube with shoulder straps. But this boob tube was 4 ft long. I put it on so it looked like one of those 1950s rock'n'roll pencil skirts, stretching from my armpits to my knees. Then the bars of hashish were wrapped and taped all down my back to my waist. Twenty bars were taped into place, then the bottom of the boob tube was lifted up to cover the bars ensuring everything was effectively folded in and nothing could fall out. I wore tracksuit bottoms with an elasticated waist and a black silk shirt with a black bomber jacket also made of silk. I wore all black because black makes you look slimmer than any other colour and I am not a slim man, even without five kilos of puff on my back.

So, all prepared, Steve and I set off for Malaga airport and my first massive adrenalin rush. I booked in at the flight desk and went through to the baggage X-ray and the Guardia-Civil metal-detecting frame. My heart was trying to imitate a Triumph Bonneville! I walked through, collected my sports bag off the X-ray roller and waved goodbye to Steve who was grinning like a Cheshire cat. First hurdle over. I walked through the concourse and sat with the crowd waiting to board the aircraft. I was sitting there cool as a cucumber when I clocked two big fat slobs in Guardia-Civil green coming straight at me.

Their pistols looked tiny hooked onto their big fat arses. They marched right up to me and spoke to the man sitting next to me, who apparently was one of theirs in mufti. I can't really describe the feeling. Many years ago, I jumped from an aircraft with a parachute on my back. I remember that feeling as being akin to committing suicide. I remember the scream I made as I jumped from the aircraft. I was now performing the loudest silent scream I had ever made. Shockwaves ran through my head and my heart was in overdrive.

After a couple of minutes, they waddled away, but I was sitting next to a camouflaged copper. Paranoia boosts the adrenalin. I was trying to control my arse because it was puttering away like a tiny two-stroke engine in my underpants. I sat there studying the toecaps of my trainers, trying to mould my face into what the Pope might look like, when suddenly there was a rush to board the aircraft. I waited to join the end of the queue because I didn't want anybody squeezing past me or touching my back.

At last, I boarded the aircraft and it took me to Manchester where the butterflies started again. Actually, the butterflies didn't stop all the way from Malaga, they just went into a frenzy when I disembarked the aircraft. I strolled through nice and easy. I couldn't believe my luck as I stepped into a taxi and said, 'Take me to Liverpool, please.'

That was my first mule job and I will tell you more about heart-stopping moments later. But now I must explain that the preparation of the puff is most important because it stinks and if you want to get past Customs, you must be dog-proof. Also, you must beware of any metal that could be in any of the quarter kilo bars of hashish. A nail or a drawing pin will set off the alarm in the metal-detector frame at the airport. So the consignment must be tested before it is vacuum wrapped. Easy: buy one of those metal-detectors those creeps use on the beaches looking for lost items.

When the bars have been checked and vacuum wrapped, they are then wrapped in strong parcel tape and dropped into a bucket of bleach to take away their smell. When the consignment is bleached, take the bucket out of the room to where you are going to dress yourself. Great care is taken to prevent cross-contamination because of the stink. Change coveralls and surgical gloves before entering other rooms where the consignment is being prepared. The bleached packages are laid out to dry and a second layer of tape is wrapped around each one. We make sure our rolls of tape and gloves etc. are in their various places before the puff is brought in for treatment. Cross-contamination will bring the dog on you for sure. I have strolled past many sniffer dogs with five kilos of what could potentially be stinking hashish on my back.

Remember 'P-six': Preparation and Planning Prevents Piss-Poor Performance. People say there's no such thing as luck. Wrong! There is, and it's all bad. It shows up when P-six hasn't been applied properly. Or when some low-down scumbucket turns grass. You will learn about grasses as the tale unfolds. There are professional grasses who report to HM Customs & Excise and to NCIS, the National Criminal Intelligence Service. I know: they tried to recruit me!

FIVE

That thought takes me back to Belfast in 1971 when I was on detachment to 3 Para: No. 3 Parachute Regiment. I was assigned to them to get some street experience before my parent unit came over from Germany. No. 3 Para were in the thick of it in Ballymurphy. I was billeted in Vere-Foster School with their 'Snatch Squad'. I wondered if they got that name because they snatched people or because they were always sniffing around fanny. A bit of both, I think. But they deserved every pleasure they got, because I lived with them and life was a blur of snatched action, snatched shite food and snatched sleep. I was an experienced soldier at the time, being a corporal and having served in Germany, Thailand and Malaysia, but nothing had prepared me for the Snatch Squad.

Pete was the squad sergeant. Two hundred pounds of romping, stomping paratrooper with keen survival instincts and mind-numbing aggression. The local Provos had already put a price on his head and their wives had priced his cock! I reckon he was the Belfast Knee-trembling Champion. The grey juice stains around his zip flies were evidence enough. He was hung like a stallion. I stole a glance in the shower one day. I thought he was having a breech birth because I thought I saw a baby's leg dangling from his crotch.

He made certain he passed on his street experience to me because he knew I was only with him for a month at most. Shortly, I was to go down to Armagh to help set up the accommodation and communications for my parent squadron and then I would be on the streets. But Pete and his band of snatchers gave me more meaningful adrenalin rushes than any white-knuckle ride could. We were always rushing everywhere: mobile patrols, foot patrols, call-outs, you name it, but whatever it was, it was done at Ducati speed.

Call-outs were sometimes initiated by the work of touts, which is Irish terminology for an informer or grass. The word 'grass' came about because grasshopper was cockney rhyming slang for copper. So grass was the word to describe a police informer.

All this activity was good preparation on top of what extra training I had already done down at Hythe and Lydd, in the beautiful English county of Kent. Plus months of fire and movement tactics during infantry training in urban guerrilla warfare in Germany. All good stuff to toughen myself and to help absorb the future shocks in life.

Believe me, I've had some shocks but looking down the barrel of a gun thrust into your face when the bloke holding it is shaking like a dog shitting pine cones takes your breath away. It is even worse when another shitting dog is pointing his pistol in your wife's face. But all in good time: I'm still in Belfast with shitting dogs. I'll tell you later about the pistol in my wife's face.

One miserable pissing-down night, we were on foot patrol in the 'Murph' (Ballymurphy). We were moving from front garden to front garden. Tactical movement like this in a street anywhere in the world is difficult. In Belfast, it is virtually impossible to patrol undetected. But the Snatch Squad defied the odds. Infiltration methods were various but this night the Provos provided us with a diversion. Somebody opened fire on the front gate so the blokes in the sangar returned fire. During this exchange, we nipped out on foot and started our patrol supposedly undetected. There were no streetlights to illuminate the area and we were all blacked up.

About half an hour into the patrol, I was crouched a couple of metres behind Pete when this shitting dog poked a pistol through the bottom of the hedgerow adjacent to Pete's head. As fast as a cobra striking its prey, Pete grabbed and turned the handgun into its owner's face and a broken finger pulled the trigger. The bullet entered the face at the philtrum nerve just above the upper lip. It tore through the palate then went up through the top of the head, evacuating brain tissue through a four-inch diameter hole. Killed by his own dum-dum bullet.

Reluctantly, I had to leave 3 Para and move to a National Trust site called Gosford Castle, just a few miles north of Armagh. I said my goodbyes to the Snatch Squad and I nipped in to thank their OC (Officer Commanding). I thought I would tell him he could make a fortune selling adventure holidays in the Murph, but as I entered his ramshackle office he looked up from his desk and said, 'Good luck, now fuck off and make your presence felt elsewhere.' Men of few words leave a lasting impression on me, so off I fucked, wondering what he meant, because I didn't think my presence was felt anywhere, least of all in the Murph.

Two scalys had come for me in a Land-Rover. They had been sent from Gosford Castle where they were installing comms (communications). Scalys, or scaly-backed bastards, is the term of endearment reserved for members of Her Majesty's Royal Corps of Signals. I believe this phrase takes its origins from the Bible. I think it comes from Genesis: God said that the lowest form of life on this earth shall crawl along on its belly and have scales upon its back. Hence 'Scaly'! The Royal Corps of Signals may possibly agree with this just to retain the kudos of being mentioned in dispatches in God's Gazette. The two scalys were lounging at the rear of the Land-Rover waiting for me.

Because I had become accustomed to doing everything at Ducati speed, these blokes seemed to move like snails. Sluggish is not quite the correct word to use but these two made the Spanish look hyperactive. I stowed my gear in the back and the driver slowly got behind the wheel. I told the other scaly to watch where he put his feet as he put his foot on the tow-hook and cocked his other leg over the tailboard, stepping on my kit. We stopped at the weapon-loading bay where we checked our weapons and loaded a full magazine to each one, checking safety catches. I was the commander so I personally checked each weapon was safe.

We got back into the vehicle and slowly moved to the exit gate where everybody was very alert. Although it was daylight, we still had to move fast because this was the Murph. The Paras on duty manning the exit knew that I was leaving so there was a loud laughing chorus of 'Fuck off, Chancer, you wanker,' accompanied by the usual fist action around a 3 ft-long imaginary penis.

Why do men of all nationalities do this? Why don't they use their forefinger and thumb like they do when having a real wank? Spanish blokes exaggerate even more. They pretend to have a 4 ft-long cock, and they are not really well endowed. Something to do with olives, I think.

The gate flew open and Scaly took off like a Scalextric Ferrari. Scalys can surprise you at times because behind this casual exterior lurks a sharp-brained technician capable of setting up NASA-quality comms, and moving Land-Rovers about at NASA speeds. I shouted, 'When we re-enter the atmosphere, the paint might burn off. Fucking slow down, you mad prick.' He shouted, 'Listen, Corp: you can fucking drive if you want to, but I'm not stopping here to change places. We'll be sitting ducks for Paddy.'

We were approaching a road junction with traffic lights at red. I asked him, 'What's going to happen at this red traffic light, arsehole?' As he slowed the vehicle, I heard the all too familiar sound of a breach block sliding a 7.62 round into the chamber of an SLR (self-loading rifle). I spun around to see Buzz Aldrin bringing his rifle up to point it over the tailboard. Buzz had his finger on the trigger and had snicked off the safety catch. His eyes were popping out just like Marty Feldman's.

Some people get a nervous tic just under their eye when suddenly stressed. Mine is just next to my sphincter muscle. As casually as I could, I said, 'Put your safety catch back on and remove your hand from the trigger, mate.' His head spun round to look at me, shouting, 'Not on your fucking life, Corp. And you, you cunt. You stop for this red light and I'll shoot you out of that fucking seat.' Fortunately, the light changed to green before the threat was tested.

We drove along for a minute or so, then I told the driver to pull in in front of a parked van which was unloading boxes of sweets in front of a newsagent's. He did as he was told and when he stopped I ordered him to reverse back up to the front of the van and keep his eyes peeled.

Buzz nervously asked, 'What the fuck's going on?'

I told him, 'I am just going into the newsagent's for the evening paper and a couple of Mars bars.'

'I don't fucking believe this,' he said. 'I had a bad feeling about coming to pick up a mad cunt like you, especially from the fucking Murph.' I knew I had to question him about that remark but not just now.

I said, 'There's two nice birds in this shop. I see them every day and I'm just about into the big one's knickers. If you fuck up my visit, I'll fucking kill you. So take out that fucking round, make the weapon safe and follow me. The little one likes a back scuttle in the storeroom and she doesn't charge for the fags and Mars bars.'

The change in Buzz was instantaneous. 'You fucking sure, Corp? A fucking back scuttle? You're fucking having me on.'

To my knowledge, everybody except the OC and the Padre had shagged these two shop girls. I didn't know what the scoop was down at Gosford Castle so I thought I would kill two birds with one stone just in case snatch was scarce.

Buzz the scaly had completely changed. A different kind of nervousness had taken over now. He actually thought it was better to leave his weapon in the vehicle because it would cramp his style. I asked him when his tour had started, and he told me he'd been in Ulster a fortnight. I told him, 'You've got to learn to fuck with a tit in one hand and your gun in the other.' He laughed and I wondered at the power of the snatch.

The van driver and the shopkeeper were checking invoices and boxes on the pavement as we went past them into the shop. 'You're early, Chancer,' he said. 'I'll be 20 minutes with this lot but the girls are there so in you go, boys.'

As we entered the shop, a harsh, high-pitched Belfast accent said, 'Will youse look at what the fecking cat dragged in.' It was Rea's voice, the little one. The big one's name was Maeve, better known as Maeve the Rave.

Maeve was quick. 'C'mon, Chancer, we've got the storeroom before he brings them fecking boxes in. Rea can take him in the shithouse.' It all seemed to be over in a flash. One minute, Maeve was wriggling out of this rubber roll-on she used to hold her guts in. The next moment, she was bent over waiting for a game of leapfrog. I had a mental flashback of the entrance to the Mersey Tunnel.

Bang, bang, slurp, slurp, fart, fart and I was wiping my cock on her underskirt. Before I finished, she went a bit weak at the knees and made some soft moans, but I can't take the credit for that because as I was banging away she was crushing her clitoris with her knuckles. She looked a bit dishevelled but I couldn't remember if she looked like that when I came in.

Buzz the scaly was all bright-eyed and bushy-tailed, waiting to go to Gosford Castle, but Rea didn't look too happy. 'Come and gimme a quickie, Chancer. Yer man was squirting before he got in.'

'Sorry, Rea, but the old one-eyed snake doesn't like a wet nest.'

'It's not in me. Come and see, it's on the fecking floor.'

'OK, let's have a look.' I turned to Buzz and said, 'You fuck off with your mate and wait in the Land-Rover and don't fuck around with that weapon.'

'What the fuck are you doing?'

'I'm going to have a cheerio shag with Rea.'

'You are fucking mad, you are.' He walked out of the shop as Rea dragged me into the shopkeeper's bog and pointed to what could have been anything on the carpet. The carpet was one of those little runners and was stiff as a board with previous droppings.

Up went the skirt, up went my cock and up went my morale as I realised Rea was in ecstasy and her fanny was noticeably tighter than Maeve's. We stomped around in that shithouse for 20 minutes squeezing the last drop from my sac.

She gave me a box of Bounty bars and said, 'See youse tomorra.' I didn't have the heart to tell her I was out of her life for ever and she would have to suffer all that heartbreaking loneliness until Pete came in and gave her a good beasting.

I had some questions to ask my scaly friends. The first one being, who had told the scaly they were picking up a mad cunt from the Murph? The driver answered, saying that there's a big

Irish corporal waiting for me at Gosford Castle and he told them I was completely out of my pram and came here from planet Zob.

The big Irish corporal was Pat Rice, whose namesake was a face in the IRA, but we weren't to know that yet because the B-Specials had been disbanded and they kept the scoop on everybody. As a nation, I don't understand why we tolerate such gross incompetence from politicians and tongue-powered numbskulls like Lord Hunt, who was a direct cause of many young soldiers being killed because of the premature disbandment of the B-Specials. The Ulster Special Constabulary (B-Specials) was formed specifically to combat the IRA, and 50 years later it was disbanded. The B-Specials should have been systematically debriefed before this took place. But ministers and the like don't care a shit about expert reports; they care only about the politicians they lick up to. So an unthinking simpleton caused 50 years of priceless intelligence to dissipate virtually overnight.

No matter what anybody says, the B-Specials owed its existence to the IRA and its containment. It was probably the most denigrated police force on the planet but it knew everything there was to know about the IRA. But we soldier boys soon figured out where the scoop lay because we knew our lives depended on it. But for now, I'm just arriving at Gosford Castle, a beautiful ornate structure of grey stone walls with impressive masonry and turrets and towers. I wondered if Robin O'Hood had ever lived here.

Pat Rice welcomed me with the usual squaddie greeting ceremony of abuse. His mouth matched his 6 ft 4 in. frame with a booming capacity resembling that of Ian Paisley, who was busy becoming famous for the size of his gob and, of course, the turds therein. Look up gobshite in the Irish dictionary and you find Paisley. Gobshite is truly an Irish word and should never be used by an Englishman except when describing politicians or scumbags.

Pat was a smashing bloke. Literally. He smashed all kinds of kit and equipment in his time. Just now, he was smashing a most beautiful ornate door to gain entrance to a room in the castle where we would spend the night. The cool silence and serenity of this beautiful ancient setting was being sacrilegiously raped by a size 12 army boot bashing its way through years of craftsmanship.

As he stomped into the room with dust hanging in the air and the doorjamb hanging in splinters, a wispy little man appeared with a bunch of keys. 'Oh, I see ye won't be needing these, then,' he said very softly. I took the keys from him because we had to open many doors to accommodate the Royal Engineers and Hussars who were going to live here. Besides, I wanted to see if there was anything of value that should be handed back to the caretaker, hmm . . .

There was only Pat and I there from my squadron, so we organised our camp beds and kit in a fashion that required no adjustments when we came back pissed later in the evening. We managed to get a window open so we could piss out of it during the night. Pat's boot made the hole.

We took the scaly Land-Rover to the nearest pub after telling them we were doing a quick recce. The scalys were very busy so we left them to it. We also left our weapons in their care. Fortunately, there was a corporal with Buzz and his mate who was quite switched on, so I explained to him not to let Buzz near any weapons tonight because we might be delayed at Gough barracks later and I didn't want to drive into a hail of 7.62 from Buzz when we returned. He said, 'OK, see you down at the pub, mate, you can give me a lift back.'

The pub was like many Irish pubs. It looked like two houses with the dividing walls knocked out to accommodate a bar. The clientele looked as though they had been knocked out as well. The landlord was also comatose until Pat's boot connected with the vestibule door.

Little shafts of dust fell from the ceiling as the door crashed into the wall, shaking the pub and its customers to life. The landlord looked alarmed as he clocked Pat, then me. He said, 'Fuck me, son, why don't ye come in!' Pat boomed, 'Two pints of Guinness, landlord, please.'

I learned something in the next five minutes that I remembered years later when I became the landlord of a pub. When two beautiful black pints with super-creamy white heads appeared before me, I remarked that it only took a minute or so to produce two perfect pints when normally it takes a few minutes longer. 'Ahh,' said the landlord, using his favourite Bamber Gascoigne facial expression. I knew a pearl of wisdom was about to appear. 'A thirteen-hole restrictor is responsible for this black magic,' he said. 'All your English pubs use nine-hole restrictors and it takes longer and doesn't create the head retention like mine does.'

I wondered what I was doing here listening to this crap. So I said, 'Well, don't restrict us any more, landlord. Gimme that black bugger here and start another brace.' I swear it was the most beautiful drink I ever tasted. Actually, I think it was a combination of abstinence, longing, legendary tales of this Irish beverage and sheer thirst. It didn't touch the sides as it flowed through my gizzard. 'Fuck me, Chancer,' Pat roared. 'Isn't that the fucking mutt's nuts, mate!'

We were making the same noises over these pints of Guinness that a crackhead would make over a half-kilo of Charlie. But cocaine was scarcer than Yeti shit then. It was something you had jabbed into your gum by a dentist. But it was coming, wasn't it?

There was a grunt from my left side so I turned to look into the most wonderful wise owl of a face, etched with the lines of outdoor living with bright blue Paul Newman eyes. I was waiting to hang on every word. He took a long suck on his pipe, which had a little aluminium cap over the bowl with lots of little holes punched through it. I was just wondering about that and waiting for more pearls of wisdom when he let fly with the loudest fart I'd heard in years.

The last time I heard a report like that was from another Irishman, actually, who dropped his arse in 1964. I have never forgotten Paddy Goan's fart in the Royal Engineers Training Regiment at Cove, near Farnborough. But Paddy Goan's arse didn't stink like this. Oh no, this caused my nasal hairs to fall out and it tarnished my cap badge.

The facial expression didn't change, though everybody else had stopped breathing for a moment. 'What have I told you about that, Billy? You stinking bastard!' shouted the landlord. 'Your fecking arse will empty my fecking pub.'

I said to Pat, 'You just can't tell, can you? He's got a face like Einstein and a brain like Frankenstein.'

Pat roared, 'He's probably in the SAS.'

I choked on my ale.

The pipe came out of the mouth. 'I am a landowner hereabouts and I'm also a water bailiff. Your squadron arrives next week and I don't need Einstein's nor Frankenstein's feckin' brain to realise my feckin' land will be trampled over and gates will be left open or even broken. The feckin' countryside will be damaged and wildlife will be disturbed.'

I was slightly alarmed that he knew when the squadron was arriving but everybody would know next week anyway. I replied, 'Just pray nobody gets killed on your property.'

He took a swig of his ale and said vehemently, 'Never feckin' happen, mister.'

I knew then that Billy was to be part of my Irish experience. Billy was full of valuable information and it would be crucial to many border operations, but not on this night.

There was a piano in the pub and it was near enough in tune so as not to matter. Later that night, I bashed out 'The Sash' and 'Wild Rover', amongst other stirring Irish hymns. At the end of the evening, everybody stood to attention while I battered the National Anthem. I was off my face with booze and remember nothing of the journey back to Gosford Castle. So the next morning I had to sit and listen to the breakdown of my exploits the night before, which included everything from shitting in somebody's floral hanging basket that was soaking in a trough overnight to pestering the pub landlady for a back scuttle at the rear of the Land-Rover.

Pat and I had lots to do. The Gosford Castle area had to be recced, so mornings were spent on foot, carefully checking dozens of possible ambush sites the IRA could use in this nightmare of a security problem. The lush countryside around Gosford Castle is ideal territory for the bushwhacker, but to my knowledge the site was never visited by the IRA or the UVF, which was fortunate for the residents because there would have been a bloodbath if it had been.

We spent many long hours learning the lay of the land and selecting sites for vehicle control points (VCPs). We also discovered many hidden culverts running under the roads, designed to enable water to drain away. Ulster is very wet and the culverts provide an avenue for moving water. Culverts are an ideal site for placing bombs under a road: a favourite IRA tactic. We were very busy.

At night, we checked the pubs. The pubs were bloody marvellous. The ale was always first class and so was the *craic* (pronouced 'crack'). *Craic* is another Irish word, which describes the atmosphere, ambience, debate and fun, all rolled up in one short word that has nothing to do with cocaine. 'Sure, the *craic* was great' or 'We had great *craic* last night' are the most often used phrases in Ireland, which describe last night's piss up.

We would always get back to our local for the last hour and have the *craic* with Billy. Billy was dour and always grizzling. I bet he ground his teeth in his sleep. But he knew more about the rivers and border areas than anybody else in Ireland. He knew everybody: farmers, priests, poachers, gypsies, bad men, good men, good-time girls and virgins. He even knew every barking dog and which houses kept geese. It was very important for patrolling soldiers not to be compromised by yapping dogs and geese warning the opposition of our presence in the dead of night. Because once the yapping starts, you can call in the Dagenham Girl Pipers and do the rest of the patrol with them leading the way.

Billy was a diamond. His information was never biased. He cared not about Catholic, Protestant or Jew. He said what he had to say without malice. As a water bailiff, he had been abused by every walk of life that carried a fishing rod or set of snares. His bitterness, if any, was usually reserved for gypsies.

You couldn't really tell when he was being bitter, he was like that all the time. But a little curl came to his upper lip when talk was of gypsies. One night, he gripped my forearm and snarled, 'Don't ye ever forget that tinkers are a breed whose lives are devoted to lying, cheating, double-crossing, plotting and generally shitting and wanking over their family and friends. So where do you think you stand with them?' It occurred to me never to ask his opinion of the Royal Signals.

The squadron arrived and everybody settled down to living in squalor. Belsen-type sleeping quarters were arranged, metal cots stacked four high, twelve cots to a room. Harry Houdini would have had problems getting in and out of here. There was an infamous cell in the Carabanchel called the 'Bronx'. That cell housed 12 prisoners in abject misery. But the Bronx was more luxurious than Gosford Castle.

I sometimes wonder which word best describes the British squaddie: flexible, because he adapts readily to any situation, or pliable, because he is fucked into all kinds of horrible holes by gobshites. Politicians, ministers and generals are a million miles away from places like Gosford Castle and Vere-Foster School. Maybe if the generals lived in the Murph they would respond differently to the gobshites.

Soldiers readily accept the conditions of war, be it in Malaysia, Borneo, Aden, the Falklands, Afghanistan or Iraq. But this was Great Britain in 1971. And why was there such a great sense of urgency to dump men in shitholes? Because the gobshites got it wrong and they couldn't care a shit anyway as long as their weekends were not affected. Also, because the B-Specials were disbanded by gobshites. That is the opinion of many soldiers, and nothing is going to change it.

If a soldier, sailor, airman, policeman, fireman, ambulance man or even a fucking dustbin man displayed the lack of skills and care that highly paid politicians and ministers often display, they would be sacked and booted out of the job. If they didn't acquire the skills in a given time period they wouldn't get the job anyway. Pressing knuckles during handshakes isn't really the skill required for the welfare of soldiers.

We'd got a new Home Secretary in 1970, Reggie Maudling. 'Dawdling fucking Maudling' we called him. Completely clueless. About as useful as an ashtray on a motorbike. Maudling also sounds like 'maudlin', so here I am sitting gazing out of my cell window in Malaga feeling sorry for myself, looking at the falling rain.

The phlegm-stained yard is getting a much-needed wash. It would take undiluted acid to properly clean it but rain is better than nothing. My imagination transforms the driving rain into snow as my thoughts take me back to a train journey I once made to Berlin in 1972.

I was locked in the train at Braunschweig, along with all the other military passengers, by the British Military Police (monkeys). The monkeys jammed wooden spars against carriage doors so nobody could exit or enter. This was the military train that ran through the corridor from West to East Germany into Berlin.

I was alone with my thoughts as the train rattled its way through the snow across the border into East Germany. It stopped for an hour or so at a bleak station in Magdeburg where Russian and East German soldiers searched its exterior. Using the biggest German shepherd dogs I have ever seen, they searched the underside of each carriage.

During the search, a British army major collected all our passports. He was then escorted from the train to an office on the platform where a hard-faced Russian officer checked each passport. I could see him from my window. Though the falling snow obliterated much of the surrounding scene, I could see his scowling face as he inspected each page, deliberately causing a delay because of his own importance. It is at times like this I'm glad my name is Chance and not Bond . . .

The snow continued to fall on this forlorn railway station making it feel like the most miserable dump on the planet. I was beginning to feel sorry for the soldiers stationed here, then I thought 'Fuck 'em, this is probably the most exciting place they've ever been to.'

The train left Magdeburg and rumbled towards Berlin. I remember thinking that this country was a giant mausoleum, a miserable deadland, a cemetery without tombstones, mile after mile of depression. Why the fuck did they search this train? Who in their right mind would want to come to this purgatory? Later, when I entered West Berlin, it struck me that the city was like a glittering jewel set in a crown of pig iron.

During this visit to Berlin, I was staying at the Edinburgh House Hotel, a military establishment used by military personnel in transit or on short-stay courses. I was here to attend a Joint Services Intelligence Wing course being held at the Berlin HQ. Everybody on this course apart from me was a commissioned officer, either army or air force. I held the lowest rank as a sergeant. However, I was far from being the lowest in intelligence. Some of these men were incredibly stupid and naive. I remember thinking that if they were our Intelligence personnel here in Germany, they were a liability. If they were used in a Northern Ireland situation they would be fucking dangerous.

The course was an anti-interrogation/anti-indoctrination instructor course, which was really all about the shit that would happen if you ever got caught by the enemy. Each of the instructors had been a prisoner of war some time during their military career so their presentations were from real life and absolutely gripping. It was a pity that some of their students were childish and should have been kicked out on the first day: leaders, my arse.

However, I was in West Berlin, possibly the liveliest city on Earth. It was Friday and I was out on the town. First, I had to visit the Heer Strasse sauna club, an old haunt of mine from previous visits to Berlin. It was a short walk from Smuts Barracks in Spandau, the home of the Royal Engineers in Berlin. I used to go to the Heer Strasse sauna at least once a week. It's the best sauna in the world.

The Heer Strasse is a mixed naked sauna with hot and scalding-hot steam rooms, warm splash pools and for the lunatics there's an open-air splash pool. There is also a restaurant but you must cover your sausage with a towel if you sit in there. The Germans are great sausage eaters, especially the girls.

One evening, I was luxuriating alone in the warm splash pool when I heard 'splat, splat, splat'. The sound of flesh smacking wet tiles was getting nearer. Curiously, I was waiting to see what was coming down the corridor from the shower room. When I saw what was making the noise, I had to duck under the water and nearly drowned myself from laughing.

A one-legged woman had arrived, hopping around the corner towards me, her large tits flailing up and down, 'splat, splat'. She stood before me as I surfaced coughing and spluttering, trying to catch my breath and regain some form of equilibrium. Her balance was absolutely perfect, because her leg was so magnificently muscled. Apart from the missing leg, she was perfectly built and obviously an athlete. I straightened my face and gazed at her vibrant form.

Amazingly, a cock-bursting erection extended achingly towards the one-legged beauty. I didn't think she could see it under the water, but in perfect English, she said, 'You are not supposed to do that in here, Englander. It must be for me because there's only you and me here.'

She dove neatly into the pool, and the impetus of her dive brought her gliding swiftly under the water so her eyes were inches away from my aching cock. She surfaced in front of me, then, moving very quickly, impaled herself on my erection. It was a tremendous experience to have a waterborne knee-trembler with a one-legged woman. Penetration was unimpeded because of the missing leg. Her internal muscularity was mind-blowing as she drained my seed sac in less than two minutes. I couldn't prevent it; she was so fast and furious, the intensity of it all had me spurting, completely out of control. Christ! Sexually incontinent in less than two minutes of laying eyes on a one-legged kraut bird with a vacuum cleaner for a crotch.

'My name is Gisela, Englander. You will take me home, where we will spend a nice weekend together.'

'How do you know I am English?'

She pointed to the tattoo on my arm. 'Self-mutilation, the Englishman loves it,' she said.

We left Heer Strasse sauna an hour later in her beautiful Borgward Isabella motor car. She drove me along Kaiser Damm Bismarck Strasse, then along a snow-covered Clay Allee. Two more turnings brought us to Dahlemer Weg in driving snow. I got out of the car and quickly went around to the driver's side to help her out. I tried to see what kind of pedal layout was fitted to enable this one-legged girl to drive so well, but it was too dark.

There was so much snow about I thought she would have a problem getting from car to house, but she simply held my arm and with a series of short hops she was turning the key in the door. This girl was amazing.

Gisela's apartment was typically kraut with heavy dark green curtains with ornate pelmets. Green, amber and brown seemed to be the main colours. Lots of green-leaved plants but no flowers. There were no floor coverings, mats or carpets. An ornamental draught excluder lying at the heavy front door was the only thing that could possibly be tripped over. The floor was shiny with vinyl tiles but not slippery. She told me this was because she got around the house on her bum. This explained the muscle control and why she had the best one-legged arse in the world.

There were a couple of false legs in the airing cupboard but I didn't see her use one during that unforgettable weekend. Nor did she use one during the following dates we had. Berlin holds many memories for me and is one of the best playgrounds in the world, but for me, Gisela made it better. She gave me reason to visit Berlin again and again. 'Auf Wiedersehen, pet,' I whisper as I return to my prison cell in the arsehole of Europe.

The rain is still lashing down and cleaning some of the snot from the prison yard as my thoughts turn to sunnier days. I loathe my cell, the walls seem to smother me, so to prevent the stifling of my thoughts, I quickly mount my imaginary magic carpet to allow my mind to take me back to a job I did a few years ago. Back to La Linea, the frontier town opposite Gibraltar.

SIX

Steve had given me instructions to meet a Spaniard in the car park at La Linea hospital. This shithole of a town is also the frontier between Gibraltar and Spain. Gibraltar is the pimple on the arse of Europe, and Andalucia, or, more specifically, the Costa del Sol, is the arsehole. That is the Spanish opinion and I tend to agree with it.

I found some shade just inside the entrance and turned off the ignition. This town is not the kind of place you can drive around to case the joints. The Guardia Civil are constantly patrolling and a British-registered car in this area could possibly raise an eyebrow. A mile away at the frontier there are dozens of British cars, but not in Centro La Linea.

My contact had been told to approach me, so I sat low and waited. A dark, curly-haired bloke came into the car park, strolled over to me and started gobbing off in Spanish. My Spanish then was about as good as my Kyrgyz. I knew my contact's name was Lito so I said, '*Nombre, nombre?*'

He said, 'Lito'.

OK, so I got my man. '*Adonde, adonde?*' I said.

He came around to the passenger side, which is always tricky for continentals because of the right-hand drive. They always have this daft expression on their face like when British blokes use chopsticks for the first time.

We left the hospital and drove into a warren of dirty little streets bedecked with washing hanging out to dry. Lito guided me through lines of washing until we stopped between them. The car was completely hidden from passing patrols by fluttering bed-sheets, towels and shirts. Lito gesticulated for me to unlock the boot, then grabbed my sleeve and we ran into a nearby house. These houses were a smaller version of *Coronation Street* houses: two up, two down, and very small. Three men appeared from the kitchen and immediately emptied three sports bags full of quarter-kilo bars of hashish all over the tiled floor. That was my cue to count them.

There should have been 60 kilos, so that meant 240 bars. I duly counted 80 into each of the 3 bags. I zipped each bag closed as it was filled. Lito whispered, '*Dinero, amigo.*' So I tossed him a plastic bag containing three million pesetas. They divided it into three piles and started counting. As each man finished counting, I jotted each sum of money on my pad and totted it up to the correct amount: no jiggery-pokery with this lot.

The three bags were ready to go, so Lito dialled a number on his mobile, muttered something and said, '*Espera.*' Five minutes later, his phone rang. '*Si, ahora.*' The three men picked up the bags and dashed to the car, placed the bags in the boot, slammed it down and banged the roof. By this time, I had started the engine and was ready to roll, but I was lost amongst all these flapping bed sheets.

Lito pointed me in the right direction, and I drove my way through, leaving him behind. I was in a side street just around the corner from the seafront. Nice and easy, I turned left onto the main road and drove along adjacent to the beach, heading away from Gibraltar, which I could see in my rear-view mirror. I drove into what could be called an industrial area: a road with several workshops and car-sales plots leading out of La Linea towards the busy *carretera* to Malaga. I had a rendezvous with Steve at the BP filling station on the outskirts of town. When I clocked him in his car, we did not speak. He drove away, then I waited six minutes and followed him. We would both stay within the speed limit and keep to 100 kph on the *carretera*. Our contact numbers were already punched into our mobile phones so if a problem arose we would be talking immediately.

The plan was for Steve to be six minutes ahead of me and warn me if he ran into a VCP, which the Guardia Civil were wont to set up on any part of this road to catch people like me. On being warned, I would take the next exit and go to one of the many locations that I had planned into my route. I had recced every single exit on this route. Remember P-six? It applies at all times.

Everything went according to plan and we RVd (rendezvoused) at the Cruz de Piedre restaurant on the outskirts of Coín. We greeted each other as though we had just met and had a drink together. I then called my wife from the public phone in the bar and simply said, 'Put the kettle on, love.'

Steve then left and drove to my house, which is approximately one mile from where we were in a rural district called Valdeperales: a scattering of *fincas* and derelict *casuchas*, small farms and abandoned shacks, on the outskirts of Coín. My house is a beautiful old *finca*, an eighteenth-century farmhouse set in ten thousand square metres of secluded greenery, surrounded by a two-metre high chainlink fence, built to keep my Rottweiler and two Alsatians in and to keep nosy spicks out.

By the time my wife had chained the dogs and walked down the drive to unlock the gates, Steve would arrive and drive in to park his car in our little car park off the drive. By the time he got up to the house and raised the garage door, I would be driving in. The gates were closed and locked behind me as I drove up the drive and into the garage. There was a window in the garage through which I passed the sports bags into the house unobserved. Then they were placed into the priest hole under the stairs. Later, I would take the car across town to where I had my journey car parked in a rented garage. This car would never be used for anything other than the journey to England with the hashish. Journey cars were always immaculate and fully serviced.

I would leave my small car in the rented garage and return home with the journey car and start preparing it for the trip to England. I used to love doing this. The petrol tank had been rearranged by cutting and making a hatch in the top of it and welding a steel plate along its length so that basically it had two separate compartments: one to hold petrol, the other to hold 45 kilos of hashish. Obviously, this was not a Heath Robinson job on the petrol tank; far from it. It had to be done with great care and professionalism, because at £2,500 per kilo, in Liverpool, my tank was worth £112,500. That price was in 1995. It has dropped a bit since then.

There are many types of car used for this kind of work, and HMC&E don't know about them all so I will tell you about the Rover 820 series, which they do know about. Also, I will only tell you about the petrol-tank pug. There are many ways to skin a cat and the enemy knows this one, so no harm done.

Before choosing your wheels, you need to wise up on a few things. Colour of car is important. You don't want to stick out like the proverbial bulldog's bollocks, so think about it. Which cars are the most popular on today's roads? *Autocar* magazine has a section on performance figures for all current European models, which also states tank capacity. Get a copy.

Don't go hard and fast on one model, choose three or four. When you have decided which model to use, find a car breaker and get yourself a petrol tank to fit your model. Get two if you can. They are jack-shit cheap so don't worry about price. Just worry about questions nosy bastards ask and have an answer ready. 'I ran over my kid's bike and the frame punctured my tank.' If you need me to tell you this, forget all about it and go back to being a screw.

Make sure the tank is completely clean inside and out and devoid of any petrol and fumes. I really do not wish to insult your intelligence but I must tell you about a bloke who put an oxy-acetylene torch to a petrol tank he had just removed from my car. The petrol tank no longer exists. The bloke was injured and concussed. The workshop roof was damaged. But worst of all, it brought nosy parkers in uniform to the scene. This goon was a corporal in 45 Royal Marine Commando and later a trooper in the SAS. He's an example of what not to do in more ways than one, because this arsehole turned out to be a grass for HMC&E and he grassed me up, good and proper.

I would never have suspected he was a grass because he compromised himself so much. I actually stayed at his nice little cottage in a picturesque little village in southern England. He introduced me to his wife, who is an ex-model. She had just had a baby. I can't name him because he grassed a lot of players and one firm I know in Australia are looking for him to give him his wages. Need I say more? I will call him 'Holmes'. But first I must deal with these cars.

You design your own pug because you know what you want to hide. But you must make sure the sender unit is intact inside the tank. That is the contraption which operates the fuel gauge. The fuel gauge must always work. When the Customs officer turns the ignition key, he is looking at the fuel gauge and if that needle doesn't work he gets a twinge in his groin.

You need to practise removing the tank and bringing it out from under the car without dragging it all over the floor. Then put it back. Do this at least six times and time yourself. You will know exactly which tools you need to do the job and you keep them separate. Use the correct tools and don't produce spanner-rash on the nuts and studs that you touch, as Customs will spot this and become suspicious that the tank has been tampered with.

Buy three extra fuel pumps. Stow one in the car, keep one in the garage at your destination and keep one at your loading location. Also, at these locations have trolley-jacks and axle-stands, a flexi-light, a spare set of the correct tools and coveralls. There are other bits and pieces but you can think about those requirements.

You must leave nothing to chance: think about what can go wrong, list the possible problems, then find the solutions. Start the list with yourself. You are top of the list of things that go wrong. Documentation, make sure you have it all: passport, licence, vehicle registration, insurance and MOT certification, all in date. I know blokes in prison who brought it on top because of documentation hiccups.

Don't get caught speeding. If they fancy you, you are finished. Have you got the answers rehearsed to any questions you could possibly be asked? Think about it. 'Are you on holiday, sir?' 'When did you first cross the channel, sir?' 'Whereabouts in Spain do you live, sir?' What you say next will determine whether or not you drive into the Customs or police workshop, or to freedom and profit. If you admit to living on the Costa del Sol then you will have a problem, because the Customs officer's loins will get warm and his little Hampton will tremble.

I used to say I was from Valdeperales. They would ask where's the nearest big town and I would say, 'Coín, of course.' I said it as though they were stupid for not knowing it. Nobody ever asked where Coín was, and if they had I would have told them it was just to the south of Córdoba. And I wasn't really lying, I just made sure I didn't say the words Malaga, Fuengirola, Torremolinos or Marbella.

This job is not easy. If it were easy, everybody would be doing it. You could be carrying 40 kilos of Charlie, smack or puff. If you think this job is easy, you will lose it and you will be put away for a long time.

What if you get caught? What is your defence? 'Not worth having one,' I hear you say. Oh yes it is, but circumstances dictate results. Lady Luck needs to be on your side, like when I got caught. I never would have been caught without their grass, I hasten to add. But the scumbag was compromised by the Customs officers; their incompetence gave him away. They arrested me and charged me before the petrol tank was opened. Only two players knew what was in that tank: me and King Rat, Holmes.

But for now, if you are a potential grass, think again. Your paymasters are not experienced or clever enough to handle you and the price you pay is very high. If you're lucky, a head-job, nice and swift, but you may receive a bit of foreplay first. Possibly have your bollocks fondled in a vice. If you are in Ulster you'll definitely get a head-job, a bag over your head and a bullet through it. Some people I know are very handy with Black & Decker drills and grinders.

We are still working on our list so what's next? Refuelling. You have to do this every hundred miles or so because you have only a part tank of petrol. Remember P-six? You will have run the tank empty at least three times during the preparations for this journey. Each time you will have used the trip-meter to see exactly how far a full tank takes you. With the Rover 820, my tank design gave me 110 miles' range. So depending on your route to Blighty, you would need to refuel possibly ten times or more before you reached the ferry port.

Think about it. Nobody goes into a motorway filling station for 12 euros worth of petrol, not unless he's bursting for a piss. Also, every gas station in Spain and France seems to have its resident Guardia Civil or Gendarmerie sitting drinking coffee looking at you. I used to drive to the pumps and make a dash to the toilets. Then I would put my grudge petrol in, as if paying my price for a piss. Then I'd drive another hundred miles and do it again and again and again.

What are you going to do if you break down? 'That depends on what breaks down,' I hear you say. So think of all the usual causes of breakdowns and let's see if we can manage the problems out of the job. I will assume you are not an engineer or a mechanic. First, when you purchase this car, before you tell the bloke to register it in your name, you instruct him to change the plugs, points, filters, oil and all belts including the timing belt as on the Rover 820. You want to keep all the replaced items as spares, except for the oil and filters, of course, so have them put in a box for you. Expect an argument and expect to pay because it's about seventy quid to fit a Rover timing belt and it takes a mechanic to fit it. So don't lark about, just pay, and make sure it is done because you'll get your money back a thousand times over once you've got past Customs.

When I bought my first car in Liverpool, I stayed with it for hours and watched all the work being done. Fuck Scousers, they'd take the pennies off a dead man's eyes. Don't forget to check tyres and brakes. Don't believe the MOT certificate. Get a new one. Check the exhaust and if in doubt put a new one on. I had an exhaust pipe break off at Pons in France. It was not a good experience. I had renewed everything except the poxy exhaust pipe.

Does it matter about which ferry port you use? Yes it does. It also matters which ferry company you use because they all use computers and you and the car are entered into said computer. But to my knowledge the ferry company computers are not linked to each other, so think about it.

Don't get lazy and use the easiest route all the time. There are plenty of lazy buggers in prison. The easiest route is Santander to Portsmouth. I never ever used it. I know players in prison who used that route. You need good maps to study your route. Give yourself alternative routes in case there are problems along the way. Be prepared for road closures in the Pyrenees mountains. They have rock falls and snow blockages. In the Pais Vasco (Basque country), there can be intense military and police activity. The Figueras frontier, north of Barcelona, has resident sniffer dogs and can be a pain in the arse at the best of times.

Because your range is about 100 miles, you work out on your map the places where you will need fuel. You think there are gas stations everywhere? Wrong. Remember P-six? Also, keep in mind that most French gas stations are closed on Sunday. Also, there are many holy days when gas stations are closed. I know you have a five-litre container of petrol in the boot but you should never allow the tank to run dry because fuel pumps choke on any shite that could be in there. Also, remember to ditch the five-litre can before boarding the ferry. Buy another when you refuel after disembarkation. Never take a fuel can on the ferry: the Customs officer's testicles will vibrate the moment he sees it.

Don't hesitate or stop at frontiers unless you are physically stopped. As you make your approach, you must never make eye contact with anybody. This also applies as you drive off the ferry. Avoid eye contact at all costs. Concentrate on the bonnet of the car and don't steal a glance at Mr Customs. If you think you can steal a glance at Mr Customs without causing a problem, then keep your screw's job.

So let's look at the map again. Now that you have chosen a route, list all the major towns in order of march and asterisk any change of direction. You don't want to be stopping to check your map all the time. Secure the list where you can see it at a glance. You will dispense with such things once you become familiar with the routes.

I will tell you about one of my favourite routes, and how I used to do it. The preparation of the car is too important to gloss over so I'll come back to that in more detail later.

I always made sure I had a good breakfast. Another good idea is to take a cooler box loaded with drinks and snacks for the journey.

I would leave my house at six o'clock in the morning and head for Madrid, taking it easy around the ring road, then taking the

E90 and following the Zaragoza signs. From Zaragoza, I'd take the E7 to Huesca, then through to Sabiñanigo. At Sabiñanigo, I'd turn right on the 136, signposted to Biescas. This is a most enjoyable drive over the Pyrenees, with absolutely stunning scenery. More to the point, though, the actual frontier crossing is unmanned.

The first French town you come to is Laruns, a beautiful tourist spot high in the Pyrenees. You can get fuel at Biescas or Laruns. In any case, you need to put your spick money away and have your frog money to hand. I used this route often so I know it well.

Depending on traffic and weather conditions, I would normally reach Pau and be in a hotel before 8 p.m. Never drive after 8 p.m. in France unless you are using a frog-plated car. The frogs have roving patrols of mixed Customs and police. They also have covert VCP teams at the entrances to the toll roads. You drive into the tollbooth to collect your ticket where you are suddenly surrounded by uniforms with sub-machine guns. Your car is taken to one side where the search team, complete with lamps and tools, gets to work after the dog has had a sniff. You will be questioned at length by experienced interrogators; these blokes do this every night, so be prepared for a serious grilling. If they really fancy you, you're goosed. They will take the car to pieces. They will also process your passport. So if you have any previous form, you should not be in this car.

So make sure you are off the road before 8 p.m. and enjoying lovely grub in a nice hotel. Make sure the car is immobilised and use a visible steering-wheel anti-theft device. Ask for a room overlooking the car park and put the car under your bedroom window if possible. Enjoy the hotel and at eight o'clock in the morning set off refreshed en route for your chosen ferry port.

When you get near the ferry port, top up the tank and ditch the five-litre container. I used to hide mine in various isolated lay-bys. I would stop and case the place whilst pissing. Then I would hide my container 20 paces from the ever-present wastebasket. You should always buy the lead-free containers because they are coloured green: easy to hide in the undergrowth. I never had the need to retrieve any of these containers but you never know your luck.

When you get to the ferry terminal, pay for your ticket with plastic. Don't use cash. Every time I used cash, I was stopped. So I figured using cash was part of a profile. It is possible a one-way ticket adds to the profile. Every time I used plastic for a return ticket, I breezed through.

There are stories about each ferry having a search team with sniffer dogs on board. They are let loose when the car decks are secured and all passengers are up on the decks. I heard that if they fancied your car they put a chalk mark on the front. I always checked for chalk marks but never found any. One bloke I knew always took a tiny piece of pollen (hashish) and thumbed it into the front tyre of the car two cars in front of him. I really don't know if tricks like that did any good. The most important thing for me was absolutely no eye contact when clearing Customs areas.

So now we are driving up the road away from the Customs areas and we've cleared the port of entry. You feel you have just won the lottery and you could beast a case of champagne. Not yet, my friend, it's a long way to Tipperary and you don't know if you have a tail. Assume that you have. What are you going to do? P-six. Remember?

One little firm I know has two vehicles, identical in every way. They operated a switch job whereby anything following vehicle no. 1 eventually followed vehicle no. 2 all the way to Glasgow, while vehicle no. 1 was being unloaded in London. This firm is still busy so invent your own switch method, I cannot reveal this one.

But let's be realistic: why should they fancy little old you? Well, I'll tell you: 99% because of a grass (information received) and 1% because you've brought it on top. I've known kamikaze types who simply throw 50 kilos in the boot and drive to Scotland without any problems. Great for them, but they don't do it 25 times each year. Sod's law will always let the kamikaze through, but the pro gets caught. Why? Because of Mr Rat, the grass.

To be successful in this game, you must be an incredibly private person. Two people will always know you are a smuggler or a dealer. The first person is your supplier. You can be as independent as you like but unless you own the farm in Morocco somebody has to supply you. And unless you are going to smoke it all yourself, you need a client. So, at least two people know you are a player. I know there are firms working with large numbers of people involved. I know firms using 40-ft trucks: imagine how many players are involved in that.

Another pal of mine, whom I'll call Dutch, runs three yachts, all coming in and out of the same port with three tonnes of puff on each yacht. He's been grafting for 16 years. He should have retired 15 years ago. The tight-fisted bastard has more money than the Queen and he's never had a problem with anybody. But his system is very cleverly done and everybody who works for him doesn't know for whom they are working.

One man, whom I will call the Adjutant, is responsible to Dutch. Each individual skipper and crewmember knows without doubt that he or his family members will most certainly die should he decide to gob off about any aspect of this particular job. Even hard bastards who ceased work ten years ago shit when they hear Dutch's name. The hard bastards of course are previous adjutants who are all wealthy and retired.

I knew crewmen who wasted a grand a night on brasses and Charlie, then stupidly said the wrong thing whilst in their cups. They all went the same way. Wrapped in fishing nets and lashed to a big anchor with heavy-gauge wire. It is not something one forgets. The other crewmembers were made to tie a strand of wire to the anchor so they were part of the execution. Anybody who refused joined big mouth. To my knowledge, there were never any refusals. He was slowly lowered into the water in complete silence. The boat was somewhere in the Mediterranean idling, waiting to get under way again. Big mouth would be submerged for one minute then brought back up so that just his head was exposed. The Adjutant would then tell everybody to say goodbye to big mouth, then he would rip the tape from his mouth so he could say goodbye to his shipmates. The mind-numbing scream would be branded onto everybody's brain, never to be forgotten. He would then be lowered to about a foot or so beneath the surface where everybody witnessed his drowning. He would then be released and allowed to descend to the floor of the Med, where we all knew big mouths with big teeth would be dining tonight while we were in our bunks. My friend is a firm believer in just rewards. There are no grey areas; you are wealthy or you are dead, simple as that.

The most despicable grass is known as a maverick. This name is used by Customs Intelligence to describe a rat who works for them as an informant, but breaks the rules because he still does his own smuggling jobs hoping they (HMC&E) don't find out and if they do, that they'll be lenient with him.

A maverick went missing recently. I hope he is in Davy Jones's locker. He was married to a brass who worked Marbella. This rat goes by the name of Marcel. He too was dropped in the shit by his paymasters.

A good pal of mine lost two tonnes of hashish and his liberty, but within two minutes of being boarded by the enemy (Guardia Civil) he knew who had informed on him. My friend is a most wonderful man who was a commissioned officer in the Royal Marines. He is incredibly perceptive and clever, as are a lot of people who live on the edge.

Most hashish smugglers who work at sea don't think of hash as being a drug so they consider themselves as being more an adventurer than a law-breaking smuggler: very romantic. So it comes as a shock when they end up in jail and it all seems so unfair. Consequently, when it is revealed that they are the victim of a grass, the bitterness and hatred for that despicable rat is very special indeed.

Another maverick is about to leave this prison where I am sitting right now. He is going out to certain death. He is well known here as Pat: an Irishman with a cockney accent, better known as Pat the Rat. His missus is an old blonde slag, something to do with porn mags, and their son is a Charlie pusher in Fuengirola. Again, it was his paymasters who compromised him. I hope to hear some news about him soon. Posthumously, of course: nets, anchors, fish food . . .

I've come back to my cell for a minute or two because I need a piss. Faces from the past look up at me as I empty my bladder on them. It gives me moments of pleasure every time I use the bog because this is where I store the evil bastards that shit on me: all in my mind, of course. Anyway, I'm off out again now; my thoughts are taking me on another journey.

SEVEN

The blonde had big tits and she had two big blue suitcases with a silver band around the middle of each. Matching, just like her tits. Steve knew her and was spluffing like Cosmo Smallpiece getting ready for a knee-trembler. Funny, really, because his bollocks are permanently empty. He fucked himself with anabolic steroids in his effort to look like Arnold Schwarzenegger. Now all his food has to go through a blender before he puts it in his gob. He was never a handsome bloke but since he had a face job he looks as though somebody has just varnished his face, and with his Stan Boardman perm, he looks like Pinocchio in shock. One day, I hope to lash him under my bowsprit.

We were in the queue at Malaga airport, checking in for the Leeds-Bradford flight. I had five kilos on my back. Steve forgot about me as he wasted his breath on the blonde we had randomly bumped into. She did tell me her name but two seconds later I had forgotten it. I helped her with the suitcases by hoofing them along as the queue moved forward. Her luggage was gobbled up by the system. She thanked me and gave Steve a little pecky poo on the cheek and waddled away to the X-ray machine and metal-detector frame. I checked in and followed her.

Steve, as usual, hovered a wee bit in case I got caught. I went through without a problem, but that Triumph Bonneville was rumbling away in my chest and 76 trombones were blasting into my skids. I'm not yet into absorbent underwear but I was considering investing in a set, and having a reinforced gusset inserted. My poor arse felt as though it should be in a sling.

As I was strolling to the waiting area, the intercom announced a delay of two hours for my flight, so I went upstairs to the restaurant. I ordered coffee and a *bocadilla* from the thief dressed as a waiter. Daylight fucking robbery for a snack. And I'm in prison for a bit of puff! Anyway, I couldn't eat my snack. I decided to leave it because I couldn't be doing with the rigmarole of pissing, and shitting was completely out of the question. I was too worried that my packets would come loose. The duty-free shop looked inviting and was a good way to pass the time. But I was scared of people accidentally touching my back and because paranoia had turned me into Quasimodo, I sat there for the longest two hours of my life.

At last, I boarded the aircraft which took me to Leeds-Bradford airport where it was pissing rain. I wondered what the attraction is that brings thousands of exotic turban wearers to this drab pisshole in the middle of 'Ee by gum' land.

I had to walk through the pelting rain to the reception areas where a big Negress who looked like a bewigged Idi Amin dressed in a Customs uniform was ushering everybody inside towards the baggage carousel. I was carrying my sports bag and was about to shoot through when I clocked 12 young Customs officers forming a guard of honour at the double-door exit. My bottle started to go, then I clocked big tits standing near the carousel.

She wasn't looking my way but I gave a big wave and pushed my way through the mêlée to join her. I stood behind her so she didn't see me. Two powder-blue suitcases came riding along the carousel. I grabbed one and shouted, 'Can you manage the other?' She gave me a big smile and grabbed the other suitcase. She had a trolley so I put both suitcases on it and my sports bag on top. I said, 'I'm sharing your trolley, so I'll push.'

As we strolled together through the guard of honour, I think I was talking in Russian or possibly kraut. I really do not remember. Her husband was waiting for her with the kids. I could read his thoughts: 'Who the fuck's this with my missus?' I snatched my bag and said, 'Auf Wiedersehen,' and dove into the first taxi.

The cabbie took me to a hotel where I stripped off the gear and put it in my sports bag, had a shower and hit the sack. I awoke early, shaved and had my breakfast. I phoned for a cab and went to the bus station and jumped on the Liverpool bus. On arriving in Liverpool, I took a taxi to the Old Bell Hotel near Kirkby to wait for my contact.

I had called Steve from a public phone when I'd got my room number. I said, 'The weather is fine. Eleven red roses, please.' One hour later, there was a knock on my door, no. 11. I let a pretty girl in who raced into the bathroom bursting for a piss. She sounded like a horse pissing. She was standing straddling the toilet with her fingers pulling her knickers to the side pissing over her knuckles.

She said, 'You'll have to drive me home. I can't fuckin' drive. I'm shaking like a leaf.' This was Steve's daughter. I suggested we have a drink and some lunch. She didn't think that was a good idea because she might throw up. She was more in danger of soiling her knickers, I thought. So I drove her straight into Liverpool with the gear in the bag she had brought.

She actually suggested writing down her address for me to drive her car on my own while she took a cab. I said, 'Sure, but you take the fucking bag in the cab with you.' I knew she would start pissing again. I had to tell Steve she must never be my contact again.

The next time I came to that hotel, I met a man called Peter Rorke. Peter was taller than me, quite slim and looked very fit. He was also very nervous. I did a lot of work with Peter, who was a very nice man, and I often wondered how he got mixed up with Steve. He was a fireman in the Liverpool Fire Brigade and very well respected. I eventually discovered that he used to be Steve's foreman in a road haulage business that Steve owned. But Steve hated him because Peter had grassed him to the Inland Revenue, fucked his business and fucked his wife. So here I was, working with two men who were sworn enemies.

Peter was living with Steve's wife and the pissing daughter was also under his roof. But all went well and we started to use the cars and everybody was happy and making money, except Peter. Peter seemed to be suffering from the stress of it all. He did not like doing this. I told Steve to change him, but he wouldn't hear of it. I felt that Peter was doing this under duress. Tragically, Peter died in his sleep during a night shift in his fire station. I'm not a pathologist, but I blame the stress of working for Steve for his premature departure into the next world. If you can hear me, Peter, ask your angel friends to have a nice place ready for me. My time will come soon enough.

I remember on the day Peter died, Steve called me to his gymnasium and said, 'The gear is still in Peter's locker in the fire station, so fly over to Liverpool and get it out of there. When you get back, we'll have a champagne piss-up to celebrate that cunt's death.' I was shocked by these remarks and saddened by Peter's death.

So now I looked at Steve in a different light. Now he was something evil, something slimy. I was looking at dogshit. To this day, I don't know why I didn't rip the varnished flesh from his ridiculous fucking kisser. I regret my inaction. Sorry, Peter.

I flew to Manchester and was met by the pissing daughter who drove me to Liverpool, where I was to go into the fire station and retrieve the gear. Peter had three lockers: one for his clothes and two for the gear. We arrived but the busies (police) were already there. One hour earlier, Peter's colleagues had opened the lockers.

The pissing daughter should have taken care of this fucking hours ago instead of waiting for me to come from Spain. She could have saved Peter's family from the shame that followed the discovery of the hashish. The response to the find was incredible. Television and newspapers carried the story for days. How could such a respectable man be involved in the murky world of drugs?

This was unbelievable to his family, friends and colleagues: a mystery to everybody who knew him. Steve was gloating. I was scheming to get away and start my own business. I'd had enough of Steve and his pissing daughter. Peter's death meant finding a replacement, which was arranged by the daughter. Peter's replacement was a completely different character whom I decided to keep strictly at arm's length. No way was this character going to know anything other than where and when.

He was introduced to me at McDonald's in Widnes. He started

to ask questions so I told him my name was Uncle and I lived in Germany. 'Oh, spraken de doyche, eh? So can I. Heinz, zwy, dry, four, five. Belsen. Munchen fucking Gladbach.' I should have said, 'Auf Wiedersehen,' and goose-stepped all over his fucking head. I at least knew he wasn't the sharpest tool in the shed. So I said, 'OK, Rommel, let's fuck off and recce these pubs I want you to see.'

I took him to three pubs in Widnes. They were all within a mile of each other. We did not go in for a drink; these were our changeover locations. We drove from McDonald's up Lowerhouse Lane to the Albion public house. I told Rommel to remember that the Albion pub was no. 1 and the word Albion would never be used. We then drove to no. 2, which used to be called the Angel and Elephant, right next to St Bede's church, where I was christened during the war. No. 3 wasn't far away in Birchfield Road, a pub called the Horse and Jockey.

I knew these pubs when they used to sell good ale. You could taste the hops then. Flavour, bite, aroma, falling-over fluid, and going home pissed, doing the splits in dogshit all over the pavements. Everybody had a dog in those days. Dogshit everywhere. Dead dogs lying in the roads where they'd been run over: the good old days.

Dogs of all shapes and sizes used to be around then. I remember Smoky. He used to wait for us lads coming out of school. He was brown and white and looked like a baby elephant without a trunk. He understood every word that was said. Loads of fun with Smoky. He shagged everything he laid eyes on: dogs, bitches, old ladies' legs, even horseshit if it was still warm. Then he'd roll in it with his feet in the air with the daftest grin on his face. German shepherds were called Alsatians then, which brings me back to Rommel.

I had his contact number so I told him that when I called I would say, 'Hello, it's Uncle. Number two at six.' That is pretty obvious to anybody, but I will explain: number two is The Angel and Elephant, and six means 6 p.m. And it would be the following day. There was no money involved in the changeover; the pissing daughter was dealing with that. I knew it was time to change jobs.

Everything was finalised so I left him at the Horse and Jockey.

I walked through Victoria Park to my house half a mile away. My mother was delighted to see me, and the kettle was on for a pot of tea accompanied by a meat and potato pie. Lovely grub. The pie was the size of a British mark VII anti-tank mine with a flaky pastry crust on top, the food that nourished the Industrial Revolution. That was when most Englishmen were slaves and you had to go overseas to see a fez or a turban.

I remember the first turban I ever saw was a big turquoise thing atop this black fellow's head who had banged on our front door, trying to sell us stuff. I stood gawping at him as he was gobbing off at me in a strange tongue.

I shouted, 'Gran! There's a nigger at the door!'

My gran came to the door and the bloke said, 'Me no nigger. I from Bombay.'

My gran said, 'What possessed you to come all the way from Bombay to this house? Piss off,' and shut the door.

Two minutes later, I opened the door to see where he was. He was in the middle of the road swatting his battered suitcase at six dogs that were running rings round him. Oh, childhood memories. Not only had I never before seen a turban, but the local mongrels hadn't seen one either. My gran didn't like people from nearby Liverpool, so the Indian door-to-door salesman didn't stand a chance. That was in the days when Fanny was a girl's name and most black dogs were called 'Nigger'. Political correctness wasn't yet born, so the terminology used for foreigners wasn't frowned upon as it is today. I went to school with a lad called 'Nigger'. His skin was darker than usual and he went all through his childhood answering to that name because neither he nor his pals thought it was demeaning or offensive at that time. My, how times change!

My mum broke my thoughts with, 'What about this poor bloody fire-bobby, then?' I shat myself. Peter had been to our house several times to help me drop the tank and take the puff to Liverpool. My mum is 82 years old but she is still the brightest diamond in the Crown Jewels. 'Oh, sweet Jesus, please don't let her cop on to this,' I thought as I tried to contain the rush of the panic wave that had just hit me. But Peter's death was all over the telly, and I knew she'd remember him 'mending' that car. 'I've just arrived, Mam, I haven't heard the news yet.' I knew I was farting against thunder.

I was rescued by my cousin Ruth who arrived just in time: 'Oh, look who's bloody 'ere! Bloody hell! How are you doin', love? Bloody hell, it's good to see ya. Ya lookin' bloody good kid. Must be all them Spanish onions. They make you fart loud, don't they? Ha ha ha!'

The next question was always the same. It harked back to my army days, whenever I came home on leave. 'When are you going back?' I told her it was only a quick visit and I'd probably be on my way tomorrow.

'Have you got tea on the go, Olive? I'm as dry as Ken Dodd's jokes.'

I left them nattering as I went to the corner shop for a paper and the *Autotrader*. I was trying to decide about buying a new journey car. I couldn't concentrate because I knew I wasn't off the hook with my mother. My mother should have been a spy-catcher; Maclean, Burgess and Kim Philby would have been rumbled long before they escaped. She can clock a faggot from miles away. I am 'Military Positive Vetted'. I am also an anti-interrogation and anti-indoctrination instructor, trained by the best. The Joint Services Intelligence Wing didn't know about my mum so I didn't receive the training to defeat the ultimate interrogator. I think Mam's favourite music is the Harry Lime theme. But for now I am trying to get my head round a Rover 820 Vitesse.

I had made up my mind to leave Steve and go it alone. But there were still 80 kilos of puff in the stash in Spain. So there were still two trips to make before going it alone. There is a trading estate at Ditton Junction, Halebank, known locally as the Bermuda Triangle, a real den of iniquity. I have a distant relative whose name is David. He is a good man and an expert with Rover cars. He is as straight as a die and reliable. I had a bicycle in Mum's garage so I pedalled all the way down to Ditton bloody Junction. I had a chat with David and asked him to get me a Rover 820 petrol tank and two fuel pumps.

He said he would locate an 820 Vitesse for me and would have a tank and pumps ready for me when I next came home. Also, he would fit a new rubber timing belt when I got the car. I got him to drive me home with the bicycle in the boot. David never knew what I did for a living. He discovered that when I hit the headlines a few weeks later. So did my mother.

The journey car I was using at this time was a Rover but it was at the end of its journey life. There was nothing wrong with the car. It's just that I used a car three times and swapped it. I would deliver my load first, then replace the petrol tank and part exchange the car for another, normally the same model, and then put the working tank on the new car. I still have working tanks hidden away in Liverpool.

I returned to Spain the next day having avoided cross-examination from Mum, although I knew it was far from over. Her day was soon to come.

I reported to Steve the details of future handovers. He didn't seem to care. It was as though he had achieved something by Peter's demise and his heart was no longer in the job. There was no sense of urgency anymore. So much so that he said we should leave it for a while. I told him his pissing daughter and Rommel were keen to do the business and I couldn't sit on 80 kilos forever. So something had to happen. He wanted to go to the London pub in Fuengirola to drink to Peter. I was disgusted with him and refused the offer, saying I had bad vibes about such things, so I went home, scheming.

It was about this time that Pat the Rat came to see me at my *dojo*. Pat was used as a driver by a dealer and unfortunately I had a meet with him to take 50 kilos in a deal. He recognised me as being a martial-arts teacher and he knew my *dojo*. So he came to see me some weeks later do to a job for an Irish firm. They wanted to move gold bullion from Spain to Blighty, supposedly IRA bullion. Also, there would be plenty of hashish to move. He arranged for a meet in a restaurant at Los Boliches.

I used one of my motorbikes to go to Los Boliches and I parked it 200 metres away from the restaurant and strolled down the *paseo* complete with crash helmet, sunglasses and a bandana around my lower face, just like any biker would do. I walked into the party with Pat the Rat at the head of the table. I clocked a familiar face at a nearby table. Pat welcomed me and started to introduce me to the Micks. They were waffling and boozing. One bloke asked me to take off my helmet and have a drink. Then it dawned on me to look at the big fat familiar figure nearby.

It was Pepe, the chief inspector of the Fuengirola National Police Station. I looked at Pat and asked, 'Do you know him?' nodding my head in the direction of Pepe. Before I got an answer, Pepe burst into a loud coughing fit which I guessed was the signal for the Keystone Cops to come galloping in. I was pleased I hadn't removed my helmet as I turned and quickly walked away, ending any possibility of a golden future with the IRA.

I didn't see Pat the Rat for a while so I didn't know what the score was with that lot. But he appeared at my *dojo* again a few weeks later with another proposition. He wanted me to meet his son-in-law King Rat, Holmes the Grass, to organise a hashish run to Cambridgeshire. They wanted me to set up a journey car to run to Wisbech in Cambridgeshire. This happened just at the time I became disenchanted with Steve. So I told them I would think about it because I was quite busy with my martial-arts school. In fact, I was about to do my final journey for Steve.

Holmes wanted to set things up quickly and get cracking. I told him it took time to organise a car so I would try to fix one up between jobs that I was contracted to just then. So I told him that I needed a few weeks to get organised. Steve wanted to stop doing jobs for a while, so he told me to get rid of the car with the last load he was about to give me. This was great for me because I could part exchange this Rover for a Vitesse and use the same work-tank, saving myself time and money.

I knew young David in the Bermuda Triangle would have what I needed in a jiffy. But this wasn't to be, because Holmes contacted me and said he wanted to use a Volvo estate. He also said the work on the tank was to be done at his workshop and he would cover all expenses.

So I dealt with Steve's final load, but because Rommel was busy doing something else, I was left with 40 kilos on my hands, which I had to store in my mother's garage. I dog-proofed this stash and locked it in a steel filing cabinet. I also left the Rover work-tank under the garage window next to the cabinet. The garage was locked and I had the key. I hid the key in the top drawer of a sideboard in my bedroom in my mother's house.

I went to Liverpool and bought a very nice Volvo Estate in charcoal grey. I had all the usual jobs done to it, then set off to Holmes's cottage in southern England. I parked on the gravel frontage to the cottage. He invited me in and told me to relax and have a drink after my long drive.

He put on a video for me to pass the time while he took the car to the workshop for the tank change. I actually thought he had a work-tank ready and it was a simple matter of swapping tanks. He left me indoors alone looking at the video he had inserted, which was *Real Executions from Around the World*. I checked the other videos in the stack and they were all similar. I should have fucked off then because anybody who sits through live executions for entertainment should have been with Ronnie in Broadmoor.

It was dark when he came back. He was injured about the face, arms and head. His wife came in with him carrying a baby. She busied herself sorting out the baby whilst he explained about the tank exploding and all the problems it caused. Also, I would have to stay overnight because a new tank would be delivered in the morning, but I would catch an afternoon ferry from Dover the next day. So I settled down to an evening of brain spattering and a general chat about his career with 45 Royal Marine Commando and his adventures with the SAS.

Around the house, there were pictures of him in his SAS uniforms in various poses, but nothing of his ex-model wife. She turned out to be a lazy bitch because she sent him out for a fish and chip takeaway. There was only baby food in the house. I was starting to develop a dislike of these people and I should have allowed my instincts to grow and get me out of there. But I needed that car because this place was in the arsehole of nowhere.

In the morning when I awoke, Holmes had already left the house. His wife was also leaving the house to visit a relative so, 'Help yourself to breakfast.' Great. Breakfast was a choice of digestive biscuits or cornflakes with iffy milk. There was a nasty stink of shitty nappies around the place. I breakfasted and had a shower and made ready to leave. I was studying a map when

Holmes came back and told me it would be another hour, everything was perfect and his engineer friend was finishing the job while we would have some lunch. I wondered whether lunch would be digestive biscuits, cornflakes or perhaps a shitty nappy. But we used his car to drive to a café on the main road to Cambridge.

We were gone for more than an hour so I started to wonder about his engineer friend, when his mobile rang and after a quick chat he said he would take me back to his cottage while he got the car. He explained that his friend didn't want to see me. Nor did he want me to see him. I thought, 'Fair enough.'

I sat indoors for another hour, then the car arrived. Holmes told me there was plenty of petrol in the tank to get down to the filling station on the motorway. I put my things in the car and said my farewell and set off to the motorway and the filling station, which, he said, was just a few miles down the road. I ran out of fuel before I got there.

My first thought was, 'How did he get into the SA fucking S?' My confidence in that regiment was waning fast. A fucking chunky in the Pioneer Corps is brighter than Holmes.

I rolled silently down the motorway with the hazard lights flashing and managed to push the car unaided onto the forecourt of the filling station at the bottom of the hill. I had a long way to go and it was all going belly up.

The wankers had not cleaned the tank before fitting it. I had many stoppages. The car broke down completely just south of Madrid. It was Sunday so I had to pay for a *grua* (breakdown truck) to take me to a workshop. I didn't have a spare fuel pump. I was thinking, 'P-six, you gormless bastard. P fucking six!' The fuel pump sucked its last on the *carretera* just a few hundred metres from a gas station. I knew I had to replace it so I walked to the gas station and explained my predicament to the *señorita*. She telephoned her cousin, who was the local breakdown man. I treated myself to an ice cream and dawdled back to the car and waited for the *grua*. The *grua* arrived and within five minutes had winched the car up the loading ramp, where it was then secured with webbing straps.

Off we went to the *tallera* (workshop) where I would deal with the fuel pump. Paco the *grua* man telephoned a number of spare-parts dealers but because it was Sunday most of them were closed and the others didn't stock the fuel pump that was required. I pushed the car over the workshop pit, but Paco then told me I should not touch the car because he wasn't insured for me to work on his pit, but I wasn't to worry because he had sent for his brother who was a mechanic working for the Guardia Civil.

I quickly recovered from my cardiac arrest and ordered him to put the car back on the *grua* and take me and it to Fuengirola immediately. No way was I allowing a Guardia-Civil wanker near this petrol tank. Paco's eyeballs stuck out like racing-dogs' bollocks. '*Puta madre, señor!*' Then he asked if he could bring his wife and son on the trip to the seaside. I agreed to the family excursion and the monstrous price he quoted me for the journey to Fuengirola.

Twenty minutes later, the breakdown truck was like an old charabanc about to depart for a day out in Southend with half the street out waving goodbye. I didn't mind, anything to get away from here. I had telephoned my wife and asked her to contact a pal of mine called Black Bob. There were two reasons for doing this: first, to deliver the car to Bob's house instead of mine because I didn't want the brother of a policeman to know where I lived; second, because I knew Black Bob had more fuel pumps than you could shake a stick at.

Black Bob is actually a white man who earned his name by being the main dealer of Afghan black at the Glastonbury Festival years ago. He is a West Country shortarse with a sallow complexion and black curly hair worn long with a short beard and moustache, looking like he's fresh out of Haight-Ashbury, California. Actually, he reminds me of a rat squinting over a toothbrush. Nevertheless, he suited my purposes.

Bob is an opportunist who has a nice little set-up for working on cars. Quite discreet, really, considering it is in the heart of Los Boliches near Fuengirola. The house is set in a re-entrant, a gully next to a stream, surrounded by thickets of bamboo which prevents nosy spicks from piping the goings on. Bob and I had worked together before so I wasn't too fussed about him clocking the car. I was later to regret this because when Holmes eventually grassed me I mistakenly thought it could have been Bob, because only Holmes and Bob knew about this tank. But Bob knew nothing about my movements; only Holmes could have grassed me and I proved this at my trial.

Holmes was becoming a nuisance. He kept on calling me from England, asking me to contact his father-in-law, Pat the Rat. Pat had a consignment of hashish ready to send to Wisbech in Cambridgeshire and he was frustrated because he knew the Volvo estate was in Spain. The problems I'd had with the petrol tank should have been enough for me to walk away from this job. I'd had problems since the moment Holmes put his shitty fingers near the bloody thing. I should have given the car to Pat the Rat and told him to find somebody else, but I was distracted by all the work I had to do.

I had a consignment to take to Middlesbrough for Tattoo John, an abusive, unrefined thug who lives in Los Boliches, plus I had an arrangement with Black Bob to start a journey to Birmingham. The Volvo estate's petrol tank was not such a good idea after all. Holmes's engineer had done a good job with the actual welding, but the hashish compartment could only hold 35 kilos. The incompetent arseholes should have made it bigger, so I had located another petrol tank in Liverpool, which I would collect after I had delivered to Middlesbrough.

I had taken 35 kilos from Tattoo John's stash and loaded it into the petrol tank. This was the first trip for this car loaded up, so after scrupulously cleaning the inside of the petrol tank and fitting a new fuel pump – which Holmes and his pal had so neglectfully not bothered to do when they had finished welding – it was ready to be cosmetically prepared.

I took the car to a steam-cleaning unit in Fuengirola and had it completely cleaned in readiness for underwaling, which was done professionally across town in my friend Tony's workshop. I then drove the car into the ford opposite the entrance to Hotel Biblos on the Coín road to soak the underside with river water. Alongside the river was a dusty track where I sped up and down for a minute or so, stopping in the clouds of dust. I then drove home to let the car dry in my garage so that I could painstakingly check every single nut or bolt that I had touched during the loading and securing of the tank.

Each individual nut that my tools had touched had to be treated so that, should it be examined, there was absolutely no evidence of it having recently been undone or touched by tools of any description. The best method of doing this is to carefully spray a tiny mist of WD-40 onto the nut or bolt head. Too much does not work, so practise first. Then take the paper bag from your domestic vacuum cleaner and puncture it with a pin, making a tiny hole so that when you gently squeeze it a tiny jet of dust can be sprayed onto the heads of the nuts and bolts, thereby hiding any evidence that the undersealing might have missed. I also used this method to hide any evidence of tampering with inspection covers and resetting electric connectors. I cover all my tracks.

Give the car a polish and prepare the inside with whatever bits and pieces apply to your reason for travelling. In my case, it was always martial-arts kit, boxing gloves, headguards, clothing, *nunchaku*, focus mitts, medicine ball and martial-arts magazines. I would call a martial-arts centre or *dojo* belonging to people I knew and tell them I would be passing through their area shortly so I'd pop in to say hello and give their students a free seminar. This would always be welcomed enthusiastically by any *dojo*, so I would plan my journey accordingly.

For this journey to Middlesbrough, I called a *dojo* in France and another in England to arrange the dates and cover my arse should I be stopped and questioned. I never gave them much notice so they couldn't advertise my coming. My timings were such that I would be on my way in two or three days' time. I would tell Susan about the seminars, which she took in good heart because she had to take my students in my absence. Susan is also a black belt in ju-jitsu and worked as an instructor with me on a daily basis. The only person who would know my departure time was Susan and she didn't know it yet.

On the night before my departure for Middlesbrough in February 1997, I told Susan to tell my students that I was doing a seminar in France and I would be back in a few days' time. In the early hours, she cooked my breakfast and packed my cooler box with my favourite sticky buns and fruit. We said our fond farewells at 0500hrs in the darkness of a sepia dawn.

I decided to take the route from Malaga to Granada, then on to Jaén to join the N1V *carretera* to Madrid. The reason for this decision was because it was raining and the *carretera* to Granada was then under construction so I knew the road would be thick with mud and I wanted it to be splashed up underneath the car: loads of it. The road to Antequera and then on to Córdoba would have been slightly quicker but hiding the evidence of my tampering was more important than speed.

The rain stopped just before I got to Jaén, and by this time I'd given the car's underside a great thick coating of mud. The journey from Jaén to Madrid was uneventful but the traffic became heavy on the ring road before I reached the N11 to Zaragoza, then on to the N123 to Huesca. From Huesca, the journey is most enjoyable with scenic beauty all around. When I reached Sabiñanigo, I joined the minor road to Biescas and then I was in the Pyrenees proper.

I filled my tank at Biescas and put my pesetas in my spickbox. I then put my frogbox where the spickbox sat in the centre console, stowing the spickbox in a plastic bag under the passenger seat so I didn't get mixed up with frog, spick and sterling. I would put the frogbox away when I got on the ferry.

I drove over the beautiful Pyrenees mountains and sped through the unmanned frontier crossing into France, where I stopped at the picturesque little town of Laruns for a snack and coffee at a super little café that I'd found the year before. Having rested, I drove down the French side of the Pyrenees to the town of Pau where I planned to spend the night, but because the traffic was light and because I had driven hard and fast, I decided to go on to Bazas where I knew a nice little hotel with a wonderful chef; so I pressed on.

I booked into a nice room overlooking the car park so I put the car under my window and immobilised it before showering and changing for dinner. Smuggling is a very risky business so I endeavoured to enjoy myself whilst working, up to the hilt, if you know what I mean.

The pâté in this region of France is the best in the world so I ordered a *foie gras truffé du chef*, which I knew to be the chef's pride and joy. It gave me great joy to see that it was available this night; this was to be an immense and rare treat. But first I had *bouillabaisse* with a glass of excellent dry wine, which the landlady said was local. It came in a cut-glass carafe just big enough to hold two full glasses. I finished my first course and waited a few minutes before the landlady returned with a fresh carafe and a clean wine glass. She poured the new wine into the new glass as the chef himself brought my second course and placed it proudly before me. '*Merci, chef.*'

'*Bon appétit*, my loverly Eengleesh gentlemen,' he said as he swiftly pirouetted and disappeared into his domain, all floppy white hat, crimson cravat and flour dust. I noticed the chef only brought out the *foie gras*, he let the landlady do everything else: they must have been married. I tasted my *foie gras truffé du chef*, which was sliced and served on a bed of lettuce accompanied by a *salade chiffonnade* sprinkled with a sweet white wine, making this possibly the finest plateful of haute cuisine I have ever experienced. I then tasted the wine, which surprised me because it was sweet but went with the *foie gras* perfectly. The landlady told me it was an old Barsac from an ancient chateau. I rounded off my dinner with a giant helping of strong sherry trifle with a large glass of cream sherry to chase it down. Thank you, Dionysus.

I left my table and went to reception to use the public phone to call Susan just to wish her good night and sling some slop and lovey-dovey down the line, but she alarmed me by telling me that Holmes had called from England asking to speak to me. She had told him that I was doing a ju-jitsu seminar in France so I wasn't available. He asked her to tell me to call him as soon as possible. I knew that Holmes would guess I was working so I felt slightly compromised but what the hell, I'd carry on and call him when I'd unloaded the car. I banished him from my mind as Susan got sloppy and the lovey-dovey drooled all over the French connection.

I popped my head out the door to check the car and climbed the stairs to my welcoming bed where Dionysus battered me unconscious with earthenware flagons of *vino collapso*, the result of long, hard driving, stress and not much wine.

I was up with the larks – shit, shave and shower, bag packed and down to a breakfast of *café avec croissants*. Strange race, the frogs; their dinners are something else, but their breakfasts are shite. I chucked my bag in the boot, then took a piece of toilet paper to wipe the dipstick before I set off for the ferry port. I planned to catch the ferry *Stena Antrim* at 1545hrs from Dieppe to Newhaven. I could have caught the later *Lynx III*, which is faster and takes only an hour and a quarter to get across the Channel, but there are more vehicles on the bigger *Stena Antrim*, so the Customs have more vehicles to cope with. So that's where I was going to be at 1500hrs.

I was quickly onto the motorway to Bordeaux, then changed lanes to get on the Route nationale A10/E05, passing Pons, Poitiers and coming off at Tours to pick up the N138 to drive through Le Mans, Alençon and up to Rouen where I joined the N27 to Dieppe. I bought my ticket and boarded the *Stena Antrim* for the three-hour journey across the English Channel to Newhaven where Her Majesty's Customs & Excise were eagerly awaiting my return to dear old Blighty.

I drove off the ferry amongst the slow-moving line of traffic streaming from the unloading ramp. Alarm bells rang in my head as two Customs officers beckoned me out of the line. I could see the main gates to the ferry terminal were closed so nobody was able to get out of here in a hurry. They escorted me into a workshop area, which was immediately locked behind me, so nobody else was being searched today. I knew I was in the shit and I also knew Holmes had grassed me.

I was asked the usual questions and the car was rummaged, but I carried on my charade of innocence just as they carried on their charade of rummaging the car to make it look like their professionalism was how I was going to get caught. What a load of bollocks. They think everybody is as daft as they are.

The car was moved onto a ramp and raised about 5 ft off the ground so their mechanic could get under it. I knew I had been grassed when the clown in overalls said, 'There's a spanner mark on this nut, and there's another one here. This tank looks as though it's been taken off recently.' The stark realisation that these bad actors were the recipients of information that could only have come from a rat of the lowest order posing in an SAS uniform who had supplied me with the tank and set me up a treat created an intense and enduring loathing, especially when the word 'entrapment' sprang to mind.

The fact that I'd paid so much attention to detail regarding spanner rash on everything I touched was beginning to anger me as the clown with the tools was saying, 'Oh look, here's another one with spanner marks on it.' Talk about overacting. These fuckers could get star parts on *Neighbours* or some other shite Australian soap opera. They continued their charade but the excitement was too great for them to do it well. The chubby ginger-haired thespian who turned out to be my arresting officer kept approaching me rubbing his hands, saying, 'Do you want to tell me what's in the tank now?'

'Petrol,' I said, continuing my charade of innocence.

He kept coming back every two minutes asking the same question, not able to contain his excitement.

Eventually, the fuel was drained and the tank removed, which was obviously heavier than it should have been. The petrol tank was then put through an X-ray machine, which showed a dark area on the screen revealing the hashish compartment. The Customs officers were trying to figure out how to get into the compartment but they were flummoxed by the ingenuity of the hide. The lid was fitted on a stepped flange and secured with countersunk screws, which were hidden by a rubberoid compound, hiding the screws and the gap between lid and flange. Sherlock Holmes with his spyglass couldn't find the lid so these fuckers were going to be here all night.

The chubby ginger-headed thespian could no longer contain himself. He grabbed my wrist and said, 'Right! I am arresting you for importing cannabis resin. Come with me now to the custodial suite where you will be formally charged with importing that cannabis.' He said this while stabbing his finger at the petrol tank, which of course was still a mystery regarding its contents. Again, the word 'entrapment' appeared in my mind. The other officers possibly twigged that their informant was now compromised, but they really couldn't give a fuck about that life; this petrol tank was much more interesting right now. So, I was marched away from the unopened petrol tank to be charged with importing cannabis, which had not yet been found. If you are a grass, or contemplating the worm's arse prospects, you need to read this paragraph over and over. Better still: write it all down and stick it to the ceiling above your bed.

The arresting officer pulled me away and escorted me to the custodial suite on the top floor of the main office building, where I was shown into a tiny room with a wide shelf with a mattress on it, obviously my bed for the night.

I said to the arresting officer, 'I bet you don't know the worm who grassed me, do you?'

'You wasn't grassed, I caught you red-handed with the drugs.'

'What fucking drugs? I haven't seen any drugs and neither have you. That petrol tank is full of horseshit for all you know.' The Customs officer's face went beetroot red. 'You don't know the fucking worm who grassed me, but I do, and I'll make sure he knows who is responsible for all the horrible things that's going to happen to his fucking household. He's a fucking dead man now and he'll be looking over his shoulder till the day he dies: which won't be long, thanks to you.'

'I have to write everything down you say, so all this will be said at your trial,' said the creep who was now spluffing and obviously disturbed, but still excited with his collar.

'Don't forget the word "entrapment" and I reckon you should go for a wank before you shoot your cocoa into your uniform.' He looked at me as though it might be a good idea to do just that. A collar is better than a fuck for these weirdos.

It wasn't so long ago that the BBC did a series on Customs officers. There was also a book published to accompany the series called *The Duty Men*. In that book is mentioned Customs Officer Darren Herbert. This man found 40 kilos of hashish in a car and became so excited he declared that he was supposed to start his holidays that night but now he was so excited that he didn't want to go! His co-worker, Customs Officer Hedley Beaumont, remarked that this was better than sex! Take note, Mrs Beaumont, especially when he starts moaning about going to work. Mind you, when he says his job is better than sex it doesn't say much for his sex life, does it?

It wasn't long before it got busy around me and they started to question me. They were so excited, it was like the Boys' Brigade getting ready for the communal shower. I shouted, 'Woah, I need a fucking lawyer here before I say a word.'

The arresting officer said, 'There's one coming, he'll be here in a minute but we can chat until he comes.'

'No, we fucking won't. I need a piss, and a cup of tea would be nice. You blokes are brewing up all fucking day long, that's why you've all got fat arses, sitting around supping tea all day. So how about a brew?'

They all looked at me in silence, then looked at a man in civilian clothes standing just outside the door. 'Take him for a piss and get him some tea and biscuits.' The man turned on his heel and walked away to another office, slamming the door behind him. I noticed that he wasn't as excited as the rest of them. He knew that I knew I'd been grassed and I guessed he was the boss here, rather than being with Customs Intelligence, and therefore ultimately responsible for compromising the informant.

At last, the brief arrived, a lawyer from Brighton who breezed in waffling about him being an officer who had served in Northern Ireland and if I went along with what was said then maybe I'd get a shorter sentence, especially if I gave the names of everybody I knew. I fucked him off out of it so they brought another one who wasn't so full of his fucking self.

We got down to making a statement, which was being recorded on two tapes. The arresting officer began to question me by asking me where was I taking the cannabis. 'I haven't seen any cannabis. That petrol tank had gold in it, not cannabis.'

'You don't expect us to believe that, do you?'

'I don't care a fuck what you believe, it's what the jury believes that matters.'

'But the petrol tank was full of cannabis, wasn't it?'

'How should I know what it's full of? You arrested me and charged me before anybody could see what was in the tank. I am a courier transporting gold for a titled person and my destination is Hatton Garden in London. I personally have not seen the contents of that petrol tank but I believe it to be gold.' The arresting officer became quite agitated and blurted, 'Thirty-five kilos of gold is a lot heavier than thirty-five kilos of hashish. You must think we are stupid.'

My brief said, 'Thirty-five kilos of toilet rolls weighs the same as thirty-five kilos of gold, so what exactly are you trying to say?'

'That gold is a lot heavier than cannabis so a tank full of gold is much heavier than thirty-five kilos of cannabis.' I could see the two Customs officers were somewhat confused and then angered when my brief and I let go our suppressed laugh.

Later that night, a team of Customs officers from Manchester, accompanied by police from Widnes, turfed my 80-year-old mother out of bed and ransacked her house. The rummagers couldn't find the key to the garage so they rang the custodial suite to let my mother ask me where the garage key was. My mother was quite upset but told me that other family members were on their way to comfort her. I told her to get whoever came first to call me at the custodial suite urgently. 'Don't worry about the key, Mam, I've got it.' She went on to say that the Customs men couldn't get into the garage because I had the key, so they would be back in the morning with a locksmith. I reminded my mother that whoever came to comfort her must call me no matter what the time was.

At 0200hrs, I received a call from a close relative. The officer guarding me passed the phone into my cell thinking it was to do with the house search. 'The police and Customs are just leaving the house now. What's going on?'

'Go upstairs to my room when they've gone. In the top drawer of the dressing table you will find a watch. Stuck on the backplate of the watch is the garage key. When the coast is clear, open the garage and remove the backpacks from the metal filing cabinet and take them somewhere safe. Under no circumstances do you open those packs, you do not know what they contain, just put them somewhere safe for me and I will tell you what to do with them later when I am in a position to do so. You will also find a petrol tank directly under the garage window. Remove it and put it somewhere it can't be found. You need to be quick about this because this phone will be bugged.' I gave these instructions to a person who has never done a wrong thing in their life.

My instructions were carried out so the next morning the Customs officers and locksmith found fuck all. The filing cabinet was empty and the petrol tank was now living in Liverpool. If the

Customs officers had bothered to inspect the carpet that was on the garage floor, they would have found evidence of my activities. It was cold on that concrete floor working underneath a car, so I had a nice thick carpet fitted wall to wall: one pass with a vacuum cleaner and I would have been in the can.

That was my only oversight, so when I got bail later on I removed the carpet during my first night in Widnes. I lost a lot of sleep over that carpet. The metal filing cabinet was taken away for forensic testing but the gear was packed properly so as not to attract dogs, so I had no worries there. Amazingly, the carpet lay there untouched until I came home and fucked it off out of there.

All of my tools were removed and a tube of sealant, which I'd used to reseal the lid on the petrol tank, was taken for forensic examination. There was no trace of anything so my thanks go to Shagpile, the Greek god of floor-coverings, for making my carpet invisible to the hob-nailed boots that trampled my mother's house.

Though my luck deserted me when Holmes grassed me, I had got rid of a working tank and 40 kilos of best Moroccan, and all this was done courtesy of the custodial suite telephone. I can't forget all those hob-nailed boots standing on my carpet, removing all the bits and pieces from the garage. Amazing.

I was taken from Newhaven Customs House to Eastbourne police station where I was processed into a dank cell. My fingerprints, photo and DNA sample were taken and a friendly bobby gave me a cup of tea. I stayed overnight in Eastbourne and was then taken to Lewes court where I was remanded in custody to Lewes prison.

This was my first experience of prison so everything was strange and ominous. I had this horrible expectation of something really offensive happening. I was taken from the prison van into the processing hall where I had to wait with several remand prisoners. I didn't wait long. A screw called my name so I went to his counter where he took various particulars. I noticed I was already entered as a martial-arts instructor on the induction sheet. I said to him, 'That's a mistake, I'm a lorry driver.' He muttered something about Customs officers and refused to change it. I was then ushered into a cubicle and told to strip off: everything. The screw asked me to bend over so he could look up my arse. My genuine anger was immediately apparent so the screw said, 'Yeah, OK, you don't look the type.'

I was then taken to the remand wing where I had to wait until another screw arrived who would allocate me a cell. 'I've got just the cell for you, matey,' he said, smirking like Kenneth Williams. 'I'm putting you in with Macormack, you'll like him.' He took me to a cell at the far end of the wing away from the screws' office. The screw opened the cell so I could put my few belongings in there on the top bunk. He then brought me out again and locked it. 'You can stay here until they all get back from the gym. They won't be long, then you'll see if there's anybody you know in here and you'll meet your cellmate, Macormack.'

A lot of loud shouting started coming from the main corridor so I guessed everybody was back from the gym. The wing door opened and men streamed in shouting and abusing each other in an effort to sound unaffected by living in this dreadful place. A couple of blokes came over to ask me who I was, which cell I was in and why I was in here. They looked concerned when I said I was with Macormack.

'Oh, fuckin' 'ell, mate, nobody goes near that mad cunt. Everybody who gets put in with him ends up in fuckin' 'ospital. 'E's fuckin' mental an' 'e's in 'ere for attempted murder. You'll need to watch your fuckin' self.'

Just then, a big round-faced bloke with short-cropped hair came over to me: 'I 'ear you bin put in wid me, mate.'

'Yeah, afraid so, pal,' I said.

'No fucker gets put in wid me so go tell the fuckin' screw you wants anudder fuckin' cell.'

'You tell the fucking screw yourself. I have fuck all influence in here.'

'The screws are playin' a fuckin' game 'coz dey knows I'll fuckin' kill ya durin' the night. I bet it's dat cunt Conroy who put you in wid me.'

'I haven't got a clue who the screw is and I don't give a flying fuck, mate. I'm in the same cell as you and I can do fuck all about that, so let's get used to the idea, because rest assured, my friend, you will get the surprise of your fucking life if you try anything with me in that fucking cell.' He now knew the score regarding intimidation; it wouldn't fucking work with me. He was also wondering how big a handful I would be should it kick off.

Macormack turned out to be a harmless bully, intimidating younger, smaller prisoners, but with me he was a gentleman, but who gives a fuck? Nothing much happened in Lewes prison that warrants an entry in this journal because the screws, inmates and environment simply did not compare to the true shitholes of Spain, one of which I am sat in right now writing this journal.

I eventually got bail and was confined to Widnes until my trial started ten months later. Nothing much happened during the ten months' bail apart from an attempt to recruit me by two different agencies that run undercover grasses who infiltrate the groups of smugglers on the Costa del Sol. I pointed out that Holmes was one of theirs and he was now in fear of losing his life, especially since I called several people who had lost business because of him. The smuggling world is quite small and since I'd been on bail and using my telephone, I discovered there are at least three other men from different groups languishing at Her Majesty's pleasure. Their intense hatred of Holmes will make it necessary for Holmes to leave the country when they get out. I don't suppose for one minute he considered the danger he has put his wife and baby in; his handlers don't care a fuck either.

In mid-January 1998, my trial date came at last, and Susan had come across from Spain so we booked into the Black Lion hotel on the outskirts of Brighton for the duration of the trial, which was to last for three days at Lewes Crown Court. At the beginning of the trial, the judge cleared the court before the jury entered to tell me and my brief, barrister Jeremy Gold, that the prosecution was based on information received and it was in the protection of the public interest that the informant's identity not be revealed. Jeremy Gold had a rant about this and said privately to me that we didn't have a chance. I instructed him to make certain I did not take the stand today, and to keep the Customs officers in the witness box so they told lies all day, because if the grass could not be mentioned they would have to lie about it and that's what I wanted them to do.

So the jury and I listened all day to the Customs officers lying about how their natural instinct for sniffing out smugglers was so good they selected only me from that great boatload of vehicles from the *Stena Antrim* roll-on, roll-off ferry. Trucks, vans, coaches, motor cars, motorbikes and pedestrians all rolled off onto the streets of England without being looked at. Mine was the single vehicle that was stopped and searched. The fact that they were working on information received was not mentioned on day one of the trial.

I stayed awake most of the night concocting my defence. I knew Jeremy Gold could not help me now. I took control of things and Jeremy knew that I held the reins so he sat back to watch me wriggle off the hook.

I was sworn in the next day and off I went: knowing the best form of defence is to attack, I started by telling the jury that they had lost a day in their lives yesterday listening to a pack of lies. Not just a little lie, but a daylong session of rehearsed lies, ricocheting off each other all around the courtroom. 'But don't forget, ladies and gentlemen, they swore on this Bible, then blatantly lied to you, because the reason I am here is that they acted on information received. I am not allowed to disclose his identity, but I'm going to tell you all about him.'

I established the fact that I had been grassed by a paid Customs informer; I talked at length about Holmes without disclosing his identity. The judge now knew exactly what was going on because he obviously knew all about Holmes before the trial started.

So now I explained to the jury how I used to take Russian gold to Mannheim in Germany for a titled person who lives in Marbella on the Costa del Sol. I used to do this regularly and occasionally bring gold over to Hatton Garden, London. I then explained that I did not know how much gold was actually in the petrol tank, but I did not have a problem with that because I was accustomed to delivering my cargo to gold-smelting plants. So I really had no reason to suspect there was anything other than gold in the petrol tank.

I explained that Holmes worked for the Baroness and was instrumental in converting the petrol tank and packing the gold inside. So this time he loaded it with cannabis instead of gold and the evil man set me up as a smokescreen for himself because he had another car on the same ferry loaded with something worth a darn sight more than a few kilos of puff. I went on about him being a maverick and explained that a maverick is a Customs informant who is rewarded for each conviction by his handlers, who are Customs Intelligence officers, and his reward is a percentage of the value of the contraband. At the same time, he continues to smuggle, hoping his paymasters will turn a blind eye, or at least be lenient with him. This particular maverick was at this moment laughing up his sleeve at the Customs because he probably watched them dancing around my car as he drove through with millions of pounds worth of whatever he was smuggling. So now he was laughing again because he would get a reward for loading my car with cannabis and using it to occupy his paymasters so he could come through Customs safely with something worth serious money. I was the smokescreen used to dupe his paymasters and they would pay him at the end of this trial for grassing me. I purposely didn't mention entrapment; the jury could think for themselves.

I spent as much time as possible denigrating the Customs officers and Holmes and underlining the fact that they were linked. At one point, I actually picked up the Bible and pointed it at the Customs officers sitting together in the gallery. 'Look at them; they all used this Bible yesterday to swear they were telling the truth to you lot in the jury. They were so taken with their informant they arrested me before the contents of the petrol tank were exposed. I stand here before you with this Bible and say that I was never shown the contents of that petrol tank by those liars over there.' I expected a reprimand from the judge but he merely nodded his head. I managed to survive and succeeded in making the jury angry at the Customs officers.

Later that day, my brother-in-law took the stand to explain away the various sealants that Customs had taken to forensics. He had actually used the sealants to fill and repair joints at my mother's house. The man has never done a wrong thing in his life. He is a grandfather who still goes to work every day. The prosecution unsuccessfully attempted a character assassination on him, but he is simply a nice man, hard working and conscientious.

He was ridiculed and laughed at by the Customs in the gallery but the jury knew he was an honest, normal man.

The judge did the summing up, making himself neutral by neither condemning me nor praising me. Fortunately, he mentioned my military career, which was exemplary, so that went down like the *Titanic* with the Customs.

On the morning of the final day of my trial, I stood on the courtroom steps nursing my baby granddaughter. Everybody, including Customs officers and members of the jury, had to walk past me as I crooned the Beatles song 'Let It Be' to the baby in my arms. One of the Customs officers sidled next to me, saying, 'You are going down, you cunt, that baby ain't going to fucking save you.'

'Your grass Holmes is going down too: 6 ft down and his baby won't save him either, you cunt.'

When the judge finished his summing up, the jury went out and the court was cleared. An hour later, we were called back in and the judge said the jury was split so we had to go back out again to do some more nail-biting. Another hour went by and we were called in again; the judge accepted an eleven to one verdict in my favour.

The feeling of relief was incredible. My heartfelt thanks went to each member of the jury except the one bloke who went against me, who apparently was a friend of one of the Customs officers who was in court. I heard this from two of the jurors. So everything came to a happy ending as Susan was thanking each of the jurors with tears of joy running down her face.

I called my mother to put an end to her grief and told her that I was going from Lewes to Spain. I wasn't coming home to celebrate because I didn't feel safe with HMC&E. Steve would send somebody else to pick up his stash, so I didn't have to worry about that. I had a beat-up Vauxhall Cavalier in the borough council car park. So we cleared off out of court and headed for Newhaven to catch the ferry, but I changed my mind and headed for Portsmouth to catch the midnight ferry to Caen, France.

I got the car into the queue and bought our sailing tickets. I went to a public phone and called Holmes: 'You fucking slimy grass, you will be dead soon.' I put down the handset and waited.

I knew he would get this number and call back. It started to ring. 'Hello, Her Majesty's Customs and Excise,' I said, waiting for a reply. 'Can I help you, please? This is Customs at Portsmouth.'

'Oh, who is actually there? Because somebody just called me from that number and we got cut off.'

'Sorry, sir, there's only plain-clothes officers here now.'

'Oh, which ones are they, who are they?'

'Well, sir, I can't disclose officers' names over the phone,' I said in my really good Australian accent.

'Put one of them on, please, I want to talk to somebody there.'

I replaced the handset without saying another word.

'Well?' said Susan.

'We're going home, sweetheart, nobody else matters.'

Sadly, of course, that wasn't to be my last experience of a courtroom, but more about this later. It's my bedtime now and I want to think about my Susan as I fall asleep.

EIGHT

The howl of pain froze the pen in my hand. Screams were coming from the hallway leading to the stinking row of lavatories. Vanessa was being raped.

I arrived on the scene and pushed my way through the silent, gawping Spaniards. Zombie, a giant Negro, was brutally thrusting his enormous dork into Vanessa's backside. He was naked apart from the shorts around his ankles.

I could see he had attacked Vanessa before the rape because blood was flowing from the transsexual's nose, mouth and ears. Zombie's left hand had a grip on Vanessa's long hair and had the head pulled painfully back. His right hand had Vanessa's arm bent back and forced up between the shoulder blades. Blood cascaded down between their legs due to the ripping of Vanessa's arsehole. The anal canal was getting the good news deep into the rectum. Zombie had stabbed Vanessa's arse with a broken brush handle before entering himself.

I felt immediate shock and anger, so with great force and accuracy, I delivered *empi*, an elbow strike, to the base of Zombie's skull. I followed this with a left- and right-hand *haito* (chop) to each carotid artery and swiftly applied *shime waza* (a chokehold) with my left forearm across his windpipe by giving him a reverse forearm smash, then putting on the choke. I pulled

114

him backwards and downwards so he sat on his arse and his shoulder blades were forced back against my bent knee. I then commenced to choke the life out of him.

I made my attack more effective by forcing my head against Zombie's head and with both hands clasped I pulled the bone in my forearm deeper into the throat, crushing the windpipe. At the same time, I was digging the knuckle of my thumb into his sternocleidomastoid muscle, enabling me to crush the Adam's apple, larynx and thyroid cartilage just like a vice crushing a walnut.

As I was choking the life out of him, Vanessa was busy shredding his scrotum with a razor blade. Zombie was a few moments away from death when I released my *hadake-jime* chokehold. He flopped backwards, banging his great head on the concrete floor. I trod on his throat with my right foot just in case he woke up. I stood looking at Vanessa taking vengeance, looking more like Hannibal Lecter by the second. Zombie's genitals looked like a jar of pickled red cabbage broken on the floor. I pushed the transsexual away from the beast and told him to get cleaned up. I guided him toward the washbasins as his countrymen ran to blab their story to the screws. I was amazed I wasn't banged up in the punishment block.

The incident reminded me of an old joke that went like this: who is the 17-st. Negro who rode a Derby winner? Lester Piggot's cellmate. Poor old Lester: a national hero banged up by the taxman for a victimless crime.

Zombie and Vanessa were taken to the infirmary. I was worried because the story coming from there was that Zombie was dead, so I was calling myself all the stupid bastards alive because I had gone way too far just to save a useless transsexual's arse. Zombie and Vanessa were still in the infirmary that night when I had a visit from a screw.

An interrogation was about to happen and the interrogator was Manuel, a Shotokan black belt whom I had met a few years earlier in La Moraleja prison, where I was the boss of the *polideportivo* (main gymnasium) and the prison martial-arts instructor.

All male staff in Spanish prisons must be addressed with the title

'Don', i.e. Don Manuel, Don Pepe, etc. I called everybody 'Jefe' which means 'Boss' and is pronounced 'Heffie'.

Don Manuel guessed it was me who decked Zombie because apart from the wreckage of his wedding tackle there were no other cuts or bruises. Because he is a Negro, my work was hidden by the natural colour of his skin, but the spick grasses had already told him everything, so I was farting against thunder by telling him it wasn't me.

Don Manuel's primary task was to discover how I had wasted that great hulking beast, Zombie. It was in the interest of all the screws because when Zombie had kicked off previously, they'd had to deal with him mob-handed. They'd also administered Largactil, better known as the liquid cosh, which is illegal in Europe, but the Spanish don't care a fuck about legalities. This is how he got the name Zombie, because the previous year he was injected with Largactil and overnight he became a zombie, getting about by using the Largactic shuffle, resembling an old codger trying to find his Zimmer-frame. Instant Alzheimer's disease, issued from the end of a needle.

Unruly prisoners are dealt with in this manner to keep them under control. I witnessed this in the Carabanchel, Valdemoro, La Moraleja and Alhaurin de la Torre, Malaga prison. I once spoke to a Negro who was on the receiving end of this treatment. I spoke to him before, during and after the treatment. He explained that from the first jab until he was weaned off it, he was in suspended animation and remembers nothing of the shuffling period. He was a noisy, funny, jack-in-the-box type fellow, full of life and cheeky as a monkey, but hard as nails when dealing with screws. That was his downfall.

One day, he kicked off with the screws; the next day he had the Largactic shuffle. They brought him out of it because he was due for release, but I spoke to him about it and he said it was great because he did his bird without realising it. Funny bloke; unlike Zombie, who, for my money, was a giant sociopath, a troglodyte looking for his club. He would grab smack dealers by the throat, forcing them to give him a fix, so the dealers wised up to this and used him to collect bad debts, thereby earning his keep. Zombie loved his work, he put the fear of Christ up everybody. He was unpredictable: one minute trying to be funny and impressive, the next, a lurching, frenzied 300-lb lunatic. I am over 200 lbs with an 18-in. neck, but Zombie puts me in the shade. His hands are enormous. When he makes a fist, his hand looks like a Hovis loaf. So Manuel the screw was truly interested in the techniques I used to put Zombie away.

I told him I had nothing to do with it, but I heard somebody had used *empi* to the nape of his neck, which was probably the knockout blow, followed by a left- and right-hand chop using the thumb and forefinger knuckle to impact the carotid artery and mastoid nerve, followed by a reverse forearm smash into the Adam's apple, applying an instant chokehold from the forearm smash, then forcing a backward takedown, sitting him on his arse using the knee to prevent backward motion and choking him out.

I told him that the shredding of the genitals was done by somebody else. I was aware of his wishful thinking as a knowing smile spread across his hard, bony face as he visualised himself in his mental *kata*, chopping and choking the shit out of the hated Zombie.

In the confines of my cell, he asked me to demonstrate *hadake jime* on him in a sitting position. For a moment, I thought there was a catch in it, but then I realised he was absolutely serious, and wanted to see just how effective this technique really is. It also told me I was off the hook. I knew I was out of the Zombie shit when I showed this bastard how to do *hadake jime*. I placed my exercise mat on the concrete floor and told him to sit facing the door. I knelt behind him, gently putting my left forearm across his throat with my radius bone pressed lightly against his windpipe on the upper edge of his Adam's apple. My knee was between his shoulder blades and I had gripped my left hand with my right. I put my head forward next to his and pulled on the choke, very carefully demonstrating how to use his shoulder as a fulcrum for my right forearm, simultaneously pressing and probing my thumb knuckle into his carotid artery, thereby completing the strangle.

There are pressure points in this area of the neck relating to acupuncture, the meridian system and *kyusho jitsu*, which is a specialised martial-arts system using devastating nerve strikes in its techniques. Alas, my Spanish is not good enough to explain all this to a thick screw, so I had to subject Manuel to a smidgen of pain. Nevertheless, I achieved my aim. I underlined the fact that I am a professional martial artist and I was free of the Zombie shit.

I then allowed him to practise the technique on me so he knew perfectly well how to apply it. Applying it is easy; getting your arm around an opponent's neck is a different kettle of fish, especially if he is a practising martial artist.

Manuel quietly left my cell but everybody on the wing knew he was visiting me. A thick silence hung in the air until the clang of the bottom gate closing told everybody he had gone. Then the normal buzz and chatter of the wing began, and the inmates lucky enough to have tellies turned them back up, satisfied that the danger of random cell searches had passed. I settled down to my writing.

The next day, Vanessa returned to the wing with an uncontrived mincing gait. Quite funny to watch, really, especially as he sat down. Zombie was doing the Largactic shuffle down in the punishment block out of harm's way.

Don Manuel is of dubious character, like most Spanish prison officers. Nearly all of them have a screw loose (no pun intended), making them unpredictable with schizoid tendencies. But they also have a superiority complex with a contrived strut reserved for the confines of the prison. In the outside world, they are considered to be as low as Customs officers, but I don't think anybody can get that low. Their machismo is only possible whilst in uniform in here, but Manuel the screw is a black-belt martial artist, so I have a little respect for him, even though he is a total arsehole. I first met him in La Moraleja prison, which is Spain's international prison, which was chosen to house the many foreigners needing a home when the infamous Carabanchel closed in 1998.

It was in that rathole the Carabanchel where I started teaching prisoners martial-arts techniques. I had two jobs: one in the gym and another in the *zapatería* (shoe-making shop). Amazing really because remand prisoners don't normally get jobs, and I was awaiting trial the whole time I was at the Carabanchel. Also, Englishmen never got the positions I had; the *zapatería* only employed Colombians and the gym employed only Spanish. But it's not what you know, is it? I have friends in high places, or maybe I should say I know people in high places who require my smuggling skills.

One of these was a wealthy Colombian whom I'll call 'Enrico'. He was in prison because as a government minister he embezzled millions of dollars. Misappropriation of government funds, he called it. Bollocks, he nicked millions and only escaped extradition because a family member became a high-up statesman in Colombia. Nevertheless, he was a good bloke and became my pal.

In my experience, Carabanchel was the darkest rathole on this planet. The screws were Spain's worst and most of them were quite homicidal. The Spanish inmates were the lowest scumsuckers I have ever seen. A day never passed without me witnessing some kind of abuse. Fighting between inmates was a daily occurrence and the drunken screws regularly beat up their own countrymen, especially the gypsies, sometimes ending with a supposed suicide. During Franco's reign of terror, many people were murdered in the Carabanchel, but it did not cease with the death of Franco. Oh no, this rathole provided the ideal human abattoir to practise the natural sadistic traits required in the training of Spanish prison officers.

I was thinking one day about why Adolf Hitler didn't bother his sick arse to take Spain. Maybe he thought he had it by proxy because Franco brown-nosed him for years. Or maybe he saw it for what it was: an annex to North Africa; a liability he did not want. But the silly bastards in Europe allowed them to join the club. Why? What a useless, poisonous bucket of shit this country really is. It is rotten from the top and about as useful as a chocolate teapot. Anyway, my opinion doesn't alter things so bollocks, move on.

In the Carabanchel, like all prisons, the prison population has nothing better to do than observe other prisoners and screws. Serious villains soon see who else is serious whilst the nutters seek fellow nutters. My skills were known by a black bloke who uses the name Kennedy, an experienced skipper and smuggler.

His comrades quickly drew me into their exclusive group which comprised two Colombians (Enrico being one of them), Rico, an Italian contract killer, and Gilbert, a frog coke dealer.

I had other acquaintances: one was an ETA terrorist from the Pais Vasco and another was a special pal called Ali Safave.

NINE

Ali Safave is a real warrior: arrogant and proud; an Iranian hit-man and heroin trafficker with more bottle and muscle than Stallone and Schwarzenegger combined. Eventually, I found he was the only man in the underworld I could possibly trust. If I ever needed back-up during hostilities, I would look no further than him. Ali is a high-grade Hapkido fighter and is as fit and hard as any world-class boxer. I enjoyed his friendship immensely.

Another man who became a good pal was Abdulla Habibullah, a high-ranking member of the Mujahidin of Afghanistan. We spent much time plotting and planning together. Great plans were made to move vast quantities of Afghan Black, the supershit from Kandahar and Mazar (Mazar-i-Sharif), which is grown in these two towns in the arsehole of nowhere.

Of course, those plans, along with many others, have been shelved for obvious reasons. Abdulla got his freedom before me and was true to his word, because when I first got my freedom he contacted me by telephone and arranged a business meeting with his uncle, a more senior Mujahidin member, who came all the way from Afghanistan to Spain to talk shop. They will be truly disappointed because I am back in prison: such is life.

My status in the Carabanchel was rising because of my influential friends. And this was the time to make my presence felt.

The first spick nonce I battered was a slow-moving, hulking moron who probably frightened his infant victims to death before raping them. I was in the telephone queue waiting to call Susan when the brute barged in front of me, abusing me in his native tongue: unusual for paedophiles, who tend to keep a low profile. The idiot turned his back to me, so I slaughtered his kidneys, grabbed his hair and slammed him on his back, cracking his head on the concrete. I quickly pulled out his tongue and palm-heeled his bottom jaw cutting off an inch of tongue.

There were a hundred Spanish witnesses so I was grassed a hundred times. I didn't get to use the telephone for a while so I was heartbroken because I couldn't talk to Susan. My spirits plummeted as each night I listened to the radio and in my despair I shed tears of sadness and frustration, which fell like little drops of acid corroding my soul with hatred for all things Spanish, especially nonces. In my book, child sex killers should be put to death.

The radio was on and I was listening to Ketty Lester singing 'Love Letters'. I realised that the pain in my heart, the despair, was the pain of yearning that could not be satisfied. Then along came Foreigner singing 'I Want to Know What Love Is'. And my heart fell to pieces with that haunting melody and beautiful lyrics. My search for solace ended when I fell asleep. I awoke in the morning to the great sound of Gerry Rafferty's 'Baker Street'. But that didn't help my frustration which I now vowed I would take out on the ever-present child-killers and perverts who were mixed in with us instead of being isolated like they are in civilised countries.

This is the only country I know where the paedophiles and rapists are given preferential treatment. The child-killers get the best jobs in Spanish prisons. What a shite system this is. Of course, it speaks volumes about the hierarchy and judiciary of this corrupt land.

There were many transvestites and transsexuals in the Carabanchel. Not surprising, really, because every Spanish television channel portrays men dressed as women wearing grotesque make-up every day and night. So the combination of bullfighting and prancing transvestites sets the tone of entertainment for the children of Spain. They grow up with all this shite. In the Carabanchel, the trannies wore their miniskirts and make-up, flaunting themselves to their countrymen, who in turn made no bones about what they had just done together in the shower room. A prison loaded with corned-beef inspectors. Macho-men my English arse! Some of these weirdos had cultivated their bodies, faces and gait so that they seemed to be more effeminate than women. They were truly unconventional with their weird clothes and hairstyles, so they were immediately recognised as being neither man nor woman: eccentric and as camp as Billy Butlin. But it was quite comical to watch them walking around the yard together with their contrived, short, mincing steps, walking like no woman I have ever seen.

One transsexual I saw here in the Carabanchel came to my wing in Malaga prison four years later. His name was Maria and he was over 6 ft tall with curly black hair and great big pouting lips with a permanent five-o'clock shadow. If you can picture Popeye's mate Bluto's mouth on Shirley Temple's face, you've about got it. This thing wore skimpy miniskirts and fishnet stockings. He was shagged every day. Every month, we were given an issue of condoms. Maria would come around on issue day with a plastic bag asking for unwanted condoms.

The screw's name was Antonio, an ex-Foreign Legionnaire paratrooper, a psychotic schizophrenic who became my friend when he discovered I was a martial artist. He approached me and asked if it was true that I was a black-belt martial artist. I told him that I had my own *dojo* here in Spain and my wife was also dan graded in ju-jitsu. It was partly his influence that got me installed in the gym as the combat instructor. I gave him private lessons for which he paid me by allowing me to use the screws' office telephone whenever I liked, much to the annoyance of the other shite screws. Antonio was the *jefe del modulo*, the boss, so what he said went.

Life was getting better. By this time, I had decked a few notorious faces on the Madrid gangster scene, so I was earning the respect that was coming my way. I eventually got my own cell, which is incredibly difficult in this rathole. I was teaching ju-jitsu *à la* prison style. In other words: head-butting, eye-gouging, throat-ripping, nerve-striking using elbows, knees, fists and boots, techniques to combat knives, coshes, bottles and baseball bats. My specialities are choking and nerve strikes; everything to achieve a quick knockout.

Multi-opponent training is great for fitness and effectiveness so I also specialised in that because here in prison single-opponent combat is as rare as a straight-talking spick. A fight with a Spaniard will always include his mates. A fight with a Moroccan will involve taking on the whole tribe. The Moroccans will always give you the good news even if they don't personally know your opponent. You will always be the infidel and if you hurt one of theirs you can expect problems from other Moroccans. So multi-opponent training is a must in Spain's ratholes.

The Carabanchel gym was quite well equipped. It even had *tatami*, so shoulder throws (*seoi-nage*) could be practised and *ukime* techniques, the art of falling without injury, could be learned. For multi-opponent training, I would use five men: one man in the centre of the mats and a man on each corner. The man in the centre would have to protect himself from the other four. But to give him a chance the cornermen could only attack him one at a time and they could only use kicks or punches.

On my command, cornerman no. 1 would attack the centreman. He must only use techniques that I have taught him and he must not use the same technique more than once during the exercise. When no. 1 had been dealt with, no. 2 would start his attack, and so on until all four cornermen had been dealt with. The sequence always gets fast and furious and needs firm control to prevent injury. It is really a form of circuit training for martial artists and is a brilliant method of developing discipline and fitness, as well as ringcraft.

The *sensei* (master) must be in complete control or this could get out of hand and become a brutal mêlée. Discipline is essential in the martial arts. Just imagine undisciplined soldiers playing with automatic weapons: this is principally the same. Take a look at Africa. Strict *dojo* etiquette was upheld in the gym, so I was called *sensei* by everybody, including the screws. Before and after each bout, the pugilists would respectfully bow to each other. Also, at the beginning and end of each lesson, everybody would bow as a mark of respect for the effort and courage of all concerned.

I discovered that inmates relish the idea of belonging to what they perceive to be an elitist club and actually enjoy the traditional ceremonies of the martial arts. Take note, rehabilitation pundits.

The *rei* (bow) is a ritualistic gesture performed throughout history by true warriors: men who lived by the sword, who killed with their bare hands. The bow was as essential as the sword in the etiquette of killing. Honour and a fearless attitude to life and death were the hallmark of even the most bloodthirsty of warriors: the samurai. Bowing survives to this day in the martial arts but is often the cause of embarrassment to new Western students simply because it implies subservience. However, the new martial-arts student soon understands that it is a formality observed and performed by men whom you really should not take the piss out of. Bowing is part of Eastern culture akin to handshaking in the West. No sense of inferiority is intended nor felt by either party. Everybody does it to show mutual respect for whatever reason: even to say 'hello' or 'fuck off'. I insist on it because it is the foundation stone of discipline and gives the participant an *esprit de corps*, which, of course, prevents things from descending into chaos. Much in the same vein as a gladiator or special-forces soldier salutes, it relates to recognition and respect. If a big hard mafioso hit-man or the likes can't bring himself to bow on my *tatami*, he gets fucked off *rapido*.

Prison life in the Carabanchel was like being stuck in the middle of the OK Corral for ever – just as it is here on *modulo* 13, come to think of it. During my lessons in every prison I've taught in, I've had to deal with all-comers: piss-taking hardmen, piss-taking cowards and anybody who wants to take a pop at the English *sensei*. Somebody always thinks he can put you away. Maybe one day it will happen to me. When it does, I will get up and give him the most respectful bow.

The other problem in Spanish prisons is that every Spaniard is an instructor. They observe and see how it is done, then as the days go by, they edge nearer to the mat and with sage-like facial expressions start to correct people who are practising on the mat. I love these blokes. I always stop the class and invite the new instructor to show me the technique. Every time this happens, I drive the twat into the deck. That gets rid of the spick instructors for a while.

One day, I was approached by an experienced boxer. He was a frog but spoke good English. He asked me how I would defend myself against the likes of him. I explained that unlike boxing, ju-jitsu is not competitive and is therefore not a sport. Self-defence does not start with the ring of a bell but with the closing of distance between aggressor and victim. As I expected, he then attacked me with a left uppercut that missed and a right hook under which I ducked and I applied *morote gari*, a two-handed reaping movement, whilst barging my shoulder into his guts. He landed heavily on his back on the concrete floor. I drove my knee into his bollocks, punched his slack jaw and moved over him to apply a *tate shiho gatame*, a full-body hold-down. I then realised he was unconscious. This man later became one of my most ardent students.

Techniques used against knives are the most popular in prison training, especially in Spanish prisons. Steven Seagal did wonders for the martial arts with his arm-breaking techniques portrayed in some of his earlier films. I use the same or similar techniques because they are ancient and effective.

A problem when teaching in prison, especially with knife work, is dealing with the clown who says, 'What if I attack like this?' as he thrusts at me from a different angle. This sucker gets hurt because I've dealt with this a thousand times and it's his attempt to look cool amongst his pals, so I possibly overdo it slightly with these twats. The clown is normally a spectator so he really doesn't matter. But they're always around the mat and it always happens. Prisoners are not paying students so I don't tolerate tossers, queers and poseurs. And under no circumstances do I permit child predators on my *tatami*.

Teaching and training kept me busy in the Carabanchel and provided the opportunity to meet good men. Most of the serious men I met were usually as opponents on the mat. Ali Safave first met me on the mat, as did Oscar Bonilla, a Colombian coke-trafficker who I enjoyed battering regularly because he was an inveterate fucking liar. The important thing for me was that it kept me away from AIDS and tuberculosis sufferers, as well as general scumsuckers. Spanish prisons are rife with disease, especially the shitty ones, and the carriers tend not to use the gym.

Summer in the Carabanchel was an ordeal. The air was thick and hot. The rats were so numerous they came out of their holes, not caring about being near men. Sleep was difficult because the night air was sultry and the spick gypsies think they are good singers. Christ almighty! Syncopated clapping and spick gypos singing like bullfrogs with cleft palates. Thank God nobody had castanets. I imagined them bursting blood vessels trying to hit the high notes. They would lie to each other, telling themselves how good they were. Listening to Les Dawson's piano is more enjoyable than listening to flamenco vomiting itself out of a gypsy. No wonder smack and hash sales were up.

TEN

One morning, I was working in the Carabanchel's *zapatería* when suddenly everybody went quiet. All of the Colombians were standing to attention. I noticed an elegant little man with an air of authority about him. As he passed each workbench, the men would start working with a vengeance. He left me till last, speaking to me in Spanglish, a mixture of Spanish and bad English.

I was surprised when he asked if I would like to use the telephone to speak to my wife. I told him I would love to speak to my wife. He then asked me to accompany him to his office where he told me to sit next to his impressive desk. He produced pen and paper, telling me to write down Susan's telephone number, which I did, then he proceeded to dial it. He then passed me the telephone and got up and walked into an adjacent room, leaving me alone to talk to my wife.

Susan answered and was surprised and excited to get this unexpected call, so we enjoyed a few moments of happiness. She assured me all was well at home but no matter how good the acting, I can always detect the hidden sadness behind the words of encouragement. We ended our call as the elegant little man came back into his office. He escorted me back to my workbench telling me he would see me the next day and I could call Susan again.

This was amazing because the elegant little man was none other than a major figure in the Carabanchel's administration, for Christ's sake! What the fuck did he want with me? I didn't know which of my influential friends engineered this one, but I guessed correctly that it was Enrico, who had big plans for the future. So now he was getting his act together and forming his team. It didn't matter that we were all in prison; these were long-term plans to be executed whenever the time was right. Kennedy (the black skipper) and I were to manage all nautical aspects of the plan.

There are millions of vessels on the Spanish coast, and consequently there are millions of skippers. But finding skippers with the bottle and experience to haul illegal substances is like trying to find Mother Teresa's thong. Enrico was stacking his rainbows for the future. The prison administrator had a Colombian girlfriend, whose family is big in an infamous cartel. So it didn't need an Einstein to figure out what the future held for yours truly.

He and Enrico were big pals and had all the contacts to do good business providing they had an experienced professional team. 'Da rah!' Yours truly and Kennedy had been selected to uphold the traditions of the Royal Navy Smuggling Arm, to transport the goods through DEA-infested waters. Anyway, it did not turn out like that because rule no. 1 in my Bible is: never work with a Spaniard.

The combat training was going well and my classes were getting bigger. The five-man, full-contact training was an excellent advertisement for my style of martial art. Every day, the audience grew. More and more screws appeared to witness the gladiators getting quicker and slicker with their techniques. These blokes had nothing better to do than get fitter and fitter day by day. At the same time, their control and use of violence was improving dramatically.

Physical training in prison is good for dissipating stress, improving physique and relieving boredom. Blokes had training partners whilst using heavy weights, but generally trained alone, achieving their own objectives in their own private world. Each man had his own system of training, some using old military routines like press-ups combined with star-jumps, crunches, skipping and burpees (where you go from a squat to a push-up position and back again and then jump up, in rapid and repeated succession). I have seen blokes complete a gruelling routine in the gym, then jog for hours around the yard.

The screws clock people like this, keeping a wary eye on them. The useless bastards keep a mental note on whom to get mob-handed with in case it kicks off. At the end of a gladiator session, I've seen white-faced screws walking out of the gym shaking their heads and praying like fuck they wouldn't meet any of these blokes in the dark.

The training continued and life was improving as Enrico started getting fresh food delivered and I was invited to dine with him in his cell. This meant I no longer dined with the rats in the *comedor*. Enrico had set up a little cooking range in his cell and one of his Colombian servants was the cook: lovely. At mealtimes, his butler had set up a dining table for four guests: Enrico, Kennedy, Rico and me. Fresh vegetables and pasta with either fish or meat was dished up every mealtime: a wonderful dining experience after suffering the pig's arse grub we were accustomed to. I remember the first steaks we had: an epicurean feast giving us much pleasure and enjoyment, ephemeral but unforgettable. A bottle of Châteauneuf du Pape, that super wine from the Rhone, was sadly missing.

I managed to keep my seat at Enrico's table until the Carabanchel closed its gates for the last time in October 1998. The disgraceful stains on Spain's knickers were being cleaned. The stains on my memory will never be wiped clean, you disgraceful, shameless bastards.

ELEVEN

We were handcuffed in pairs and loaded into Guardia-Civil prison buses with no windows or effective means of ventilation. We were pushed into metal cubicles approximately one-metre square. This was very cruel and unnecessary because two men in handcuffs trapped in a metal container can't really cause much of a problem to their keepers. Thank God none of us suffered with claustrophobia. We were stuck in there for hours while this cruel contraption transported us to La Moraleja Centro Penitenciario near Palencia, in the north of Spain.

I wish I were God for a day. I would put the Spanish judiciary, all prison officers and Guardia-Civil officers, every fucking member of the Spanish government and hierarchy including the King into their own prison transports, handcuffed in pairs, then give them a six-hour ride with a bag of stale bread and a bottle of warm water. I would love to do that to that corrupt bunch of faggots. As you can see, I try not to mince my words nor create grey areas when writing about holier than thou, evil, cruel, compassionless bastards who are beyond reach. Perhaps you think I'm being a tad over the top. Bollocks, the most senior officer in the Guardia Civil is languishing in prison as I write. He must have been grassed. His name is Roldan. The word Roldan is an anagram of *ladrón*, which in Spanish means 'thief'. Roldan deserves to be imprisoned in a place like the Bronx, along with 11 other prisoners, 20,000 cockroaches and plenty of rats, but I try to be realistic . . .

I often wonder how a member state of the European Community, where there is so much supposed concern for human rights, gets away with so much shitty treatment of its prisoners. Though I am pretty certain Roldan will never be treated like a normal prisoner, at least the bastard is locked up. Anyway, stop this bus, I want to get off.

La Moraleja was a brand new prison with plenty of amenities. The cells had a nice new shower stall and a nice new lavatory. Compared to the Carabanchel, this was the Ritz. This is where Spain dumps most of its foreign prisoners, so apart from the screws, there were not many spicks here. Great, because as I've said, the spicks are not too fussy where they discharge the contents of their noses, throats or arseholes, so there was a marked difference to the floors and ablution areas compared to prisons containing Spanish inmates.

Later, when I got the job in La Moraleja's gym, one of my tasks was keeping the place clean. The job was easy because there weren't so many Spaniards to gob and shit everywhere. Even the Africans respected the cleanliness, but they still stood on the toilet seat to shit.

When I was processed into La Moraleja, I was taken to *modulo* 8, which is the remand wing. I was banged up with a bloke from Guatemala who spoke good English. Everybody called him Guati but his name was Roland. He was a good cellmate, a nice chap with a great sense of humour. He was a fitness fanatic and was delighted to hear about my martial-arts teaching. He would be joining my class when I got started. But first I had to find the lay of the land and see how the mop flopped around here.

After a few days of strolling around the yard, I was bored shitless, so I decided to do some training. I ran a few laps of the yard, then I dropped and pushed some press-ups, did ten star-jumps and ten burpees. Then I practised my stances, *zenkutsu dachi* and *kiba dachi*, holding them very deep for a long time. I then practised my blocking routine using *jodan uke, chudan soto uke, chudan uchi uke* and *gedan barai* in sets of 20, then doing many sets of combinations of blocks and kicks. I did dozens of *mae geri*, *mae keage*, *mawashi geri* and *kansetsu geri*, building up a great sweat.

Perspiration poured off me as I worked at blocks, kicks and punches. To the onlooker, it appeared there was a strange man in the yard, kicking an imaginary opponent, then striking the invisible man several times; then more invisible men would arrive and the action would repeat itself many times. I expected to receive a comment or two, but not the abuse I received from a group of young bucks smoking dope. This was made up of possibly a dozen bollock-scratching Colombianos, lying in the shade at the far end of the yard. The yard had about 150 chatting blokes in it, but now there was a hostile silence, thick with malevolence. The pack leader looked like Bluto. He pointed his finger at me shouting '*cabrón*'. He again pointed his finger, imitating a pistol shot, blowing imaginary smoke from the end of his finger.

That broke the silence as the yard erupted with laughter. I walked to the centre of the yard pointing my finger at him but instead of firing an imaginary pistol, I beckoned him with my forefinger. The silence dropped heavy again, a bit like the OK Corral. All that was missing was the roll of drums. The dopes started to get to their feet, dusting their jeans and stamping their boots, all trying to look like Lee Van Cleef. Quite pathetic, really.

I was alone in the centre of the yard. The lone Brit: knowing this was my moment. After the next few minutes, I would be king of the wing or in hospital. My credibility as an Englishman is much too valuable to be shat upon by a wetback from wankerhood. I could read him like a drill manual. I knew exactly what he would do. But right now he was being egged on by his cronies, who were all keeping him company as he strutted towards me. I used my open hand to halt them and pointed to Bluto to single him out, but it was meaningless: they all wanted a bit of me.

I sensed a movement behind me and quickly glanced over my shoulder to see Ali Safave standing ten feet behind me wearing his gladiator smile. I knew my back was covered. I always try to work on instinct, understand the body language, be prepared, stay loose, welcome the adrenalin: it's my life force. I knew Bluto wouldn't hesitate as he got within his striking range.

There was no dialogue, just a massive roundhouse punch, whooshing over my head as I ducked beneath it. I was in my fighting stance as I stepped forward with my left foot, swinging a mighty crutch blow with my right fist, wrecking his bollocks with my first knuckle and thumb knuckle, just like a bricklayer's mash-hammer. I stayed strong in my long stance as I then swung my right arm from the crutch blow into a looping forearm smash across the back of his neck. This was easy because, as expected, he'd doubled over with the crutch blow. I then came out of the long stance by driving my right knee into his heart, bringing him upright with his head back exposing his windpipe, which I smashed with my right fist. I finished with two very hard punches to each eye.

I needed to advertise for my combat classes. Everybody had seen that I'd used only one arm to do the job, and they realised I could have done this with one arm tied behind my back. My cred was assured.

Ali swept past me viciously decking two young bucks and grabbing a third by the gizzard, driving his knee up into his bollocks. The remaining *compadres* set about tending the wounded, thinking medics don't get attacked; the Geneva Convention . . . bollocks. Ali and I set about decking as many as we could. I took a kick in the guts and a couple of blows to the head but felt nothing as we wiped the floor with the lot of them, exploding the myth that Colombians are hardmen. Without guns, they are fuck all. I do realise, though, that without Ali it might not have been such a good day out.

A few days later, I was installed as the *jefe del polideportivo*, the boss of the gym. My influential friends were helping me again so I got the gymnasium job. This meant that I had to move off the wing and go to *modulo* 5, which is the workers' wing. This was great because everybody had a job, so there weren't so many ponces and dippers to cope with. I was banged up with an American by the name of David Midcap from Akron, Ohio: a most wonderful companion, a gentleman whom I am proud to call a friend. We understood each other very well.

David is a big, strong man, standing over 6 ft tall. His brown hair is very long so he keeps it in a ponytail, and he is one of the few men who can do this without looking stupid. He is a good weightlifter and a college wrestler and is very skilful on the mat. He uses lots of judo techniques which make him quite effective when ground fighting. He isn't violent by nature so was reluctant to finish a scrap with something nasty, unlike me.

One day, we caught a Nigerian thief rummaging through our gear. David asked him why he did this because David was always kind to this piece of dogshit. I pulled him out of there and punched his fucking lights out. I finished by breaking his fingers and dislocating his thumbs. The blokes in the infirmary were pissed with me but gave Dogshit the good news while fixing his hands when they were told he was a thief.

The gym was well equipped with lots of weights, wall-bars, *tatami* and a punch-bag. I had to be strict with the punch-bag because everybody wanted to punch it bare-knuckled, leaving blood and skin debris on the bag. AIDS and other shitty diseases are rife in Spanish prisons, so care needs to be taken to avoid contamination. Blokes with AIDS would punch the bag leaving their blood for the next man to punch into, then a couple of weeks later this bloke would wonder why his dick had dropped off and why when he bent down to pick it up his eyeballs had fallen out. This may have been a new prison paid for by the European Community but there was no segregation from life-threatening diseases and paedophiles. So really it was just another shithole, a brand new one.

The prison wasn't yet full but there were about a thousand inmates, which gave me personally a hectic schedule. I ran three combat classes each day: two in the morning and one in the afternoon at 5 p.m. This was because each *modulo* had its own times for visiting the gym. The rule was that only one *modulo* could visit the gym at a time because inmates were not allowed to mix with those from other *modulos*. Business-wise, this was great for me because I became the go-between for the *modulos*. So if Fritz on *modulo* 2 wanted to sell his gear to Hans on *modulo* 3, it was done through me. I was on a good earner, but it meant that I had to open each package in case heroin was being pushed through me.

One of the screws guessed I was at it and wanted some of the action himself. So one day he asked if I could sell some booze. He brought vodka and gin in big plastic bottles. The gym was like a Bottle & Jug, a fucking off-licence! It became more like a *souk* than a gym. Hash and booze were changing hands faster than a Scouser with a speech impediment playing snap.

Philipe, my pet screw, was working well with the booze, and the drugs were coming in on family visits, stuffed up the wives' and mothers' fannies. There were whole nine-bars coming in, so there were some big fannies out there. Not surprising, though, because some enormous items were smuggled in on visits. I sometimes wonder why none of the smaller spicks escaped from the visiting rooms.

I needed to earn because soon I was to be temporarily transferred to Valdemoro prison to go to trial in Madrid. I needed pocket money for that excursion so I worked hard and took many chances before I went. I wound down the business in the gym and came to an agreement with Philipe that we would re-open on my return. Philipe took his holidays at the same time as my departure, so everything died the death because David was now responsible for the gym and he wanted nothing to spoil his release date. He would be going home soon so he would not take chances with his remission. There would be no dealing until my return.

Another memorable journey handcuffed to a lunatic in a square-metre cubicle took me to Madrid's Centro Penitenciario, Valdemoro prison. On arrival, I was pushed and shoved from the bus by the bullying Guardia Civil into the reception area, where I was verbally abused by a fat screw shouting about Gibraltar belonging to Spain. The fingerprint and mugshot ceremony was performed, and I was issued with a dirty mattress and shoved into a holding cell to spend a lonely, chilly night in this daunting vault, which stank of weeping concrete. The following morning, I was processed into the foreigners' wing, *modulo* 9, where the first person I said hello to was the most wanted man in the United Kingdom.

TWELVE

Kenneth Noye is a quiet, unassuming man who prefers his own company to being surrounded by lesser villains. I found him to be kind, clever and a gentleman. I enjoyed his company during the time I spent in Madrid and we discussed many things. He would join me during my walking exercises around the yard and we trained together in the weights room in the *polideportivo*.

Mr Noye is Britain's public enemy no. 1. He is also a cop killer. He killed DC John Fordham, who was a member of the police C11 close surveillance team, working at Hollywood Cottage, which was Kenny Noye's home. They were investigating Kenny Noye's part in the famous Brinks Mat gold bullion robbery. DC John Fordham was wearing camouflage kit and a balaclava mask when he received ten stab wounds from Kenny Noye on a cold January evening in 1985. When I met him, Mr Noye was facing extradition for the killing of a bouncer by the name of Stephen Cameron in what is now the famous 'road-rage' killing. Mr Noye told me that Cameron was a bullying thug and the only glimpse of heaven he got was when God laid him on his back in readiness for his journey to hell.

Kenny Noye was always dressed in a navy blue tracksuit which looked as though it was tailored to fit. He looked healthy and hard at all times, as befits a man of his reputation. He was quite reserved and quiet, but never boring. His eyes were penetratingly vibrant, never soft, never revealing what he was thinking: snake eyes. However, he was always happy talking with me and he never showed any of the traits the press are always keen to put out about him.

At first, I was impressed with the underfloor heating in my new cell. I was told about it by one of the other Brits but I found it hard to believe until I jumped from my bed to find the floor pleasantly warm. But so did the myriad cockroaches that appeared. I was in yet another unhealthy, vermin-filled spick shithole.

Heroin was used openly here, but seemingly only by the Spanish. I didn't see any other nationality openly using heroin in Valdemoro. The junkies always used the tables near the *economato* and though they found the means to finance their habit, they constantly begged for coffee or cigarettes in a most intimidating manner. It was my first day on the international wing and I was threatened by a snarling spick junkie as I queued for coffee. I was next to be served, but as I shuffled forward a dirty hand gripped my forearm and a greasy, unshaven face loomed into mine, snarling, '*Cinco cafelitos, hombre.*'

I splattered his nose with a hate-driven head-butt whilst turning his dirty hand into *kotegaeshi*, which I used to throw him into his angry *compadres* who were about to come to his aid. Kenny Noye was by my side in a flash with two other Brits, ready to take on anybody who fancied their chances. There was an immediate backdown and everybody sat down again, gawping at the bleeding shitpile unconscious on the floor. Spick smackheads are as weak as piss, they really should not intimidate strangers, but had I bought him the five coffees he snarled for, I would have been a target for every junkie on the wing.

A small Arab standing nearby walked over and pushed the shitpile onto his back; he was grinning, then laughing loudly as he started a kicking frenzy into the unconscious face. Nobody tried to stop him. The face was unrecognisable as the screws frog-marched him away from the unconscious gypsy. The gurney soon arrived and the shitpile was removed. I didn't see the gypsy or the Arab ever again.

Lunch-time soon came around so I joined the queue for my first meal on the international wing. I could smell pig, so I thought maybe we were having gammon or some kind of cooked ham. I moved forward with my *bandeja* as the cigar-smoking server ladled a scoop of stinking pig gruel onto it. I imagine the pig was slaughtered in the cauldron in which it was cooked because of the layers of scum and the nauseating stink. I tipped my *bandeja* into the waste bin and made do with some bread and a bit of salad.

I was looking for the English table when I heard a shout: 'Chancer, over here.' The English table was at the far end of the *comedor* so I made my way through the rows of tables. I could feel the eyes on me: some of them wary, some of them hostile, none of them friendly. As I passed the clogs' table, I got a bit of friendly banter and the kraut table treated me with typical Teutonic grim looks until I said *Mahlzeit* as I rapped my knuckles on their table. I then received a chorus of *Mahlzeits*.

'*Dieses Essen ist Hundefutter*,' I said as I passed them, meaning that the grub here is dog food. I didn't intend it to be funny but the krauts guffawed and sympathised with '*Scheisse*' and '*Ja, giftig Schwein*'.

I moved on, passing several tables of Arabs, a few Moroccans nodding in recognition. The Italian table was noisy as bottles of olive oil and piquant sauces were handed around. Kenny Noye pointed his plastic fork at the empty seat across the table from him, nodding me towards it as he chewed a mouthful of salad. Nobody on the table had pig. I sat down and introduced myself to everybody with a flurry of handshakes. I had met Kenny Noye and Alex, a ginger-headed ex-publican, earlier that morning.

This was my first day on the international wing and I'd had aggro already and there was more to come later in the day, but for now it was question time on the English table. Everybody talked the usual shite, like how they all got fucked over by a spick, and how no one was working with fucking spicks any more. Except for Kenny Noye, everybody was in for handling cannabis, but their stories are not for this journal.

I noticed a big bloke on the next table looking at me. He nodded and said hello. I returned the gesture and Alex looked at the big chap and said through the side of his mouth, 'Have fuck all to do with 'im, 'e's a fuckin' grass.'

'Who did he grass?' I said.

Kenny Noye looked at me and said, 'We reckon 'e's Old Bill, put in 'ere to get around me. 'E's askin' too many fuckin' questions.'

'What's he in for?'

'No fucker knows,' said Alex. 'Just keep fuckin' clear of 'im.'

I started to eat my pathetic salad and became a tad concerned about my diet so I asked, 'Is the grub as bad as this all the fucking time, or is it just today that's shite?'

Alex, talking between chews, said, 'It's shit every day but we get by with tuna and cold meats from the *economato*.'

'Don't worry, we won't let you starve, Chancer,' said Kenny Noye.

We finished our crap lunch and strolled around the yard in a group, everybody chatting to each other like we had just come out of the pub. I noticed the closed-circuit television cameras following our progress. 'I see we are being piped,' I said to nobody in particular.

'They're always on Kenny,' said Alex, as he brazenly gave the nearest camera the finger. 'Fuck you, spick tossers,' he shouted, vigorously jerking his middle finger at the camera.

'They never come out into the yard unless they're tooled up and mob-handed,' said Kenny Noye. 'There's never any aggro in the yard anyway,' he said. 'That always kicks off in one of the *salas* like this morning.'

'You mean we have more than one *sala*?'

'Yeah, there's the noisy fucker that you know about, and on the other side of the screws' office there's the entrance to the quiet room which has a small library and tables and chairs used for writing. Everybody goes in there to read or write.'

'Where are the showers?'

'There's two in there,' said Kenny Noye, pointing to a door near the corner of the yard.

'Only fucking two?'

'Yeah, but there's more next to the screws' office, but they only open them after six o'clock.'

I really felt like I needed a shower, especially after being so close to that fucking sack of shit who tried to intimidate me this morning. I imagined he had head lice so I couldn't help scratching my head every few minutes. 'I'll dash down after *siesta* bang up and get a shower,' I said, as the siren wailed to tell us to get inside so the screws could lock us up for the afternoon.

I was busy sorting out my kit and bedding most of the afternoon. I put my towel and shampoo in a plastic bag ready to run like hell to the showers, then prepared to write a letter to Susan. I wrote to Susan every day and I telephoned her whenever I could. The siren wailed again so I tidied up and grabbed my bits ready for the dash to the showers. The crash bang of the big sliding bolts drew nearer, then it was my door. Crash went the bolt and I was through the door like a whippet, momentarily alarming the screw who looked incredulously at me as I raced away, running down the stairs three at a time.

I ran across the yard through the door and along the corridor passing stinking lavatories on the way. At the end of the corridor were the two showers. Somebody had beaten me to no. 1 but no. 2 was empty so I quickly stripped, leaving my clothes across the back of the plastic chair on which I sat to remove my trainers. Naked, I stepped under the shower to welcome the lukewarm stinging spray. I was shampooing my hair, looking down to keep the soap out of my eyes when I saw movement to my front. Being a bit bashful, I turned my back to whoever was out there and continued rinsing my hair. That was the moment the first kick hit me. Somebody had kicked my arse and was now screaming at me to get out of the shower. I turned to see who had kicked me whilst at the same time washing the soap from my eyes as the second kick came in, which was aimed at my bollocks.

I love kickers. I've trained for donkeys' years against kickers. They always lose; the untrained ones haven't got a chance. The groin kick was well aimed but too slow. I grabbed the heel of the shoe and lifted it above my head, pulling the kicker into the shower. I stepped into him, sweeping his other leg from under him, thereby crashing him onto his back on the concrete floor, where I quickly gave him an open-fingered *nukite* thrust into his eyes. I hit both eyes with my spread fingers, and felt the softness of them as I poked them into his head. That was when I felt the knife. He stabbed me in the knee, wildly slashing to his front. I had the advantage of sight so I grabbed the knife hand, turned it back against the joint (*kotegaeshi*) and broke his wrist. Somebody grabbed his hair and pulled him out of the shower stall where he was half in, half out with his trousers wet through. I stepped out to grab my towel but the man who pulled my attacker out of the shower came at me growling and spluttering with his hands trying to grab me. He looked just like my first attacker, with hairy forearms sticking out of the baggy sleeves of a blue denim shirt, his jet-black hair long and greasy. They looked like brothers, resembling Anthony Quinn the film star.

I backed away from the wet area, moving in the direction of the stinking lavatories. He rushed at me screaming so I stepped half out of his path, grabbing his throat at the same time as I transformed his linear energy into circular momentum to ram him backwards into the steel stanchion on the corner of the row of lavatories. I felt good about the satisfying crack of skull against steel as I rammed his head into the web of the upright girder. I punched his lantern jaw twice, hearing a loud sickening crack as my second blow drove into the open jaw. I finished him with two very hard punches to each eye.

The first attacker was sitting next to the chair which had overturned so my clothes were now wet on the floor. He was rubbing his eyes, which were streaming with tears and tiny streaks of blood. He still couldn't see and was in agony with his eyes and broken wrist. The knife lay out of reach in the shower so I quickly dressed and put my bits in the plastic bag. As I was doing this, an Arab went into the shower and pocketed the knife, a big grin on his face. He pointed to my knee which was bleeding. 'Elastoplast, my friend have,' he said. 'Come quickly before *funcionario* come here.' I stooped to deliver a crushing blow just under the ear of the arsehole who first attacked me, knocking him out.

Fortunately, the only witnesses were Arabs. Thank God there weren't any spicks in the showers. I went with the Moroccan to his friend's table in the quiet room where he gave me a large plaster from his sports bag. 'You are from La Moraleja prison in the north, yes?'

'Yes,' I said. 'Why?'

He looked at me proudly and announced, 'I am the brother of Mohamed Rubio.'

I knew Mo Rubio. He was the king of the wing on *modulo* 7 in La Moraleja. He also ran the *economato* and all things bent on that wing. Later, I had dealings with two Moroccans who used the *nom de guerre* Mohamed Rubio. They were both big players in the hashish game. But for now I got my knee mended and I had some new Moroccan friends.

It didn't take long for the screws to find Pinky and Perky in the showers; the first spick in there would have reported to the screws in an instant. The screws thought they had been fighting each other so they were removed to the punishment block when the *enfermería* had finished with them. The bloke with the knife who first attacked me was an Italian who was awaiting extradition for killing a Roman Catholic priest. The priest was murdered with a knife in some kind of ritual killing, which took place in his own church. He was mutilated and his genitals removed and forced into a slit in his throat. The priest was a member of a respectable business family, the head of which is *capo di tutti capi* (boss of bosses) in Reggio di Calabria, in the south of Italy. So the priest killer really did not want to go back to Italy.

The last meal of the day got under way and the Italians seemed unperturbed about the two empty places at their table. They all turned to me and nodded respectfully. I'd obviously done them all a big favour so there were no hard feelings. They knew it was supposed to be me lying bleeding in the showers.

My trial happened and everything turned to ratshit because the spick that was paid to take the burn reneged at the last minute. This is another story, so suffice to say that I had warned my colleagues not to trust the spick, so it came as no surprise to me when it all went belly up. I was sent back to La Moraleja alone to await my sentence. My colleagues were sent to different prisons, which suited me because they were no longer my colleagues. I hope I never set eyes on any of them again.

Yet again, I was subjected to a horrible journey in that contraption they laughably call a bus. I was glad to get back to my cell with David in La Moraleja. I quickly took command of all things bent in the gym and got Philipe busy again with the booze. I was back in business; things were back to normal and now I could look forward to my first *permiso*. A *permiso* is a six-day leave of absence from the prison, normally reserved for inmates with a record of good behaviour who have served their qualifying percentage of sentence. If my sentence wasn't too steep when it came in, there was a chance that I'd qualify. In the hope of this, I kept Philipe very busy, as I'd need enough money to pay for the journey to Malaga if my ship came in.

Within a few weeks, I was called to La Moraleja's *comunicación* block to receive this sentence. The clerk of the court from the Audiencia Nacional (high court) in Madrid had come to La Moraleja with a batch of them, and mine was amongst them. Every prisoner had to be escorted by a screw wherever he went within the prison walls, but because I was in charge of the *polideportivo*, I was deemed to be trustworthy, and because the visitors' block was very close to the gym, I was allowed to go alone.

When I arrived at the visitors' block, I pushed the buzzer and the duty screw operated the electronically controlled sliding gate to let me in and allow egress to six prisoners and their escort prison officer who was trying to calm them down. It looked to me as if their sentences were far in excess of what they'd expected. The sense of foreboding was rapidly spreading across my heart as I anticipated receiving the same bad news myself. I need not have worried. 'Creestoffur, *venga*,' cried the little man from Madrid, beckoning me to him from behind the armoured glass partition. He slid a sheet of paper through the gap between counter top and glass and said in English, 'Sign at the bottom, please. You are lucky: no *multa* (fine) and you only got three years.'

'Thank fuck for that,' I said. 'Did everyone get the same?'

'No, the men with previous convictions got nine months more than you. Goodbye, *amigo*.' He passed me my copy of the sentence and off I went back to the gymnasium to show it to my pet screw, Philipe.

He told me that now I had my sentence I could apply for my first *permiso*, even though I had served not quite one year of the three years handed down to me. I asked what I needed to do to apply and he told me not to worry, he would speak to the *educador* (social worker) himself to sort things out for me.

Spain is a very slow country; the *mañana* syndrome weaves through everything. It took them approximately ten months to get me to trial, several weeks to decide on my sentence, and then from May to December to arrange a *permiso*. After umpteen interviews with social workers and a psychologist, they decided to give me my rights. The shrink, a cruel young woman in need of treatment herself, told me that Paco, my co-defendant, had already had *permisos*, as was his right. She then asked me if I or my wife would be disappointed if she stopped my *permiso* because though I had been granted one, she hadn't quite decided whether or not to cancel it. Why do the Spanish do this? A supposed professional psychologist purposely inflicting mental anguish and distress (I witnessed much of this mental cruelty). There is definitely something wrong with a nation whose national sport is the slaughtering of bulls in a public arena, which is televised across the nation daily. After what she thought was a suitable period of time spent doing my fucking head in, I was told my *permiso* could be taken in December 1999. Philipe told me not to worry because the shrinks were new so they created distress in order to gain experience. Hmm . . .

I was given a choice for my *permiso*: Christmas or the Millennium celebrations. I chose the Millennium because there will only be one of those in this life, so I wanted to spend it with Susan. The journey from Palencia to Malaga is a long pain in the arse, but I would have walked all the way to be with Susan for New Year's Eve.

We had the most wonderful time during that *permiso*. I was so happy and in love I will never forget the turn of the century, the showers of champagne cascading down from the upper windows in the old town square in Coín. The fun and laughter was infectious as we danced ourselves to a standstill in the early hours of the first day of the new century of the new millennium.

The year 2000 was upon us, though, and I was going back to prison. A stiff upper lip and a heartbreaking goodbye saw me off at Malaga airport, but I felt I didn't have long left to serve. There was a light at the end of the tunnel, but it was on the front of the train that was hurtling towards me. Don Manuel was transferred to La Moraleja.

I returned to Palencia and there to meet me at the station was Philipe, my pet screw. He told me Manuel was lodging with him and would be working in the *polideportivo*. This was not good news. It meant Philipe had to be extra careful with the booze and I had to be really cute because Manuel had the eyes of a shithouse rat. He missed nothing and had a nose for all things iffy. I know this isn't exactly end of the rainbow stuff, but I needed to make a living and not be a burden on my Susan, who was struggling to keep everything together in Coín.

There was CCTV in the gym, which was controlled from the screws' office. There were also monitors in the control tower and the director's office, so at any time there could be three sets of screws piping the gym. The camera was always focused on the *tatami* whenever I had a class. Between sessions, I did bag work and that camera never moved off me when I was training. I don't know what Manuel was thinking but he kept me under observation at all times. He is a dan-graded *karateka* so my ego tells me he was getting pointers from my workouts to improve his own performance. All the time he was looking at me he wasn't looking at others, so I organised my business by hiring Guati to be my runner and bagman. The business flourished until the day I gained my freedom and most of my time was spent on the combat mat so my thanks go to the cameraman: Manuel the screw.

On the day of my *libertad*, Philipe made his biggest mistake; he trusted one of his countrymen, a spick prisoner whom he thought he could do business with. You guessed it: he was grassed and lost his job. The spick, whose name was Debaño, was set up with a plum job. He could have made loadsadough, but in typical Spanish tradition he scurried to the director's office where he promptly fingered Philipe. Had Philipe been Debaño's father, he would still have grassed him. Such is life in this rat-filled country. The Inquisition started in the year of our Lord 1233, but I reckon the Spanish were grassing long before then.

THIRTEEN

Prior to my release from La Moraleja, Kennedy had gained his freedom and had moved into one of my holiday apartments in Coín. This plan was hatched in the Carabanchel because Kennedy had nowhere to live. We had become good friends so I gladly put a roof over his head. Besides, we had things to do.

I was finally freed on 18 May 2000, when I was processed out of La Moraleja prison near the little town of Dueñas in the Palencia region. I was in a daze as I packed the last of my kit and gathered up the magazines and bits and pieces I was giving to my pal Captain Peter Smith, who now worked in the gymnasium. I borrowed a baggage trolley from *ingressos* (reception block) where I had been banged up for my last month prior to release and took Peter's inheritance across to the *polideportivo*. I said my farewells and tried to be cheerful, but I couldn't shake off the feeling of foreboding. It must have been stress causing this perverse anticipation, making me think that somehow I was not going to leave here today. At last, I was escorted to the prison gates and ushered through by a familiar screw, but I didn't remember his name as he said cheerfully, '*Adios*, Creestoffur.' I stepped into the sunshine and briskly walked away from the prison towards the sun: due east, on the lonely country road to Dueñas, where I would catch a bus to Valladolid railway station where the train would take me to Madrid, where I'd change for Malaga.

La Moraleja is approximately three miles from Dueñas, in the arsehole of nowhere, so the taxi I'd ordered earlier met me on the isolated country road just a few hundred yards from the prison. The taxi honked as he passed me then turned around in the road and stopped where I was standing. I threw my bag onto the back seat and joined the driver in the front, who was shitting himself because I looked like the Wild Man of Borneo with masses of hair and fucking great bulging muscles. I breathed a massive sigh of relief as we sped away. I did not bother to look back as I experienced the magical, exhilarating sensation of fleeing the cage. The journey to Malaga was uneventful but the butterflies raged in my stomach when the train slowed and glided past familiar ground as it entered Malaga proper. I could feel my heartbeat increase as the train slowed and pulled into Malaga railway station, where hundreds of people milled around the platform. I searched the sea of faces as the train shuddered to a halt; I couldn't see my wife. As I stepped down from the train I spotted a flash of blonde hair to my left; there she was, searching the hundreds of faces, looking for mine. People seemed to clear a path for me as I urged myself through the throng of happy, laughing Andalucians. I made my way to my lovely, tearful Susan who was now crying with joy as her searching blue eyes found mine. We embraced in the cool early evening as silence enveloped us while hundreds of noisy commuters and travellers milled around us on the station platform. The stress melted away as we held each other and our hearts melded into the mysterious bond of natural duality, an energy of love that chased away all other feelings and sensations of the moment. I was so euphoric, I don't remember leaving the station, but I'll never forget our moment of recognition and the reunion of spirit that happened on the first day of what was to be an all-too-short honeymoon period for me and my wife.

Another great, noisy, happy reunion took place when we arrived home and Roxy, my lovely Rottweiler, was first to greet me at the gate as Max and Sammy, my two German shepherds, noisily bounded down the gravel driveway to add to the yelping joy of recognition. Their glee pierced my heart as I tried to push aside the subtraction of two years from all of our lives, but the moment of heartbreak ended there as Kennedy and his missus joined my dogs in a most joyous greeting. Before long, all four of us were kissing and hugging in a ring-of-roses huddle, dancing around a tray of glasses and a bottle of champagne.

Susan had spent many hours preparing my *libertad* dinner. She had cooked and dressed a beautiful poached salmon which she served with a delicious lemon sauce, making the last of Kennedy's champagne taste slightly metallic, but bollocks; Susan had really pushed the boat out with superlative wines to accompany fresh roast chicken and my favourite cut of beef – roast aitch-bone. Kennedy's contribution was some shite from the Caribbean, which was very colourful and spicy, but he did pay for the wine, so bless him.

The following day, though, it was straight back to business, as Kennedy had sea charts and maps all over the show. Several jobs had been stacked up in readiness for my return home. I needed money, and work was being chucked at me from all directions. Kennedy had prepared a job running out of Puerto Duquesa to Morocco and back, so I sorted out my kit and checked Kennedy's coordinates to work out fuel requirements and other logistical necessities. I then fought with my conscience over the fact that I'd just come out of prison vowing never to go back and I didn't have two halfpennies to rub together: what was I to do? Should I try to rekindle the martial-arts business or should I make use of my two years of study in the university of crime?

All the valuable contacts loomed onto the screen of my conscience, pushing and shoving to take centre stage. The devil got into me with a vengeance: 'Don't throw away those two years; blokes would pay millions for your contacts. No spicks are involved and nobody knows about this job apart from Kennedy and the bloke in Puerto Duquesa. You know the Moroccans are safe as houses, you know the beach team on this side of the Med and you also know the boss on the Moroccan beach, so all's well.' I should have said, 'Get thee behind me, Satan,' but I didn't. It's a strange power that makes you think you're fireproof and forget two years of hell in a Spanish pisshole, just to come out and pick up where you left off as though you've just had a fortnight in Blackpool.

I now had to consider the restrictions placed upon me by the *libertad condicional* rules, because the final year of my sentence wasn't just scrubbed for good behaviour. Oh no, I had to sign on at Malaga prison every month, as though I was on probation. If I missed just one signing on, I would be put back into prison until my sentence ended in May 2001. So with this in mind, I studied the plans.

Checking equipment and charts is second nature to me so we were soon ready to go. Our first job was supposed to be a quickie but it unfortunately became a fiasco and I became illegally stranded in Morocco. That doesn't sound serious but it is, especially when you are fucking skint in a foreign land.

Kennedy and I were in the Lidl supermarket in Churriana, a little town near Malaga airport. We were buying food for our journey to Morocco when my mobile phone rang. It was Mariano Alcantara Oliva: part African, part Portuguese, part Martian, or possibly from the planet Zob. Mariano had also been resting in the Carabanchel so he was no stranger to me. He was the 'Jim'll fix it' for the illegal launching of RIBs (rigid inflatable boats) in the Estepona area of the Costa del Sol. He was very well organised, with the Guardia Civil in his back pocket. The police were paid to look the other way during launching and recovery operations with smugglers' RIBs. Also, the police were paid for information regarding the whereabouts of Customs cutters and police patrol boats. It is debatable who makes the most money in this game: the police, or we smugglers who risk our lives at sea.

The message was short: '*Venga, toda listo, dos horas. Hasta ahora.*' We had two hours to meet the launch time, so we had to move it. We loaded our supplies into the Range Rover and set off to Coín to pick up our sailing gear.

I normally enjoy the drive through the mountains from Coín down to Marbella. It is a beautiful part of Andalucia, driving past the picturesque villages of Monda and Ojen, but I was too busy checking our gear to notice the scenic beauty of the place. Opposite the entrance to Puerto Duquesa Marina is a car-sales lot called 'Story's Cars'. This is Mariano's front. He hasn't sold a car in years. This is where the RIBs are given their final prep before being loaded onto a truck then taken to the marina for launching.

We drove into the car lot to find our RIB already loaded onto an articulated truck, all ready to go. It took a few minutes to clamber up and stow our gear securely. This was the only chance to secure everything until we were well out to sea. From now on, everything moved like shit off a shovel. Our RIB was a 9-metre Valiant with two 200-HP Yamaha outboards on the transom. She was fuelled up and ready to hit the water, which was only a short drive away across the road in Duquesa Marina.

Mariano was his usual abusive self, charged up on a yard-long line of Charlie, hurrying us along so he could get back to his pisshead cronies in his local boozer. I drove the Range Rover across to the marina and waited for the truck to arrive. The RIB would be craned into the water right next to the *gasolinera* where the legal craft tank up.

Every fucker knows what's going on around here, so why we needed to fuck around like Laurel and Hardy with that piano, I don't know. We might just as well have behaved like the locals and taken all day about it; the Old Bill had been paid anyway.

As the truck came into view, we raced into our sailing gear faster than a fire-bobby getting his gear on. I was sweating my bollocks off as I put on a woolly hat and sunglasses in case there was a smart bastard with a camera taking holiday snaps. Everything happened fast now, just like the *Keystone Kops*. We climbed up onto the truck to fix the slings and eyed them onto the crane's hook. The crane lifted the RIB from the truck out over the water and lowered away. We then jumped aboard, unslung, rapidly started the engines and fucked off. I quickly checked everything was shipshape as Kennedy steered us out of the marina into the open sea. We cleared Puerto Duquesa at exactly 2 p.m.

Our RIB was brand new so we kept our speed low in order to run in the engines properly. Had there been any patrol boats in the area we would have had to speed things up. But the Guardia Civil were earning their bread today; we had a clear run out to sea. Our rendezvous on the Moroccan coast was eight hours away so our engines would be well run in long before we got there. The sea was kind to us for about four hours, then she blew a force four at us for an hour or so which wasn't any bother, then she settled to a Lake Windermere ripple. The RIB had a 1,200-litre fuel tank fitted so we had no fuel problems. Our problems would happen at the RV.

On reaching our GPS position, we called in to our contact to tell him we were at the RV. We were 500 metres from the beach. Our contact was a man called Omar, a very wealthy, stupid Moroccan, dafter than Tommy Cooper. Generally, Moroccans are lovely people who behave sensibly away from their home crowd. But in their own little village surrounded by their own tribe they tend to show off a tad and revert back to wankerhood. Omar was the big man in his village and here was the chance to show everybody just how big he really was, especially with the infidels.

He told us to come ashore where he had a big fire on the beach. We told him there were dozens of blazing fires on the beach. He then said to come in where the car headlights were flashing. Alas, there were several cars flashing headlights out to sea. There must have been a flotilla of smugglers coming ashore this night. Eventually, he came out to us in a *patera* (a traditional wooden Moroccan fishing boat) with about 20 of his tribe on board, enthusiastically waving and shouting greetings. They came alongside, a tub full of happy idiots, led by the daftest bugger in Africa.

Omar jumped aboard and sent the noisy *patera* back to the beach, and then said he wanted to take us in. It was his RIB, he'd paid 15 million pesetas for it, so when he said he wanted to take it in to his beach to pick up his shit, we got off the jockey seat and he got on. I did tell him to take it easy because 400 horses driving such a small craft can get a bit tough on the reins if you gee them up. He was beaming and yelling to his tribe when he slammed the throttle forward. I fell to the deck as the RIB leapt forward with incredible acceleration. We were lurching around so fiercely I could not get to my feet. Then I was introduced to rocky Morocco, a line of rocks just a few yards offshore.

My body seemed to be numb with shock as my elbow grew like a balloon; then came the pain. My knees, ribs and especially my elbow were ablaze with pain. The RIB was written off across these rocks upon which Omar had spent his childhood. Omar's teeth were knocked out so that saved me a job. Blood was flowing from his hairline and his left ear was missing. The thought occurred to me to rip the other fucker off to balance him up.

Kennedy was unharmed, not a scratch on him. He came to me and helped me to my feet, concerned about my growing elbow. I don't remember getting from the rocks to the beach. We climbed a cliff to some kind of shack where a beaten-up old Mercedes car was waiting. Within minutes, we were driving through rock-strewn passes at breakneck speed in pitch darkness. Hours later, we stopped at a village where we speedily transferred from car to house.

As the car sped away, we were shushed into silence and led through the darkness to a candlelit room. I was led to a mattress where I lay down and immediately fell asleep. Two seconds later, I screamed awake with an icy, deep pain in my elbow. Kneeling next to me was a grinning, befezzed old wizard, muttering, '*Mezyena bzef, mezyena bzef. Tawil balak.*' (Everything's OK, calm down.) Apparently, he had fixed my dislocated elbow as I slept. The pain was subsiding now and I actually felt better.

I was offered a glass of steaming liquid with a bouquet of mint leaves sticking out of the top of the glass. The glass was a tall slim-jim glass and the bunch of mint stalks reached the bottom of it. I gingerly negotiated the hot drink over my swollen bottom lip and the flavour of mint tea and honey was so good I asked for more.

Kennedy was sleeping on a nearby mattress so I quietly asked the old man for some food. My Moroccan language skills are shite, but I know the word restaurant is universal so I whispered, '*Restaurant, por favor.*' The Wizard of Fez replied, '*No. Pero yo traigo pan y miel.*' He stood upright and smiled proudly at me with a twinkle in his eye. I know that look; it means, 'I'm smarter than you, Mr Englishman.'

With arms akimbo, he stood looking at me looking at him. His yellow *babouches* (Moroccan slippers) were peeping out beneath his fawn-coloured *djellaba* (hooded garment). His fez had gold thread woven into the arabesque design. In the dawn light, I could see he wasn't as old as I'd previously thought. The cut of his beard beneath those oily brown eyes conjured up a vision of Osama bin Laden; more a caricature than a portrait, definitely a problem at international airports.

He reached behind his head to pull the hood of his *djellaba* over the fez, then disappeared through the bead curtain, allowing the weak dawn light to flicker into the room. Off he went to fetch some bread and honey. The light from the rising sun was strengthening and glimmering through the closed louvres, which I was about to open, but I was abruptly stopped by a stage whisper saying, '*No, no abrier. Venga, comida ahora.*' Bin Laden's stage whisper awoke Kennedy with a start and a fart that could waken the dead.

Bin Laden convulsed into fits of laughter, which quickly accelerated into a consumptive coughing fit that became quite alarming. I slapped his back with my good hand as he coughed up a dollop of phlegm the size of a tennis ball which he gobbed out through the beaded curtain. I thought, 'Christ, if anybody steps on that they'll never get away.'

We breakfasted on mint tea, bread and honey. ObL told us that Omar would be here when he got out of hospital later in the day. He said the tribe were patching up the RIB and would have it loaded in a day or so. We gave each other knowing glances, which meant, 'Get fucked, Omar.'

ObL informed us that Omar had several broken ribs (no pun intended), a broken collarbone and other minor injuries. This news made me feel better because now I hated Omar and wanted to kill him. Kennedy felt likewise. Kennedy and I discussed our predicament and decided to seek help from other contacts in Morocco. We had to act fast before Omar appeared on the scene. He could muddy the waters for us if he suspected our fuck-off plan.

We questioned ObL about the area we were in. He proudly told us we were near Aknoul. We asked ObL for more food to get rid of him so we could make a phone call. Kennedy used his electronic diary (which handily encrypted everything he entered into it) to find the number of a colonel we'd be working with in Nador. They were talking within a minute. After a quick explanation of our whereabouts, the colonel told us to be ready to move at midday prompt.

We had our kit ready to go and my elbow was cooling nicely as I lay on the mattress thinking about what would happen next, when ObL entered, carrying the most delightful lamb stew. He explained that this was a favourite nosh of the Rif Berbers hereabouts. He talked a lot about his tribe, explaining that Berbers were the main inhabitants of Morocco and they used three dialects. His dialect was Riffi, he proudly told us. He gobbed off about how great they all were and I was getting interested in his geography-cum-history lesson when it dawned on me that Omar was one of these arseholes, so the interesting chat became rat diarrhoea in an instant. However, the lamb stew was memorable.

Just before midday, a car horn sounded outside our shack. There was a little Austin 1100 pulling up near the door. The car door opened and the colonel shouted, '*Venga, ahora*!' We picked up our kit and dashed to the car, throwing everything onto the back seat. Kennedy scrambled in with the kit as I got into the front passenger seat. The colonel rammed the gear stick into first and with a screaming engine and clutch we bounced over ruts and rocks with a vengeance.

Nothing was said until we reached Aknoul, which was only a five-minute drive from the shack. We stopped at what looked like a bus stop, where the colonel told us to get out and follow him. Grabbing our gear, we followed him around the corner to an air-conditioned Land-cruiser complete with chauffeur and drinks cabinet, a palace on wheels. I suppose this is exactly what it was, because I later learned it had been made for a certain Arab royal family. I realised I had entered a different circle of friends.

Setting off on the journey to Nador across the Rif Mountains sipping cold drinks, we explained our adventures with Omar to the colonel. Typically, he laughed his ragged head off, but when the driver joined in the laughter, he beat him savagely about the head. We were speeding at the time. A vision of having another accident with a Moroccan at the controls almost ruined my gin and tonic. In that moment, I realised that the colonel is a dangerous man. I read it in his cold black eyes.

We ensconced ourselves in one of the colonel's many apartments in central Nador, a noisy, bustling, dirty town just a few kilometres east from the Spanish enclave of Melilla, the Spanish penile wart on the dick of Morocco. We renamed Nador, calling it Plastic City because everywhere was littered with flimsy plastic shopping bags. No matter where you went, they were blowing around getting snagged on weeds, which were everywhere. Nador is merely a Riffian town with nothing to offer the tourist. Consequently, there was nothing to catch one's eye, especially fanny, which was all jealously hidden beneath *djellabas*. So: boring, boring, fucking boring.

I have no wish to be disrespectful of any faith, but I had terrible thoughts about what I would like to do to the gizzard of the muezzin in the minaret at Nador mosque. He used a sound system, which seemed to spoil the romantic notion of being called to prayer, shattering my childhood image of a haunting song calling the shuffling crowds to the mosque. That was how I would have liked it to be. But a rude awakening in more ways than one was what I got.

There must have been a lot of holy buggers in Nador, as the calling to prayer never ceased, or so it seemed. Eventually, we persuaded the colonel to move us away from the incessant wailing. But before we left, we met many interesting people. Whilst in the apartment in Nador, we were supplied with dope, booze, food and servants to see to our every need. One day, the colonel informed us that we would have a dinner that evening to honour a special guest.

The servants were busy preparing all kinds of things, cooking, polishing and cleaning, reminding me of an old army saying: 'If it moves, salute it. If it doesn't, paint it.' The guest was a senior member of the judiciary, one of the prosecutors. So if we were ever up in front of the beak in Nador, it is likely this was one of the bastards who would try to jail us. The prosecutor, a small man with a bad limp, was the brother-in-law of the colonel, so everything was kept nicely in the family. We met other brothers-in-law, high-ranking officials, up to their bollocks in the hashish industry. But tonight we were having a beano with a prosecutor.

The dinner was reminiscent of the Last Supper, with the colonel sitting at the head of the enormous table. The prosecutor was to his left, with me, feeling like John the Baptist, on his right. The resemblance to past events ended there, except perhaps for the beano at Sodom and Gomorrah. The prosecutor was presented with a bottle of single-malt whisky of the most expensive kind, which he kindly passed around the table after first filling his own glass.

The servants placed before us enormous platters of succulent fish, cooked to perfection in Riffian style. There was no cutlery: fingers only. Superlative wines accompanied each course and with this delicious fish came a cold bottle of Chablis, a steely, dry, excellent partner for this dish. Meat followed the fish and full-bodied reds followed the dry whites, which in turn were followed by fruits and desserts accompanied by Château d'Yquem, Eiswein and vintage port. All too good for pricks like the prosecutor who was off his face with foot-long lines of Peruvian flake, the ultimate rocket fuel from South America.

The servants swiftly cleared the table and served the hashish. We had several grades of pollen to choose from. A servant gave me a lump of *tbezla* with the thumbs-up gesture, indicating it was the best. *Tbezla*, sometimes called *chicha*, is the finest of Moroccan hashish. The everyday Moroccan calls his shit 'kif' regardless of what grade it is. But Europeans tend to classify and assign different names and grades to everything. The low-grade cannabis resin that goes to Britain is generally known as soap, nine-bars or *alpaleado*. But now the British market is growing for the various higher grades of pollen, which is normally reserved for the Netherlands.

Not so long ago, there was just soap and pollen, but now because of all the clever fuckers involved, various names for different grades have been invented, demanding different prices for different grades, facilitating cheating like never before. Pollen hardly worth jack shit is being sold as *chicha* and there is now so much jiggery-pokery there's fuck all trust anywhere in the game. It reminds me of the premium ales business in England: lots of names for various brews, but basically the same piss.

Some of the frequently used names these days are: *placa*, sputnik, zero-zero, pollen, *tbezla*, *chicha* and *burbuja*. There are more, but I don't want to add to the confusion; suffice to say that *tbezla*, *chicha* and *burbuja* are arguably the same grade, and the most expensive.

We were relaxing and chattering, feeling great and chilling out, when one of our servants, a tall, big-boned old girl with a face like a camel, came into the room. She brought a big silver platter of sliced meat for us to pick at. As she bent to put it on the low table in the corner, the prosecutor shot his hand up her kaftan, rummaging for one of her holes. I thought it might be prudent to get my meat now before he put his hand into it after feeling around the old girl's beef curtains.

Camel-face put up a token struggle and scurried off into the kitchen with the prosecutor in tow. We all staggered to the kitchen to see the source of all the shrieks and laughter. There was the prosecutor, performing a frantic back-scuttle with Camel-face bending her knees so the short-arsed prosecutor could hide the sausage without it slipping out and slapping her orange-peel textured thighs. His little hands were clinging to the cellulite as his hairy arse was trying to get some rhythm.

I sometimes wonder how many sorry bastards this cretinous prosecutor has sent to die in those horrible Moroccan prisons for crimes that pale into insignificance in comparison to what he was getting up to here. Actually, Camel-face was being raped, no matter how funny it looked. But, like all states where religion is strong, crimes against the state and Islamic law seem only to apply to the lower castes. Punishment and accountability had problems climbing over all the money. I suppose it depends on who pisses on whose fireworks: look what happened to Roldan, the Roman Catholic head of the Guardia Civil in Spain. Whose fireworks did he piss on? Anyway, fuck him.

There were many dinners with special guests. During those first two weeks in Nador, I dined with and observed the prosecutor, senior police, naval and military officers and three members of the Moroccan parliament snort Peruvian flake and behave like hooligans. One of the MPs was often on TV. I would look at him in his sober suit, distinguished and elegant, and I would smile to myself as I recalled his hairy Arab arse wobbling as he rogered one of the houseboys on Kennedy's bed. I am no angel, but I knew I was near the devil when I was with any of these fuckers. Paradoxically, I felt safer by knowing them; they were my insurance policies if things went belly up over here.

Collectively, these people controlled the movement of hashish and illegal immigrants in their respective areas. They owned the farms where the hashish was grown and prepared for export. They controlled all movement on land and sea. No significant cargo moved without their permission. Police, soldiers and sailors were used to help load cargoes and escort craft safely out to sea. Lots of shit makes lots of money, but the real profits went to the respectable gentlemen in ivory towers. Hashish cargoes, human cargoes, they didn't care a fuck just so long as they got their kickback.

The going rate for loading and sailing out of Sebkha bou Areq is seven million pesetas (approximately thirty-thousand pounds sterling). This is the lagoon that fronts Nador. There is only one entrance to this lagoon, which is a bottleneck easily controlled by a few soldiers. When you are loaded, you must await the commandant's permission to leave. You will be given a window of opportunity to get out of the lagoon into the open sea. This departure time is normally between 0100hrs and 0500hrs. If you haven't paid your seven million, expect to be shot to pieces. You will not get out alive. Normally, you would not sail with less than 1,500 kilos of hashish on board, so seven million pesetas doesn't knock such a big hole in the overall profit.

Opinions differ upon whether or not the police, army or navy get paid to look the other way on the North African coast. It is my opinion that if they are not paid and you expect to move substantial amounts of hashish, you will not be onto a winner. I'm not talking about 10 or 50 kilos; I'm talking about 10 or 50 tonnes. You may think the Moroccan coast is desolate in places; I agree with you, but try it large and you'll wonder where all the ragheads have come from.

Nador became intolerable with all the wailing and singing. It was worse than listening to singing Spanish gypsies and syncopated clapping. So the colonel took us to his farm, 30 km from the Algerian frontier near a small town called Berkane. This place, with its silent beauty, was such a contrast to living in Nador. We were on a real farm, complete with dairy herd, fruit, vegetables and miles of juicy grapes. The vines ran in parallel lines as far as the eye could see. I ate so many sweet grapes that my poor arse was crying, 'Please, no more fucking grapes, blowing this trumpet is killing me.'

Actually, being a grape addict is quite healthy, but it didn't help my dad. On the day he died, I was at his hospital bedside eating some of his grapes. In those days, there weren't any seedless grapes, so with a mouthful of pips I asked my dad, 'Where do you put your pips, Dad?' My dad was ever so funny. He gave me his favourite facial expression, the one he used on the rent man, and we laughed our silly heads off. My hero died later that day. I love you and I will miss you for ever, Dad.

The farm was terrific. There was a swimming pool and a Jacuzzi set in beautifully kept grounds. The servants kept the gardens, house and pool in pristine condition. The pool and the surrounding area had the most beautiful arabesque designs, all worked with mosaic tiles. Elaborate patterns, winding around each other, simply beautiful.

I spent lots of time in the pool keeping myself fit. Being surrounded by luxury can lull you into complete inactivity, especially when you are treated like a king. Lounging around in the hot sun is second nature to everybody and can change you into a deckchair potato in no time. I also spent lots of time exploring. I really enjoyed nosing around the farm, exploring outbuildings, looking at animal husbandry, seeing what goes on in the milking parlour, avoiding the ever-present booze and drugs. Unlike Kennedy, who was flying the Milky Way, high on Peruvian flake, *chicha* and the finest Scotch, stopping occasionally to dip his wick into Camel-face who followed and picked up after him all over the fucking place.

I was impressed with this place. It was fit for a king. In fact, the main house was more like a palace than a farmhouse. Everything that could be gold-plated was gold-plated, but this captivating ensemble carried the mark of the philistine. The colonel's touch was everywhere. He kept the fucking labels on every painting, vase and tapestry. Even the chandelier still had the Marbella shop label stuck to its base. Every wall-hanging had the supplier's name attached and the library shelves were filled with phoney books. I tried to pick one up and a yard-long row of fake hardbacks came away, revealing they were all hollow inside. But let's not allow little things like that shadow the opulence of this palace in the arsehole of nowhere.

We were wined and dined, pampered and spoilt by the servants who were obviously instructed to keep us happy. Here we were, waiting to go to work, being treated like film stars between takes. But now we were getting bored waiting for the colonel's new RIB to arrive. The colonel was hiding us at his farm because he knew there were plenty of his town-folk looking for us. There were many tonnes of hashish to export and everybody knew there were two skippers here somewhere and skippers are scarcer than Biafran cookery books.

We discovered people were trying to find us when a visitor arrived. One fine morning, we were surprised to find a new arrival at breakfast. An elegant Italian gentleman introduced himself as Maximilian.

Max is a nice man, a clever man, who speaks several languages very well, especially English and Arabic. His bespoke tailor lives in Milan, his cobbler makes the most beautiful hand-made shoes in Tuscany, his wristwatch is Patek Philippe, his perfume is an exclusive Chanel *pour monsieur* and his breath is a blend of Himalayan yak and Shetland pony: possibly the cause of his watery eyes. He made my eyes water when he got too close.

However, a good man to know. He told us that during his overnight stay in a hotel in Nador, many of his business contacts asked if he knew our whereabouts. He said he knew nothing about us until he met us this morning at breakfast. He now told us we were in great demand in Nador. Max had business with the colonel, who was using Max's haulage company to take 12 tonnes of mixed-quality hashish to Rome.

Max's mobile phone was constantly ringing. I was lounging around the pool when his phone rang. He answered, speaking French for a moment, then passed the phone to me, saying, 'Someone for you.'

I took the phone expecting the colonel. 'Hello, who is it?'

A familiar voice said, 'Iz zat you, François? Zis iz Rouge. Jimmy!' he yelled.

Now I know this sounds daft but my name in Morocco is François and I speak very little French. Rouge speaks little English but calls himself Jimmy. However, we both speak German so we have developed a good business relationship over the years. He was ecstatic about finding us. He told me everybody had heard about the fiasco with Omar and had laughed their heads off.

Jimmy knew the colonel was hiding us at the farmhouse near Berkane. He asked if we could be on the road outside the main entrance tonight at 8 p.m., where he would meet us to take us to dinner in Oujda, Morocco's easternmost town, 15 km from the Algerian frontier. I confirmed 8 p.m. prompt.

There is a gatehouse manned by sentries at the main entrance to the farm. This is approximately 1 km from the farmhouse. The gates are always locked and guarded. Before we set out, I watched Kennedy fire a line of shite up his nose. I realised he was now dependent on cocaine. Nobody can envisage the consequences of cocaine addiction. But in this game, death is the usual outcome: not by the drug, more likely by the bullet. Trafficking and addiction do not mix well. I felt a quick stab of sadness and disappointment at the state of Kennedy. It soon departed, but I knew one day it would return with a vengeance. My rock, Kennedy, was crumbling, but not tonight.

In pitch darkness, we crept past the gatehouse. A beam of light shone from the window opposite the gate illuminating the lock, which was open. We got ourselves through the gate and in the silence, heard snoring. Was this handy coincidence anything to do with Rouge, I wondered? The only illumination we had now was from the occasional passing headlights. A big black Mercedes limousine sitting wraith-like in the shadows suddenly came to life nearby. Like a silent hearse, it came gliding towards us. The two nearside doors clunked open as the interior lights exposed two grinning Moroccans dressed in Western garb flashing gold- and diamond-linked white shirt cuffs and glittering Rolex wristwatches.

Rouge and Abdul el Ouassini arriving at the fucking Oscars ceremony. Our attempt at a covert exit was shattered by a deluge of excited greetings in wog, frog and kraut, with most of the noise coming from a gleaming, gold-filled gob: Jimmy's.

Jimmy's business partner, Abdul el Ouassini, is a short, oily-looking character with a wonderful Arabic nose. The nose is massively convex beneath two seal-like watery eyes lurking under shaggy eyebrows, epitomising my vision of an Arabic warrior of long ago: a flashback of scimitars, dashing headgear and betassled camels. He would have looked more the part than Omar Sharif in *Lawrence of Arabia*. Actually, he is just another wog scoundrel whom I could trust just about as far as I could dropkick Lawrence's camel. He had tonnes of hashish and needed to sell it pronto. This was the real reason for dinner.

Dinner was sensational. We drove to Oujda to find a restaurant near the centre of town just off the Boulevard Mohammed Derfoufi. The restaurant was very French and specialised in fish. Antique silver servers were used to bring succulent fillets of several species of Mediterranean sealife, cooked to perfection as only the best Moroccan chefs can do. The dishes were garnished with shellfish, of which the texture and flavour were superb. This lot was washed through the gizzard with three bottles of Moillard 1972 Puligny-Montrachet, the most delightful amber nectar to come out of a French bottle.

In contrast, we finished the dinner with a super-light crêpe Suzette. And just to be different, I ordered a bottle of Katlenburger Erdbeer Schaumwein, a light, sweet, sparkling wine from the Harz Mountains of Germany. This is actually a strawberry wine so the flavour is perfect for bitter-sweet crepes. In a previous life, I was a member of the Guild of Sommeliers and also a member of the British Institute of Innkeeping. I am entitled to use the letters BII after my name if I wish. But I was now a smuggler with an expensive palate and had no need for such decorations.

Jimmy and Abdul gave us the outline of their plan to move 30 tonnes of hashish from Nador to Alicante in 15 2-tonne consignments. We argued various aspects but eventually closed the deal amicably. This was more like it, a decent job with plenty of money up front. The problem now was getting back to Spain. I needed to return quickly to Spain to organise a new RIB big enough to carry a 2-tonne cargo and enough fuel to take it from Nador to Benidorm. This also meant I needed to do a recce to the north of Benidorm on the Alicante coast. I'd have to recce the unloading point, the approaches and any possible escape routes I may have needed. The unloading point had been used by Jimmy the previous year, so I was really going over his old ground.

My priorities were quite clear: get our passports stamped with an entry stamp so we could get out of Morocco, contact my marine-engineer friend Paul in Malaga to start the RIB construction, recce the RV near Benidorm, then put the show on the road. The entry stamp on the passports is essential, so the passports were given to two Moroccan policemen who went on a ferry from Nador to Almería. They did a bit of shopping, then returned to Nador and somehow got our passports entered into the Moroccan computer. The passports were stamped and the corresponding computer number was written across the entry stamp. This cost Jimmy and Abdul an arm and a leg (so they said), but fuck it, they were millionaires.

We were still under the colonel's roof so we laid plans for our extraction and subsequent journey to Malaga. When we received our passports, speed was of the essence because the colonel's RIB was threatening to arrive presently and that would cause many problems because the colonel's shit was ready to be loaded and he would expect us to sail within hours. When Jimmy brought the passports, we had already packed our gear and we were ready to move instantly. Jimmy was delighted, so immediately called the airport at Oujda and booked us on the afternoon flight to Casablanca.

We grabbed our gear and one of the servants drove us down to the main gate, where Jimmy waited with his Merc. We told the servant the colonel could contact us when he got his shit together. In the mean time, thank you very much, see you soon.

We had a couple of hours to kill before our flight, so Jimmy took us to a restaurant he knew in Berkane. He had a vested interest in this restaurant because one of his many brasses ran it. We could have had one each for dessert, but by the time we had finished eating we had to rush to catch our flight. She might have been on the game, but by fuck she could cook. We had *couscous bidaoui* with *djaja mahamara*. That is semolina cooked with seven vegetables and roast chicken stuffed with raisins, almonds and more semolina. Absolutely splendid and it sticks to the sides. For pudding, we had *m'hencha*, which is an almond-filled cake drenched in honey. After that lot, neither of us could have handled a brass. Anyway, we had to dash.

Jimmy dropped us at the airport, giving me a wad of peseta notes, then departed after assuring us people were waiting for us in Casablanca. Our aircraft was a twin-prop Moroccan Airlines jalopy but gave us a good ride over the Rif Mountains to Casablanca. A tall, distinguished-looking Moroccan, resembling a suntanned Christopher Lee, awaited us, complete with a posh-looking name card advertising my name. He informed us that there was a change of plan. He had booked us on the next flight to Gibraltar so that scuppered Kennedy's plans for a heavy weekend in Tangier, which was where we were supposed to go from Casablanca. I telephoned Susan, asking her to meet me in Gibraltar at 7 p.m. that night. Great! She was all excited and so was I.

We passed through the concourse where we had to be stamped out. My heart stopped for a moment as the creep in the kiosk checked my entry-stamp number against the computer entry number. 'Short stay?' said the creep inquisitively. I merely nodded, holding out my hand to retrieve my passport. I was truly relieved when I boarded the aircraft and flew out of there. Moroccan officials are permanently sinister looking, which makes me uncomfortable.

My spirits rose as rapidly as the tiny twin-prop aircraft that lifted me out of Morocco. I happily pictured my wife in Gibraltar anxiously awaiting my return. The aircraft landed and I could see Susan waving to me. Lovely Susan: my pride and joy; my blue-eyed blonde with a heart of gold; my fount of strength and the safe haven where I find my equilibrium and peace of mind. My cares disappeared as I held her in my arms. Neither drugs, booze nor food can equal the sensation of holding your loved one. Nothing can equal this feeling of togetherness.

We loaded ourselves into Susan's car and off we went to Marbella to dump Kennedy amongst his exotic friends. I didn't expect to get any sense out of him for a couple of weeks. I didn't need him anyway, but before we reached Marbella he asked Susan how was she getting along being alone at the farmhouse because he thought she looked tired.

'I don't sleep well when Chris is away, so I've started to take Night Nurse,' said Susan.

'Christ, love! Are you all right driving?' I said, as Kennedy started to sing the reggae song 'Night Nurse'. It hit me like a bolt from the blue because I didn't realise how my absence and the worry of danger were affecting her.

'Drop me here, bro,' said Kennedy as I was thinking about Susan's remark.

'This will end soon, love,' I said as Susan stopped to let Kennedy out. I wish now I had ended it right then.

I told Susan I would be disappearing up my own arse in a minute because of the hectic preparations involved with Jimmy's job. But this weekend was for us to spend together without a care in the world. That evening, Susan and I had a super romantic dinner at my favourite spick nosebag joint, the Bohemian restaurant in Coín. The food is excellent, the selection of Rioja and other Spanish wines is the best in the region. Even the house wine is memorable with its damson bouquet, robust and long on the palate: great with beef olives.

The maître d' is a total arsehole, wearing a permanent frown on a face that would stop a clock. He is a great lumbering oaf and the only thing missing is the hump. He's a combination of Boris Karloff and Manuel of *Fawlty Towers* fame. Still, he's a source of inverted merriment, a treasure, and the place wouldn't be the same without him.

We had a smashing night. I had Susan in stitches as I laughed at myself explaining the carry-on in Morocco.

FOURTEEN

A weekend of joy and love sped by as I shared my time between Susan, Roxy my Rottweiler, Sam and Max my Alsatians, Charlie my blue and gold macaw, Dicko my parrot and Big-gob my mynah bird. I also took my Honda CB 750 custom bike with its four snarling exhaust pipes for a blast around the mountains. Then I fired the dust off my Honda Magna 65, a V-4 1,100cc Japanese knicker-wetter, which really turns heads. I felt like Tarzan on Monday when Susan woke me with a great English breakfast steaming on the table. Bloody great!

I rode my Magna 65 out to the Guadalahorce industrial estate near Malaga airport. It didn't take long to get there but I had to clean the dead bugs off my Raybans when I arrived at Eduardo's marine workshop where my pal Paul works. This is the Aladdin's cave where RIBs are made to order. But first I had to case the joint, ensuring no spick secret Old Bill were lurking in Ford Mondeos, jeans, black bomber-jackets and Raybans. I don't know why they didn't just wear a uniform like the rest of the wankers.

All clear, so I roared into the workshop, cut the motor, parked on the side-stand, removed my helmet and waited for the abuse. 'Fuckin'ell, where've you been, Chancer?' It was Paul, the best marine engineer in the world. Everybody then welcomed me: Eduardo, Keith, Pepe, Paco and several Moroccan clients who were inspecting their new purchases: gleaming new RIBs all ready to scream off to Morocco to collect the beneficial herb.

The Moroccans acknowledged me with nods and knowing smiles, awaiting their chance to proposition me, an occupational hazard when near RIBs and Rockys. Finding an experienced RIB skipper prepared for work is like trying to find a virgin in Ibiza. And here I was, standing in front of them with their shiny new RIBs. I nodded at them, saying, '*Mas tardes, amigos, mas tardes*,' then entered the office with Paul and Eduardo to explain my requirements.

Paul informed me he had three hulls in the workshop now, the best being a Narwal 9 metre, which was being prepared with a 1,400-litre tank. We bashed lots of ideas about and discussed several engine set-ups. I decided on fitting two Suzuki EFI 225 HP outboards on the transom, enabling the 'shit off a shovel' effect required for this kind of work. Actually, it was Paul's suggestion but my decision. The choice of these engines was governed by the fact they are 40 per cent more economical than the normally preferred Yamaha 250's carburettored engines, which of course was a crucial factor with Abdelmajid's job.

The problem with fuel-injected engines is that they run on lead-free fuel, which for some unknown reason is not favoured by the Moroccans who buy these RIBs. Somebody once told me the quality of lead-free fuel in Morocco is shite. Maybe, but if Rouge bought lead-free fuel from Melilla and brought it to Sebkha bou Areq, that would solve the fuel problem. Extra fuel takes up precious deck-space and is life threatening. This fact was highlighted yet again just recently when two tonnes of happy leaf, passing the sentries at Sebkha bou Areq, suddenly diverted to a lunar course due to a crewmember lighting his kif. Adios amigos for ever.

So, I started something new. I chose EFI engines for my job, maybe changing things for the good. I also ordered Recor filter and water separation units to be fitted alongside the normal canister filters ensuring only clean fuel would be piped to the injectors. Paul and I fitted a four-seat jockey seating arrangement, which actually formed part of the fuel tank. But the two rearmost seats were replaced with a stainless-steel compartment housing the batteries, accessible cut-out switches and a small toolbox. The helm was fitted with a small Navionics plotter, a compass and a holding bracket for a GPS. I installed four waterproof cigarette-lighter sockets to run my extra bits from, so the whole thing was exactly tickety-boo. The mutt's nuts cost around 16 million pesetas to prepare, but this beast could catch pigeons. This craft would suffice until I got my hands on the Crompton 12 metre that Paul had ordered for me. Time was of the essence right now so the 9 metre would do to start the job off.

The RIB took three weeks to build, so I spent most of this time working in the workshop with Paul. He had several projects in various stages of completion, so whilst waiting for parts for mine, I mucked in and assisted in the build of the others. All this time, I had to dodge propositions from other Moroccans. Wonderful deals were tempting me away from Rouge. But I bolstered my reputation by refusing politely and explaining the rules.

One of the business conditions whilst working with Rouge was not to undertake any jobs or favours with anybody else. This was a normal requirement for obvious reasons, but I will explain: if I was to work with somebody who was under surveillance, the observers would follow me, thereby enlarging the surveillance net, ensnaring others whilst enhancing the reputation of the Old Bill, who really did not deserve an iota of kudos from the likes of me.

The nice thing about these propositions was the realisation that I would never be out of work. One proposition I had was from a man I knew in prison: a very well-placed man, a serious and highly respected mover of vast quantities of Morocco's finest herbal remedy. His name is Mohammed Rubio.

My RIB was practically finished. There were a few things to adjust but there was a delay due to a component being sent to the wrong address. I had had enough for today. I was tired, hot and about to fuck off on my favourite death trap to boost my spirits with a high-speed scratch through the *campo*. But first I did an about-turn so hard that I wheelied against the flow of traffic in this one-way street because I had just clocked Raybans and bomber jackets lurking inside a Ford Mondeo opposite Eduardo's workshop. They were obviously waiting to follow me, which was very difficult for them now because they were going with the traffic and I was not. The Ford screeched away, burning rubber through the traffic flow as the hairs on my neck prickled: nature telling me to fuck off now. I dropped a cog and roared out of there like Roadrunner with a rocket up his arse.

Police drivers are good, they've done the courses: regular, advanced, super-advanced and solo. But to catch me on this kamikaze flying bollock they needed to be a nano-solo-astro jockey with three bollocks. I scratched around the corner, narrowly missing oncoming traffic, a cacophony of blaring horns and fist-waving spicks enthusiastically encouraging me to commit suicide as they reached for their mobile phones to grass me. It wasn't important; I was using a phoney registration plate anyway, so bollocks. My best chance of losing them was by sticking to the *campo* roads, avoiding the *carretera*. I was aware I had committed no offence. They needed to locate my house to facilitate surveillance on me. Obviously, they'd guessed what I was up to and wanted to get in for the kill. RIBs capable of 75 mph are not used by fishermen. They also wanted to see my associates to enable their net to be cast wider.

I was alarmed that they had fingered me so I was thinking fast about further precautions. I knew I would lose them in the *campo* but just to make sure, I headed for the hills, using tracks no car could follow. I checked the sky for a chopper, realising I didn't rate such expensive surveillance, but one never knows, does one?

Actually, it took them a year to find my house and that was with the help of a grass. But right now I was roaring through Cártama, a dusty little place 15 km from my home, and looking for a track I once used that takes me to El Rodeo on the outskirts of Coín. From there, I had a choice of tracks hidden by hedgerows and trees.

Before long, I'd made it to safety. I sat astride my Magna 65, gazing down on my home from the high ground a mile to the south. I'd found this observation post (OP) three years ago when I'd recced the area on foot. I could watch unobserved from where the cart track contoured the hillside.

I was just inside the entrance to an olive grove where my bike stood hidden by the lush foliage. The gentle hum of the busy bees collecting nectar nearly sent me to sleep in the hot afternoon calmness. I used my sea binoculars to scan the surrounding roads and tracks for hidden vehicles in the vicinity of my home. There was a metallic clicking sound as my bike cooled after the thrashing I'd given it. The powerful roar of the four-cylinder engine with the screaming rush of air was in great contrast to the serenity now surrounding me in this spectacular spot south of my home, nestling on this Spanish hillside.

I kicked down the side-stand as I got off my bike. I needed to calm down before I went indoors. I didn't want to alarm Susan so I relaxed in the bole of a nearby olive tree to settle my mind and recover my equilibrium. I longed for a cool refreshing swim as I surveyed my swimming pool, shimmering turquoise blue in the evening light. The tranquillity was bringing me back to earth when my mobile phone rang. It was Paul at Guadalahorce. 'All the parts arrived for your job just after you fucked off. I've been calling you but you've obviously not heard it because of that noisy fucking bollock rocket you are riding.'

Paul wanted me to come back to the workshop, telling me we could have the RIB finished that night. He was surprised by the lack of urgency I expressed when I told him I had problems at home. However, I asked him to have it prepared and ready for launching in three days' time. He assured me it would be done: good old Paul.

The solitude in the olive grove gave clarity to my thoughts as I planned my next moves. Tonight, I had to inform Rouge of my planned timings. And most importantly, I needed to spend some quality time with Susan before the start of my next adventure. I stayed in the OP for another hour, scanning my home. I then rode around for a while, checking the various approaches to my front gate. I telephoned Susan, asking her to open the front gate so I could ride in unhindered. I watched her through my binoculars from the high ground to the south. Two minutes later, I flashed past her, then she locked us in our private little world called Casa Budo.

As I sit in my Malaga prison cell, the greenery of my idyllic hillside home and the drama of that escape from the police triggers another memory. My mind takes me back to Malaysia, to 1965, when my pal Geordie and I were being chased along the coast road from Terendak to Malacca.

FIFTEEN

The Redcaps were chasing us because we had just trashed a brothel-bar in a punch-up with four Australian soldiers who should have known better than to get bolshy with two lunatic Brits. We were British soldiers, riding British motorbikes, pissed as British lords.

We thrilled to the roar of our bikes as we flashed past the jungle greenery, screaming through *kampongs*, sending chickens clucking and flapping in all directions, and sweeping through bends in the jungle road sending frightened dogs yelping into attap huts as our motorbikes rocketed towards Bukit-Bahru. We were headed for the Chogi-bar, an isolated shack which served as a pub for the handful of Brits who chose to live out there.

We were both riding Norton Dominators, those famous twin-engined adrenalin jabs from years ago. The Redcaps were in a long-wheelbase Land-Rover so they had no chance. However, we knew we were in the shit because these Norton twins were probably the only ones in Malaysia. Besides, every fucker knew us.

The *mamasan* at the brothel-bar knew we were from the lunatic squadron: 11th Independent Field Squadron, Royal Engineers. Stationed at Terendak Camp, the home of the 28th Commonwealth Brigade, 11 Squadron was an outstanding squadron of combat engineers composed mainly of sappers from commando engineers, paratroop engineers and engineers from the SAS whose mother regiment was Her Majesty's Royal Engineers. There was also a troop of Royal Australian Engineers. Fuck knows where they came from. Who cares? We were a minor unit but won all the major unit trophies for rugby, boxing and every other game worth watching.

Our SSM (squadron sergeant-major) was built like a brick shithouse. He was over 6 ft tall and was incredibly fit. He dominated the tennis scene at our squadron and he was also very tasty with his fists, which were like rugby balls. We knew he was going to leather us for breaking the code of conduct: no fucking about, no giving the squadron a bad name by brothel-wrecking and punch-ups, no record of violence for this outfit. No, that was reserved for the rugby pitch or the boxing ring. To my knowledge, this military unit never lost at anything, which was amazing considering it was a minor unit of possibly 200 men of whom half would be away serving in Borneo or Thailand whilst the remainder would support the brigade. Nevertheless, the half-strength squadron won everything, except, perhaps, for chess tournaments.

Geordie and I had got totally shit-faced in the Chogi-bar, then crashed out in the chinks' hammocks out back. The Redcaps duly arrived the next morning and immediately clocked our bikes stupidly hidden behind the NAAFI hut. We were then sent for and presented ourselves to the sergeant-major, who quietly mouthed, 'You fucking nobheads.' The Redcaps marched away smirking, knowing our fate.

We marched over to the headquarters office, then stood to attention in the roasting sunshine outside the officer commanding's door. The door flew open and out came the brick shithouse. 'Remove headgear and belts,' he roared. We whipped off our belts and berets, dropping them on the laterite ground to gather the red dust of Terendak. 'Quick march! Lef', rih', lef', rih', lef', rih',' he screamed as we clattered into the OC's office. 'Mark time!' he screamed, using lots of unnecessary decibels. 'HALT!'

I forget the old man's name but he had a Churchillian face with red, droopy lower eyelids. He offered his brief view of our fatherless lives, which was quite funny really. I had a problem keeping my face straight as he reminded me of a stoned-looking orang-utan I saw in Malacca zoo. I wondered if he would break into a wank like the big monkey did.

He asked if we would accept his punishment or go to courts martial. We accepted his punishment, which was to carry out some shitty jobs around camp that needed doing. This of course was the secret Masonic code which gave the brick shithouse permission to practise his combat skills on me and Geordie. He knocked fuck out of us behind the tennis courts. No facials, short and sweet, lots of body pain, no hard feelings, now fuck off.

Later that day, we rode our bikes down to the Strip, which is the name given to the cluster of brothel-bars a mile out of camp on the Malacca road. As soon as we roared along the Strip, waking everybody up, the *mamasan* of the trashed shack came wobbling out onto her veranda, waving us away.

Geordie threw a hot ball of buffalo shit, which smacked into the middle of her painted face, silencing her instantly, as most of it went down her throat. I was choking with laughter as we entered the adjacent bar. Ripocoi, a monster Maori, grabbed me in a friendly bear hug, breathing a mixture of curry fumes and Bacardi rum in my face. The Kiwis were great fun. They always played those Polynesian ukuleles when they were on the piss.

Those sentimental haunting songs would screen the lurking violence which often erupted between choruses. For now, though, a joyous gathering of lunatics was noisily getting pissed. This memory is abruptly interrupted though, and I'm brought crashing back into the shitty present.

SIXTEEN

My cell door opened with a clatter. '*Fuera, fuera!*' the screw screamed as he stood glowering at me. It was another shakedown: a cell search.

There are teams of screws called *cacheros* whose sole job is to perform body and cell searches. They are a soulless bunch of weirdos, pretty much the same as HM Customs personnel, but these bastards get rough. They know all about me so they came mob-handed with fucking big sticks. '*Fuera, ahora, rapido, hombre. Fuera!*' I marched out of my cell and stood facing the gallery wall with my arms outstretched and my legs apart, a standing, spread-eagled posture enabling a body search minus the token pushing and pulling much loved by these scabrous cretins.

The goon with surgical rubber gloves was aching to frisk and pat me down. A nonce in uniform, the worst kind of sexual predator, was about to touch me. This pervert was the infamous Don Juan, the *jefe servicios del cacheros*. He looks up arseholes like a dentist looks in mouths, and just as often. I had already decided to shit if he tried to look up mine. I flinched as the white hand touched me. He noticed the involuntary jerk of my elbow, realising that this was the instrument of destruction that would wreck his face should he step over the mark.

The wing was in complete silence as the *cacheros* trashed my

176

cell. The pervert, Juan, cautiously finished his frisk without getting too personal with my arse. Two big bastards with truncheons guarded him as he searched me. Thank Christ for that, he's normally alone and these witnesses would keep him at least partially in check. Nobody else was getting the good news, which indicated victimisation. I had been grassed for some unknown reason by a malevolent spick.

I could not see what was happening in my cell, but they were trashing it thoroughly and making lots of noise. The rest of the wing was shtum, not a sound anywhere. Everybody knew the Brit was getting the treatment.

I asked if I could help find the magic keys, or maybe there was a pneumatic drill hidden in my bed. The ungrateful *hijo de puta* glared at my smugness and knocked my bog roll into the lavatory, rendering it useless. A newspaper lay on the floor with a picture of King Juan Carlos of Spain looking up at us. I smiled and pointed at it. They all knew what I would wipe my arse on next time I needed toilet paper. I burst out laughing. There was a communal sigh of relief as I laughed, taking the tension out of the cell. They are all yellow bastards at heart, knowing somebody would get hurt if I kicked off.

Every time I am in a situation like this, I pick my targets in readiness to defend myself. Normally, I target eyes, necks, bollocks and guts. Like a good poker player, I have everything sussed in a moment as I automatically prioritise targets, keeping myself on red alert until the situation changes. Then I go back to my natural state of amber alert, because this is a rats' nest where malevolence is ever present. Relax here at your peril. Attacks come always from the rear. Spicks will never attempt a frontal attack unless they are mob-handed. God should have given us wing mirrors.

The pervert screw told me I possessed heroin and was now the main dealer on this wing. I told him he was talking bollocks, there was no shit in my cell, nor *dinero*. I glared at him as I told him to tell his gypsy informer that if he ever drops his guard when he's visiting the shithouse, I'll be removing his voice box. Don Juan's eyes told me I was right in choosing a spick gypsy as being the grass. When it comes to apportioning blame, my instincts are quite reliable. I knew the screw would tell the grass, especially as they found nothing.

It did not take long to locate my grass. I knew the culprit would look at me each time he went for a piss. He might not be the type to visit the showers so often but he had to go for a piss, so I clocked each gypsy as he entered the pisshole. Sure enough, every time Francisco Nunez Pacheco went to the toilets he checked my whereabouts before entering. I had my rat. He couldn't hide the fact he was studying me, but I could not let him know I knew. Every dog has his day and Pacheco's day was fast coming.

Every day, there are six or more men jogging around the yard, all strung out to avoid the walkers. I jog every morning so it was normal for me to be exercising at this time. I ran with Geti, a Romanian hard-case friend of mine. I had clocked Pacheco, who was strolling up and down the yard with three of his breed. I awaited my opportunity to strike. One of his group walked away to chat with somebody else, leaving my target on the end of the line of three abreast. This was my chance. I punched Geti jokingly, prompting him to race me. We dashed forward with a burst of speed coming out of the bend at the south-east corner of the yard, racing into the straight towards the north-east corner of the yard.

It was beautiful; Pacheco was right in my line. I was pounding along with Geti on my left as we approached Pacheco on my right. The other joggers had entered into the spirit of things and had accelerated with us, causing a stir on this lovely morning. Everybody heard the smack, then the beautiful scream as I broke four of Pacheco's ribs. His right lung punctured with splintered bone as I delivered the most powerful in-flight *chudan empi uchi*, an elbow strike which in layman's terms is similar to, but not quite, a forearm smash.

Nobody witnessed it apart from Pacheco himself, who knew during that final second it was too late for him to avoid me. His eyes transmitted complete hopelessness in that moment of recognition, lovely watery brown eyes showing the red contour lines of the heroin map across the whites, exposing his terror an instant before impact. I had concentrated all my energy into my elbow; the speed, distance and timing were perfect. Geti was trying to run with me but was laughing too much as he realised what I had done. He knew it was me as I gave him a knowing wink as we both doubled over laughing and trying to catch our breath at the same time.

The yard was in uproar. *Payos* (non-gypsies) shrieked with laughter when the gurney appeared to take Pacheco to the infirmary. Knowing where the blame would fall, I had secured my witnesses. I was having a good day out. There was only Pacheco's word to worry about and that's worth jack shit. 'Revenge is sweet,' sayeth the Lord. So don't allow anybody to tell you otherwise. Wonderful, satisfying vengeance. Go for it. Each time somebody shits on you, shovel it back as hard as you can. I try to live by my wits, my skills and my daring. I never shit on anybody. So revenge is the antidote for the gnawing negativity created by being shat upon by an unworthy coward. Turning the other cheek will never be my code in life. I leave that philosophy to life's victims.

Every screw in the prison knew about Pacheco's demise, so it didn't come as a surprise when Don Manuel came to see me. He wanted to know how I broke four ribs in a crowded prison yard full of grasses and got away with it. I lied, telling him it wasn't me. But it must have been somebody's really powerful *chi* to break four ribs with one strike. The silly bastard actually believed me.

He is a Shotokan black belt and he's into all that theatrical shite, believing he has a certain mystical aura about him. He tries to walk like John Wayne or Robert Mitchum but it looks like he has piles. He is quite mad and something of a poseur is our Don Manuel. I don't usually badmouth fellow martial artists, especially black belt grades, but this man is a screw in a Spanish prison so that makes him different because he is a bully, just like 90 per cent of the screws in Spain. Maybe he looks at his work in prison in a similar way to the way I look at my existence in here; the difference between my violence and his violence behind these walls is that his violence is purely bullying and my violence is survival.

Martial-arts philosophy gets bashed around a wee bit within

these walls, but so does everything else. God's laws tend to be ignored a tad but I personally try hard to stay afloat on this tide of intimidation, dirty tricks and this country's xenophobic attitude. I am so pleased to have my own cell where I can kneel and pray, or lose myself in meditation. My cell is not quite the well of silence enjoyed by cloistered monks, but I have trained myself to become oblivious to the hum and buzz of the wing, enabling my mind to wander in my pursuit of wisdom. I now realise that time spent in search of wisdom is never time lost. Meditation provides me with avenues of thought that Western scholars might treat contemptuously simply because it is something beyond their comprehension, or maybe because it seems not to be sourced from the Sea of Galilee.

Prison gives me the time to delve mentally into avenues that freedom seldom has time for. I have learned to develop eclectically in the privacy of my cell by ruthlessly separating wishful thinking from problem solving, realising that my mind combines experience and intuition to enable a sharper focus on my problems, thereby eliminating the 'what if' syndrome. I developed an ability to use mental and breathing techniques from various disciplines like Zen, Tibetan tantras and Chinese Zhan Zhuang.

I have the time to augment my minuscule knowledge of exotic practices simply by pondering the myriad philosophical mysteries. This is how I believe a martial artist should devote some of his or her time, not only to the practice and execution of painful locks and strikes but also to removing the blinkers of the parishioner and investigating the various paths available to us along our Way.

I study books that Susan sends to me every week. Susan has to send books because though we have an extensive library, it is run by the Spanish, so it doesn't really work. Lists have to be submitted for whichever books you require but the lazy spicks can't be bothered to get off their arses to get them. Spick inmates always receive their books but foreigners like me are merely *giris* so not worthy of the effort. Thanks to my lovely Susan, though, I have plenty of books in my cell.

The moment I step out into the maelstrom of Spanish flotsam, all noble thoughts disappear instantly as I meld in with the tide of human scum. I try my best not to be infected whilst attempting to live harmoniously with the prevailing population of sodomites and heroin salesmen. Anything to do with heroin is acutely alien to me, unlike most prisoners, who succumb to the constant temptations of the pushers. Moral fibre is a rare commodity indeed, especially amongst the Spanish inmates.

I look at some of the killers and nonces here and wonder about Christ's great question: 'What has a man profited if he shall gain the whole world and lose his own soul?' I am now looking at a monster who is playing *pachis* (a dice race) on a table with three of his countrymen. He raped and killed a young girl and here he is throwing dice on a table with his friends. He looks like any other Spanish gypsy and I suppose like most of those in here, he couldn't care a monkey's fuck about Christ's question. Though on his sweaty back he does wear a large tattoo of Christ wearing his crown of thorns with that familiar lamenting facial expression so loved by the Hispanic races.

I think about Christ's question and wonder how far down one needs to go to lose one's soul and then I remember my parish priest Father Kelly warning us kids that should we enter any other church for whatever reason we would lose our souls to the devil. I wonder how Christ feels about that interpretation of his question as I feel right now ready to rip the flesh of Christ's face off the back of this soulless bastard sitting here laughing and playing the dice.

He catches my eye, then averts his gaze as he interprets my loathing, his shoulders hunching in an effort to become invisible to my open hostility. I am pleased that he is frightened of me and is now cringing uncomfortably, knowing my eyes are boring hatefully into the back of his head. Is having that feeling a more serious sin than visiting a different denomination church?

The gypsy dirtbag knows I would love to take his life just as he took the young girl's, but he can't understand why, because I am in here with him so we must have something in common, especially because *modulo* 13 is the domain of the truly revolting inmate. I search the faces of the other three bastards playing *pachis* and they remind me of characters from Robert Louis Stevenson's *Treasure Island*, all earrings and bandanas with lashings of sweat and grime. These creatures are the friends of Francisco Nunez Pacheco, possibly the lowest scumsucker in this dreadful place. Their dark looks go well with their dark souls.

SEVENTEEN

The gypsies on the wing were a bit miffed with me because their source of smack was in the infirmary. Another reason for unrest was because the dirty deed was performed by the lone Englishman: an isolated, individual upstart with no back-up and no support. The impudent *hijo de puta* must be taught a lesson. He must be stabbed to death by a gypsy to restore the status quo.

The plot to kill me was not a well-kept secret. The perpetrators talked openly about it amongst themselves, each volunteering to be the glorious restorer of gypsy dominance, the hero of the hour whose name shall live for evermore amongst snot-nosed children living on earth-packed floors. Other gypsies were looking at me with pity in their eyes as though I only had one leg or something. Maybe I don't have long to live, but these primitives will not be the cause of my demise. I set about discovering exactly who was going to kill me.

Pacheco was a crap guitar player but the noise of the syncopated clappers surrounding him hid the fact. My guess was the syncopated clappers were to be my assassins. I guessed correctly. Several people tipped me off about my impending doom. I heard three gypsies were to kill me very soon. A Romanian friend told me he overheard three blokes planning the dirty deed whilst chasing the dragon in the shithouse. I now knew exactly which three nutters to deal with.

The best form of defence is attack, and it is imperative to be absolutely savage when doing so. You must deliver a good hiding never to be forgotten, ruthlessly inflicting lasting pain: broken bones, torn ligaments and dislocated joints. Bushido: the Way of the Warrior. Smackheads are at their lowest in the early morning. They feel like shit until their first fix. My assassins were each under surveillance by my little group of friends, their every move watched by professionals. One such is Karlos 'Jackal', a serious man, an educated man of letters: ETA, to be precise. Karlos is serving two twenty-four-year sentences for terrorist activities against the state. He was a journalist until his writing skills got him into trouble. He sent a government official a letter bomb.

Karlos speaks good English so it was no surprise when he came to my breakfast table whispering, 'Zey arr in ze sheethouse sniffling ze brown stuff. T'ree of zem.'

I calmly left my table and strolled to the doorway of the *comedor* where a screw stood idly surveying the diners. Breakfast was shit scran anyway: coffee, bread and jam, so I wasn't missing much by leaving it unfinished. I walked past the screw, taking the left corridor leading to the toilets. I quickly checked who was in the vicinity: all clear. I could hear voices in the lavatory section so I crept in to find the Three Stooges in a huddle, holding silver foil with a cigarette lighter beneath it scorching the heroin and taking turns to sniff the fumes. They were huddled next to trap no. 2, the second lavatory in the row of four. Fortunately, the bogs were empty; there were only the four of us.

I picked my moment just as Curly was taking his sniff. I banged each of his kidneys in quick succession. Grabbing his mop of greasy black hair, I yanked his head back. I gave his protruding Adam's apple a crushing *haito uchi*, the base of my thumb hacking into his windpipe. That left Larry and Mo looking at me through glazed organ-stops. An open-fingered *nukite* into each pair of eyes rendered them helpless. I needed to work fast to prevent the screams that would attract the screw. Mo went first. I punched his throat as hard as I could, sending him into trap no. 3, sitting him on the filthy shitter. Larry took a *mae geri* to his pubic bone, sending him backwards, cracking his head on the tiled wall. I gave him *kin geri*, a groin kick hard enough to send his nuts up to his lungs. He lay in the piss, out cold. I quickly entered trap no. 3 to give Mo the good news, breaking his ribs on each side, then breaking his collarbone. I pummelled his eyes enough to blacken them for weeks. I then revisited Curly and Larry, giving both of them broken ribs. I swiftly applied *ude gatame* (arm lock/crush) to each in turn, dislocating their elbows. Now that's what I call a good trip, smack at its best, a memorable day out.

It took approximately one minute to sort those three out and as I came out of the toilets Geti and Karlos were coming in to help me out. They did an about turn and the three of us walked through the *sala* into the yard. I couldn't believe my luck: my friends were the only witnesses, nobody clocked my activities.

Vanessa came mincing over to me five minutes after the gurneys had taken the stooges away. '*Qué tal, guappo? Pareces censado.*' ('How're you doing, handsome? You look tired.') I told him I wasn't tired and to fuck off or else he would need a gurney.

The inevitable visit from Don Manuel soon happened. I argued about smack wars amongst rival dealers but he was having none of that. He knew it was me but had no grounds to do anything about it. The same went for Curly, Larry and Mo, as they couldn't remember who or what had hit them. They shouldn't have fucked with the lone Brit. Knowing that these three Spanish gypsies would most certainly have stabbed me, possibly taking my life, erases any feelings of guilt or remorse that would have naturally followed such happenings. I don't strut around the *pateo* bragging, as they would have done. I sit quietly and write to my darling Susan.

EIGHTEEN

I was feeling good now, so I cranked up my training routine and started to diet. Malaga prison isn't exactly an epicurean hideaway on the Costa del Sol, but fruit is available every day, not quite gourmet quality, but edible – sometimes. My fruit intake grew as my friends gave me theirs when they learned about the diet and my training.

I missed breakfast and jogged for an hour instead. I would then do a one-hour bag workout in the gym. The gym here is roomy but poorly equipped. Everything seems to be cobbled together from scrap iron, especially the weight benches and the Smith machine. Every week, something has to be re-welded. The whole thing is typically Spanish; even the welder is a Spanish inmate and what he knows about welding could be tattooed on an ant's arse. The punch-bag is also a Heath Robinson affair, tied together with string and rope, looking like Albert Pierrepoint (the famous British hangman) has just left it there. The gym is all we have to maintain our muscles, so there used to be a dedicated group of blokes trying to keep some semblance of order. I was one of them. I was soon to become the boss of this gym, too.

In previous prisons, I had prominent roles in gymnasiums, so I wasn't surprised when I was made gym boss on *modulo* 13. Don Manuel was instrumental in this because he knew me at La

Moraleja. It mainly happened because I was always pestering the screws to open it up. Eventually, it dawned on them to appoint somebody who could possibly control things in the gym and account for the equipment. So I was approached by Don Manuel, Don Roberto and the *educador*, Don Francisco. Francisco was a nice man, a caring man. I actually liked and respected this Spaniard, a rarity in Spanish prisons, harder to find than Christ's bones.

The three of them explained my duties, which included a count of weights, bars and skipping ropes. Also, there was to be a no-smoking policy, which gave Manuel and Roberto perverse pleasure in telling me to maintain because every spick over the age of five years smokes. To uphold a no-smoking rule, even in the gym, would be problematic. I needed big 'No smoking' signs. The *educador* found some in the infirmary. The serious fitness freaks were the Romanians, so I recruited them to help uphold the no-smoking rule. I got them on my side by telling them they could help me clean the gym at the weekend when it was closed, thereby allowing them a training session on Saturday and Sunday when access would otherwise have been denied.

On my first day in charge, I put the biggest no-smoking sign at the entrance to the gym: no mistaking this. The Romanians were the first in for training. They are all big lads, especially Daniel, who stands at 6 ft 8 in. in his socks. Daniel is boxing fit and has fast hands. I've studied him doing bag training; he's a hard hitter with both hands. He slots in the occasional vicious head-butt as he works the bag. He endures a gruelling daily workout with punch-bag, skipping-rope and free weights. This requires terrific self-discipline, which I admire, but am wary of, because this man is totally focused when destroying anybody that upsets him. However, receiving pain from me during training does not affect him; he takes it in good heart just like any other martial-arts pupil.

I do inflict quite a lot of pain on him because he tests the technique. In other words, he attempts to escape from painful locks and strangles causing stress and strains on muscles and joints. I have choked him out a few times simply because he fought so hard to escape strangleholds. This is good training for me, exposing any crap restraining methods and iffy techniques.

This man respects my methods. He values the fact I am teaching him how to wreck a human being quickly with his bare hands. I taught him the best way to practise his head-butts. This is something I've worked hard at over the years of bag-work, developing an effective and demoralising method of neutralising the most ardent attacker.

As with all strikes, distance and timing are crucial. But unlike a kick or a punch, the head-butt is truly difficult to avoid once it has been initiated. That is because a head-butt is not normally launched unless the user is sure of a hit. A head-butt is not the same as heading a football into a goalmouth. No, the head-butt is a deliberate, dynamic, focused thrusting of the head into the target in an attempt to cause tissue trauma deep into the point of impact. Many muscles are employed in a face-wrecking head-butt, so to be an exponent of this devastating strike, you need to learn how to deliver the good news effectively. A leather, heavy bag is required and must be clean of knuckle skin and blood, scrupulously so around the area of head impact, for obvious reasons.

It takes possibly three weeks of daily training before the face becomes conditioned to the pounding it receives. The bruises and the blue and yellow shading which appears around the nose, eyes and cheekbones soon disappear. Be prepared to buy some new shirts because your neck will grow thicker. I have an eighteen-inch neck thanks to head-butt training. Whilst training, always imagine the punch-bag is a man. Concentrate your thrust deep into the impact area. Develop speed of thrust rather than power of thrust; there's a difference. The weight of your head is sufficient to impact itself hard enough without you trying to add power by using neck muscles to add impetus; it doesn't work like that. It happens naturally for me now; my neck muscles merely provide the nodding action required to angle my head for the impact. Whilst training, control the bag by keeping it stationary for each strike. Don't try to head-butt a swinging bag. Don't worry about the stinging around your face; if your nose and cheeks sting a tad, then you know you are achieving penetration with your forehead.

Develop your head-butt to follow a blocking technique. Imagine the bag is an attacker punching you with a big John

Wayne punch. Defend with an *age uke* or an *uchi ude uke* or whichever block you naturally use. Follow the block with a head-butt; get into the action and make it effective. Start moving around the bag and you will find you are using your forward foot to initiate the thrust of your head. This is fine to begin with but you must practise with your feet in a casual rather than a fighting stance. Adopting a fighting stance always telegraphs your intentions. Also, train yourself to respond from grabs.

If you begin head-butt training, use it as your warm-down at the end of your training session. Start with 20 attempts at getting it perfect. Take your time, stay loose and focus on delivering the good news to that bag. Twenty is enough to start you off; stay with 20 a day for the first week, then start to gradually increase to 50 a day. I do a minimum of 100 a day.

Arguably, an elbow strike is more penetrating, although I do more damage with my head than my elbow. If you do get hit with *empi*, though, you will wake up with a crowd around you. This is what happened to one gypsy after slagging Daniel in the gym. It was all over before I could intervene; Daniel is amazingly quick. The gypsy, a long-haired snot-candle by the name of Kiko, was demonstrating his dislike of no-smoking signs. Deliberately exaggerating the opening of a cigarette packet and making a big deal about asking his fellow shitpiles for a light, he caught Daniel's attention, who said politely, '*Por favor. No fumar aquí, amigo.*'

Kiko, pirouetting dramatically, started spitting abuse into Daniel's granite face. Supported by his cohorts, adding abuse to this obviously planned day out, Kiko thrust his face nearer to Daniel; bad move, *amigo*. Daniel's fists became a blur as Kiko's face disintegrated. An audible crack echoed around the gym as the cheekbone broke when Daniel finished the pummelling with an *empi* strike, followed by a slurping sound as the *nukite* finger flashed in and out of the eye socket. The final blow was an incredible *oi zuki*, right fist under the sternum, turning off the lights in Kiko's central nervous system, guaranteeing an infirmary bed for the night.

The flamenco charisma and bullring machismo from Kiko's *fuerte hombres* had dissipated in a flash. They were now shitting bricks because a wall of Romanian muscle was between them and the exit. It was now or never. I decided to underline the no-smoking rule with a loud *kiai* and a devastating *empi* strike to the heart of Kiko's adjutant, a big turd called Paco. Whilst England was preparing Paco for the infirmary, Kiko's pals were getting the treatment from Eastern Europe. The Romanians and a Sicilian capo, Jimmy Gallante, were busy kicking and punching the no-smoking rule into the Andalucian shitpile on the gym floor. The message was quickly understood about not smoking in the gym. My next objective was to get no-spitting signs made.

Spanish housewives and mothers must be continually scraping up the nasal droppings of their menfolk. I've watched them gob at the dinner table so I imagine they gob in the bedroom. I expect it won't be long before I see somebody piss under the table. I suspect that being surrounded by snot and gob gives them a warm feeling of home. So it is not surprising when you do the splits on somebody's phlegm anywhere in this filthy prison. And you really do slip and slide when visiting the toilets. As the day goes on, the situation worsens; a visit to a lavatory cubicle puts a scar on your memory for ever, so most people stand outside and piss through the doorway, thereby helping to clean the floor. Unlike the indigenous population, I have trained my body to perform ablutions in my cell, thereby avoiding the need to use the communal cesspit.

The gymnasium was to become a sanitary sanctuary for the fitness freaks, so the *no escupir* signs were displayed and obeyed because any dirty bastard gobbing in the gym was sure to be decked by a flurry of European boots. We soon had the gym cleaned up. Neat bleach was used to purge the toilets and all surfaces were scoured. We made it usable and exclusive to gym regulars who maintained the place.

Time was going by easier now because I was doing a lot of meaningful training and I had a hard group of serious villains in my combat class: men like Geti, who helped me enormously in planning a route from Turkey across the Black Sea into Germany via the Danube, and Jimmy Gallante, a wealthy mafioso, who was well placed amongst the jet set. Jimmy and I planned a super job operating out of St Kitts in the Caribbean into the Emerald Isle. This job would involve the use of a famous 21-metre yacht belonging to a dandy member of the royalty.

The job is an absolutely cracking little number (no pun intended). Every facet has been carefully studied and planned in minute detail. I daydream about skippering this yacht, but that is all it will be: a daydream. There will be no more skippering of yachts for me, for I have given my word to the big Skipper in the sky and to my precious Susan that there will be no more sailing close to the wind for me. I will strike my own sail and allow the big Skipper to guide me through the remainder of life's voyage.

However, thoughts of the sea take me back to Casa Budo where I am kissing Susan goodbye as I begin my lone adventure on a sea journey I should never have undertaken.

NINETEEN

Paul had a problem with the Suzuki engine set-up, holding the job up for a further week. I was gutted. Fortunately, Rouge held back the cargo in the Rif hills so it wasn't much of a problem for him. The problem arose as I arrived for the launching. My heart was set on sailing that night so I wasn't thinking straight when another man at the workshop offered me a journey that very night.

Charles Gurnel, a Frenchman, was with Driss bin Massoud, a Moroccan, in Eduardo's workshop ordering a new RIB. They heard my outburst with Paul and guessed what my problem was. They had a job arranged for that night but were unhappy with the Moroccan skipper so propositioned me.

They gave me the details, telling me the RIB was ready to be launched at Torrox, a little town one hour up the coast from Malaga. I rapidly considered the proposition, checking coordinates, discussing refuelling arrangements at sea, cargo, money: bollocks, I'd do it. So instead of going home to spend a few extra days with my wife, I chose the adrenalin trip. I stupidly ignored my instincts by going to Torrox with them.

I knew the boatyard and the greasy bastard who owned it. This man had launched me several times in the past. He is Spanish so I refused to trust him. I checked with Gurnel that he knew nothing about this job: not even my return and recovery time. Semi-satisfied, I got on with my kit check. I connected a water-hose to the water intake on the Tohatsu 150 HP outboard motor and started her up. Whilst warming up, I connected in turn each of the fuel lines from the three fuel tanks. This was a small craft at only 6 metres long, but ideal to carry a cargo of 700 kilos. She only had one engine so I was breaking my own rules by using a RIB without two or more engines, but there was a 9.8 HP Tohatsu auxiliary engine stowed, so I had some back-up if the 150 died. I could at least get home with a 9.8 outboard.

After satisfying myself all was shipshape and with everything secure for a high-speed trip, the Valiant 600 was launched. Driss gave me two mobile phones in waterproof plastic bags, the kind that permits use without removing from the bag. The sea conditions were perfect for a fast ride: no swell, not a ripple, great! The Valiant floated away from the launch trailer into deeper water. I hit the starter and quickly brought her up to 25 knots, heading due south. I checked everything was secure on board, then opened her up to 40 knots. The sun was falling over the horizon when I took a south-westerly heading, turning towards Capa-Negro, just east of Ceuta on the North African coast.

When leaving shore in a fast RIB, I always experience a strange sense of freedom and foreboding. There's exhilaration, but when darkness falls, trepidation comes with it because of unseen dangers, especially debris. Then comes teeth-gritting acceptance of danger as man and RIB hurtle through the night, a vessel of screaming stress. The RIB becomes part of me, like a limb. My feelings grow towards the craft because I live or die by her performance. If this one had failed me between now and my return to Spanish shores there would have been a great chance of losing my life. Anybody who says this game is easy is a liar. I nearly died as I narrowly missed a massive baulk of timber not two metres from my prow.

The gods of the sea smiled on me this night. Sea conditions could not have been better. There was a slight swell as I roared into Moroccan waters, but nothing to hinder me. I arrived at the rendezvous position two miles out to sea from Capa-Negro at midnight.

One of the mobile phones rang so I cut my revs and dug out the phone from my parka pocket. The engine was ticking over quietly as I answered the phone. Rapid Arabic flowed in my ear. I shouted, 'Fuck, fuck, fuck, you raghead fucking twat. Speak English!'

Shocked silence for a moment, then an oily voice said, 'Ah, Englishman, where are you?' I knew this preamble; I'd experienced it before. 'I am at the rendezvous alone. The *patera* should be here. It's midnight, time to give me my cargo,' I said.

A pregnant silence for a moment, then he pulled the usual Moroccan trick by saying, 'Ah, Englishman. There is a change of plan. You must come into the shore at the new GPS position which I will now give you.'

I then told him about my change of plan. I informed him that I would circle this RV for a further 15 minutes, then I was going home. He said, 'You can't, you haven't enough fuel. I have your fuel here on the beach. You cannot go home, Englishman.'

I said, 'Fifteen minutes, Abdul, and I'm gone.' I hung up on him.

The sea and the night sky were incredibly beautiful. I cut my engine and relaxed to the sounds of the sea. It was then that I noticed a school of dolphins playing 'catch the Englishman', super creatures grinning at me with their effusive greetings, giving out little squeaks and snorts of happiness. In my imagination, I thought they were giggling at me. It was a moonless night but the starlight shone on the dolphins' spray, creating a phosphorescent glow on the flying droplets. Such moments will live with me for ever.

Leaning over the rubber sponson, I reached out my hand, hoping to touch one of God's better creations. But they teased me by swiftly gliding towards my hand only to dive gracefully under the boat. The ringing phone disturbed our fun. The dolphins, seemingly annoyed by this rude interruption, sped away. 'Where are you, Englishman?' It was the Moroccan's oily voice. I imagined his teeth gnashing as he spoke. I replied, 'I'm at the rendezvous, Abdul. You have another ten minutes before I fuck off. And don't tell me about fuel. I can get to the nearest Spanish beach without your help.'

Another silence, then a stream of Arab curses as he vented his spleen at me. Then, through gritted teeth, 'Stay right where you are, Englishman. My *patera* will be with you soon. Possibly 20 or 30 minutes so don't go away.'

I answered, 'Get on with it, then. You have fucked this job because you didn't follow instructions. You Arab cunt!' I switched off the phone and checked my bearings to see how far I had drifted from the RV. Five minutes later, I was circling my station awaiting my cargo. Half an hour later, the *patera* arrived with five grinning bin Ladens and one Arab spiv dressed in jeans and leather bomber jacket. He was obviously my travelling companion, put on board to make sure the cargo went to the right people. I said, 'Shucks, Gabby!' That's what Roy Rogers would have said because here were five Gabby Hayes each wearing a fez.

They drew alongside to transfer the cargo into my vessel. I roared at them to load it properly but I might as well have spoken to a passing whale. I raced for'ard shouting my brains out, grabbing a bale of hashish, throwing it back into the *patera*. I then explained how the lot would go overboard if they didn't load it properly. They all looked at the spiv.

I shouted at him. 'What's your fucking name?' His hands came palm up in front of his chest as though he was about to juggle two invisible watermelons. 'No spikka Eengleesh,' he said. 'OK. *Nombre*. What's your fucking *nombre*?'

Fortunately, he spoke a little Spanish and told me his unpronounceable name. 'Oh, fucking hell. Fuck it! Your name is Billy. *Te llama* Billy. Me François,' I said, poking my chest.

Two minutes later, everybody knew the score. The cargo was stowed securely and Billy was filling my aft fuel tank from the 20-litre *jarafes* (plastic fuel canisters) which the Gabby Hayes quintet was passing over to the Valiant. We stowed the extra fuel and I could now see that the Valiant was overloaded. The buggers had put 34 30-kilo bales onboard a 6-metre RIB. By the time I had finished counting the bales, the Gabby Hayes quintet had cast off my painter and, leaving Billy with me, distanced themselves, sailing rapidly away without a care in the world. Unlike me. I had to decide what to do about a six-metre RIB with more than one tonne of hashish onboard.

I decided to make an effort with my cargo rather than ditch part of it. I shifted into forward gear and slowly headed north at five knots while Billy organised himself and found a comfortable bed on top of the cargo. I opened my picnic cooler box, taking a sandwich and a bottle of water from it. Billy immediately dove into my cooler box, ransacking it like a Biafran refugee. I grabbed his collar and yanked him up out of my box. I was now angry because he was here with nothing and I had enough food only for me. I explained that he could have some water but he couldn't touch the food. I knew I was talking to a ravenous hyena near a dead pig, so I relented and gave him two chocolate bars and a packet of biscuits, telling him that was it, no more. We settled down again as I took a north-easterly heading and opened the throttle.

I was just about hitting 20 knots when the engine dropped revs and became erratic. I slowed and put her out of gear but there was no response from the throttle. I guessed it was an electrical problem but now wasn't the time to start farting around with an electrical system that resembled tumbleweed stuffed into the helm. I switched off the ignition and sat there thinking about the non-existent plan B. Then I remembered P-six and silently called myself a gormless prick. I could see the whites of Billy's eyes as he realised just how much of a tub of shit this boat really was. But his panic disappeared as I switched on the ignition and started her again. She roared into life as sweet as a nut, so off we went again.

The engine ran sweetly for ten minutes and the problem returned. I came to the conclusion there was some kind of cut-out preventing the engine from labouring too much. It must have been a Spanish idea. Again, I considered shedding some of the load, but valuing my reputation, decided against it. I have never lost a cargo nor fluffed a job. This was my livelihood, but this journey might have killed me.

We had just got under way again when Billy pointed to a light a couple of miles off the starboard beam. My stomach lurched as silent alarms clanged in my ears and I tried to figure out its course. I frantically pulled out my binoculars from my backpack and focused on the light. I couldn't quite make it out, but I knew it was coming for me. As the light came nearer, I could see it was a warship, a naval vessel, but from which navy? It was coming right at me when the engine conked out. Billy was about to throw the hashish overboard so I grabbed him, telling him to be quiet and lay low. I would say when to ditch the shit.

The warship stopped approximately 1 km south of me. I then heard a loud metallic clunk as the biggest searchlight in the world illuminated the sea. Thankfully, there was a slight swell and we were low in the water so we were very difficult to detect, especially on a moonless night. However, they knew we were nearby because zodiacs were being lowered from davits near the stern of the warship.

As the zodiacs were lowering away, I could see men on board. It occurred to me that the ship could not move whilst lowering zodiacs and crew. They were suspended above the water, so bollocks, I'd be off. I leaped into the jockey seat and started her up. I headed due north at full throttle. Now was the time to ditch the shit but I didn't think about it. I was wondering how far I could get in the next ten minutes before the engine died again. I made a mental note here to kill Charles Gurnel on sight, the lousy frog bastard.

I headed north for five minutes or so, then I turned east, making a dog's leg. I was prepared to zigzag all the way to Italy but the engine croaked, so we lay wallowing in the swells. Ten minutes later, two zodiacs raced by, 200 metres off the port beam. They didn't see us, many thanks to the gods of the sea. I sat there waiting for the mother ship to run over me, but she didn't because the most beautiful sea mist came over us, obliterating everything. Oh, what a lovely fog. I started her up and headed east at about 12 knots. The engine ran smoothly for two hours, then I increased the revs so she cut out again in protest.

I told Billy we couldn't get to the unloading point before dawn so we would stay out at sea until 2300hrs tonight. I would be able to phone Driss later when we came into range. So now we'd get some sleep. We bedded down on the hashish and I fell asleep to the sounds of the sea. I awoke to the sounds of Billy screaming, '*Tiburón! Tiburón!*' which means 'Shark!' I scrambled to my feet to see the sea around us churning with moving beasts. There was the sound of a massive fart as a blowhole vented the breath from one of these great creatures swimming around us.

This beast of a fish was 4 ft away from me and several others were nearby, wondering why Billy was making so much noise. I shut Billy up, so these giants of the sea got bored and buggered off, possibly looking for another Moroccan comedian. Silence again, so I thought I would have a snack. I opened my cooler box to find it empty. The thieving wog bastard had eaten everything as I slept. The greedy, selfish, bloated dollop of camel shit had gorged all my rations. There was nothing left to eat and I was hungry.

There was a paddle lashed to the sponson, which I took to Billy's head, knocking him unconscious with one blow. I then went through his pockets, finding two chocolate bars. This was all that was left from a box loaded with chocolate, sandwiches, biscuits and a flask of hot soup. Where was the empty flask? The gutsing bastard must have thrown it overboard when he emptied it. I thought about putting him over the side. I should have done, too, because later he would steal more from me, causing me great problems.

I started the engine and headed east. The sun got higher, making short work of the mist. Billy started twitching. Eventually, he sat up, rubbing his head, wondering where the bus was that had run over him. He sat sorrowfully eyeing me as I slowly took the wrapping off the first chocolate bar. I made a big deal about eating it and drinking my water. I knew he was thirsty but the case of water bottles was next to my leg with the paddle lying across it. He pointed to the water and gestured for a drink. I said, '*No agua para ladróns puesto mi barco. No agua para ti. Hijo de puta.*' He lay down with his back to me so I couldn't see his face. The sun was hot so his thirst was raging.

An hour later, he propped himself on an elbow to look at me with the most pained expression and asked for water. I grabbed a bottle of water and threw it intentionally over his head into the sea, where it landed with a splash. He nearly dove in to retrieve it, but thought better of it. I took a fresh bottle, had a big swig, smacked my lips then put it back with the others. I strung out the water torture for another hour or so. Then, because I'm a big softie, I tossed him a litre of water, which didn't touch the sides as it poured down the thieving bastard's throat.

I slowly chugged through the Mediterranean Sea, heading eastward until I was 40 miles from Torrox. I then turned north and sailed another 20 miles nearer to the Spanish coast. It was from this location that I tried the phone. Driss was ecstatic. At last, he'd located his precious shit. His concern was not for me or Billy, it was for the cargo.

I quickly made the arrangements to unload at 2300hrs at RV no. 2, which was Algarrobo beach, not far from Torre del Mar. If there were any problems on Algarrobo beach, then RV no. 3 would be used at Nerja. I then closed the phone. There would be no more contact between us unless there was an emergency.

I planned to do the final 20 miles at 5 knots, so I hit the starter at 1900hrs and slowly headed in to the Spanish shore over flat, calm waters. I had explained everything to Billy and instructed him to keep his thieving eyes peeled for patrols. This is the most dangerous part of the job. This is the part where most people get caught. My plan was to move slowly, making the RIB more difficult to detect. It is my belief that fast-moving craft are easy to detect because they are eye-catching and because they leave a big wake.

The journey to the RV was slow and uneventful. I was correct in my guess that the Guardia Civil at this hour would be in the bars, on the piss till midnight. They do not expect to see any sign of *traficantes* till after midnight. It was a doddle. The sun dropped slowly over the horizon and darkness fell. The sea was like a millpond as I brought the Valiant into shore. Not a soul could be seen on Algarrobo beach as I tilted the engine before the hull crunched lightly on the beach. I had cut the engine to prevent prop damage so now there was only the noise of the sea.

Suddenly, there was movement as the unloading party appeared from nowhere. Billy leapt off and six Moroccans leapt on. They frenziedly tossed 34 bales of hashish onto Algarrobo beach. I was sitting on my jockey-seat waiting for the push that would float me into deeper water, when Billy climbed back aboard.

My backpack, containing my equipment and binoculars, was

attached to the GPS mounting on the helm. Billy grabbed it, yanking it off the helm, taking the GPS and my bag with him as he jumped ashore. At the same time, the RIB was pushed away from the shore, and I knew I'd have to lower the engine from its tilt position and bugger off. I started her up, slowly riding astern, clearing the beach quietly using low revs so as not to attract attention. I checked up and down the beach, then out to sea, all clear.

Cursing that thieving bastard, I headed south, slowly increasing my speed. When I was well clear of the shore, I opened her up, racing across the sea like a bounding greyhound free from its trap. No restraints, light as a feather, screaming curses at that lowlife as I realised the GPS had gone with the bag. My change of clothes, my charts, my binoculars, the RIB's documents and the GPS had been stolen by a man with 34 bales of hash worth over a million pounds in his charge. This ridiculous theft would change my life forever.

I was soon to discover how. But for now I was thinking about speaking to Mohammed Bukr bin Essa the next day to get my things back. He was the boss of the overall contract, which was the eventual movement of 30 tonnes. I had merely brought across the first tonne.

My plan had been to stay 20 miles out to sea, then come in to hide the RIB at Torrox at 0900hrs in the morning. So without my GPS, I decided it would be prudent to stay within sight of the lighthouse at Torrox. This I did, so I cut the engine and set-to with scrubbing brush and washing-up liquid, cleaning all evidence of recent employment. I checked my watch at 0040hrs. I don't remember falling asleep but 20 minutes later I was awakened by gunfire and a raging sea. I thought I was having a nightmare as I awoke bathed in strong light. A vessel was bearing down on me with somebody firing a weapon in my direction. An amplified voice was shouting staccato instructions at me in Spanish. The sea was crashing all around me.

During my 20-minute kip, a squall had whipped the sea into a raging tempest. I was so fatigued, in such a deep sleep, it took a combination of gunfire, raging sea and a harsh searchlight to awaken me. The searchlight was dazzling but I managed to catch the line somebody threw at me and tie it to my painter. The RIB was pulled alongside a sleek Customs patrol boat as I was ordered at gunpoint to jump onto a scramble net draped over the side.

Leaping from the RIB, I grabbed the net with both hands but an angry wave sent the RIB crashing into my legs dangling below the net. Fortunately, the rubber sponson absorbed the impact but my calf muscles were now numb, so the hands that pulled me aboard thought I was pissed because I couldn't stand properly. The hands held me upright for a moment, then the man with the gun indicated for me to go below, wagging the pistol at me, looking as though he did this every night. I was helped below, then treated with noisy hostility by the gunfighter, his body language straight out of a spaghetti western, but more like a spaghetti nautical as the sea bashed us.

Without invitation, I sat on the floor to massage my calves, ignoring the gunfighter who was spluttering like Sylvester the cat. The senior officer suddenly appeared and told me he was taking me to La Caleta for questioning. He caught me studying his radar equipment so ordered me to lie facing aft. The radio operator was busy asking police in the area if they had found any hashish or illegal immigrants on this sector of the coast. I realised I was still in the shit but remained confident because the RIB was clean.

The engine pitch changed so I guessed we were coming into port. All movement ceased and the noise abated, leaving only the hum of various bits of equipment. Men were shouting to each other outside, then came the clump of boots on the deck above me. My arse was kicked by a burly spick slob dressed in semi-nautical uniform of black boots, black trousers, white shirt with black tie and one of those heavy-knit pullovers with epaulettes with the silver paraphernalia of rank much loved by armchair warriors. In passable English, he asked me where had I been since the day before yesterday. This question exposed the boatyard grass.

I told him a story about going to Fuengirola to pick up some spare parts for various engines I was working on and then spending the night at home. Early yesterday, I said, I worked on two boats in Fuengirola and last night I took some oil, filters and tools to a tourist fishing boat 20 miles out from Torrox. I had left them and was returning to Torrox when I developed engine problems about ten miles out. I was working on my engine but the sea conditions changed dramatically after midnight, putting me in great danger. Thank God I was rescued by this patrol boat. I would have perished at sea if they hadn't arrived in time.

He asked for the boat papers. I told him I would bring them tomorrow after I'd spoken to the owner. He was standing over me with his right boot pressing on my hipbone. I was lying on my side, looking up at him and his two shipmates. Three more Stooges. They were telling each other this crafty English *cabrón* must be skilful to survive that terrible sea, but there are no reports from the police so we have nothing on him apart from him not using navigation lights. The *cabrón* must have thrown his GPS overboard, his boat is clean so we have *nada*.

They questioned me further and when I told them I earned my living teaching martial arts and I had black belts in karate, aikido and ju-jitsu, the boot was respectfully removed and a chair was offered. The atmosphere changed instantly.

Now the Three Stooges were affable loons, behaving as though we were all good pals. The man with the boot was the senior rank and was possibly the ugliest man in the world. His face was like that of a bulldog licking piss off a nettle. His breath stank like a polecat's lair. God bless the woman who slept with this awful bastard; she must have had chronic sinusitis and been totally blind. They were getting jolly now and I half expected booze to appear, but bollocks, I was tired and wanted my bed. They wanted to talk about Singapore and everywhere, but I was falling asleep.

I made a big deal about checking the time and standing to leave and asking had they finished with me. To my utter amazement, the Three Stooges stood up, as did the captain and two crewmembers. In unison, they snapped off a very smart salute. Coldstream Guardsmen couldn't have done it better: up two three, down two three; regulation timing for a military salute. I returned the compliment with my Boy-Scout dib-dib salute and got myself off that fucking tub.

The Valiant was moored alongside the patrol boat, which was named *Fenix*. The captain escorted me off his vessel, telling me to bring the Valiant's papers to the office in Malaga on Monday, then I could remove the Valiant from La Caleta. I thanked him and walked away.

Strolling along the quayside, I dialled Susan to come and pick me up. The poor girl had been up all night wondering where I was. I explained how to get to La Caleta and that I would be at the Ship roundabout. That is the big roundabout with a brightly painted fishing smack sitting in the centre of it near the entrance to the port. It would take an hour for Susan to get there so I strolled out of the port heading down the road towards the roundabout. I looked at my reflection in a shop window and was shocked to see how bad I looked. I was reeking of petrol, damp with sweat and sea water and looked just like a terrorist with a camouflaged parka, face-veil around my neck and a balaclava-style ski-mask rolled up on my head. The only thing missing was the RPG 7. If a patrol car clocked me now, I would have had a repeat performance of the last couple of hours. I arrived unmolested at the roundabout and took shelter in a shop doorway out of the driving rain.

At 0430hrs, Susan arrived and she quickly pulled off my headgear and parka, telling me to strip and put on my tracksuit, which she had brought in the car. She also produced a flask of hot coffee. This girl is a diamond and I will love her for ever. I drank some coffee and in the luxurious warmth of the car and the familiar scent of Susan, I started to fall asleep as she chattered on about leaving this stupid and dangerous life behind. All she wanted was to be with me constantly. We could live in a croft in the arsehole of Shetland breeding hairy ponies just so long as we were together. She hated the separations and could not understand my quest for adventure and the reasons why I risked my life at sea. Had I listened to her when she first started telling me off about it, our lives would have been so very different. What a fool I've been putting her through such trials and tribulations for a bit of extra money and excitement.

TWENTY

The wailing siren awoke me so I got out of my prison bed and got ready to start another day in hell. I was eating my bread, alone at the table, when Karlos the Cackle came over to tell me that ten new prisoners were coming on the wing this morning. 'None of zem iz Eengleesh,' he said. 'But one of zem iz a crazy swecko, a cop killer from Sweden. Ze screw, he say he putting him wiz you, Chancer.'

I left my bread and jam to see which screw was *jefe de modulo* today. It was Roberto. I asked him what was all this bollocks about putting a swecko in with me. I told him that I don't smoke and I live alone. I don't want anybody sharing my cell. He spoke very little English but liked to practise, so he answered me in English as I spoke to him in Spanish. The end result was Roberto telling me to fuck off.

Peter Ackerman is a big young Swedish man, 6 ft 2 in. tall and 225 lbs of hard muscle and foul gas. His flatulence is legendary. He is a good man but his arse lets him down; the stink from his arse could halt traffic. The only upside to this was that whilst he lived in my cell, I didn't see any cockroaches. Peter is one of those blokes who needs to gob off all the time about his cop-killing spree in Sweden in an effort to elevate his standing in here. He is a man who constantly seeks the limelight; consequently, he tells

204

atrocious lies. His tales of adventure make Harry Potter seem positively dull.

Actually, he was in here because he was caught with a couple of kilos of hashish in his apartment. The cop-killing story was a load of bollocks to boost his status because if it were true he would be in Valdemoro prison awaiting extradition to Sweden instead of stinking this place out. Besides, he lacks the killer instinct. He has a problem with violence. When it comes to breaking bones, he hasn't the heart for it. Ackerman will retaliate in self-defence but lacks the spirit for a pre-emptive strike. Cop killer my arse.

It wasn't long before Peter latched on to my loan-sharking business. My prison wealth was due to my banking acumen. My business principles are no different from those of any High Street bank. I lend money for a price. The only real difference in principle between banks and myself is the fact that my loans go exclusively to drug addicts; they are used to purchase drugs. Another difference is that banks never lose. They have all kinds of mechanisms for default: I have only my fists. Sometimes I lose money but generally I am on top. Some weeks I can net 500 euros, other weeks only 100 euros. But I never *really* lose money.

The occasions when I've lost money happened when blokes were removed from the wing for bad behaviour or when somebody was unexpectedly released. Nobody has blatantly refused to pay me and walked away. The few who tried that regretted it instantly because I rigorously allowed my fists to do the talking. I never argue about loans. Blokes owe me or they don't owe me. They must pay on the day or there's a problem. I explain explicitly to each of my customers the consequences of default. Absolutely nothing is left to the imagination regarding the results of non-payment. So the few who've tried it on must have thought they were tough enough to frighten me off. Each defaulter ended up paying a 50 per cent penalty after receiving a very painful thrashing, the like of which they had never experienced before. As a punishment to them and a deterrent to others, I scarred an eyebrow on each defaulter, leaving a visible gap in the eyebrow from a head-butt. They will remember me every time they look in a mirror.

Peter Ackerman asked me about loan-sharking so I explained

how it worked for me and how strict one must be to make the business work. I explained about dealing with defaulters. He nodded sagely, making a big deal about smacking his fist into the palm of his hand, saying, 'I'll fucking kill 'em!' I also explained about trespassing on my territory, poaching my clientele. I condescendingly agreed to send him any new beggars whom I wouldn't give the skin off my shit to. He happily rubbed his hands, imitating Ebenezer Scrooge at a sole-beneficiary will reading.

Every new Spanish inmate blatantly begs the moment he sets foot in the place. This is a ploy to stop his countrymen from pestering him. The beggars are soon sent to me. Their sob stories inevitably involve a mother and a funeral. The spicks have this notion that Europeans melt in sympathy at the sound of '*madre*'. When I hear the word '*madre*', I visualise a Spanish crone hobbling into the visitors' block with her big fanny packed with dope. This scenario will live with me for ever. *Madre* = big Spanish fanny.

It became natural for me to adopt a funereal facial expression as I told them all in the nicest possible way to fuck off. I have cultivated the most impressive hangdog expression, which I hope may be of some use to me later in life. I would point to Peter, sending the beggar to his bank.

One of my rules regarding loans was never to lend money to a new bloke until I observed him getting paid on *peculio* day. Payday was Thursday on *modulo* 13, so every Thursday I would position myself where I could see who got paid and how much. Also, it put me in a position whereby my clients could pay me before they blew their *dinero* on smack. Peter quickly adopted my rules and was happy making easy money. The rules were simple: you borrowed 10, you pay back 15 on payday. If for some reason you don't pay on payday, then you pay double next payday. If I don't believe your story, I split your eyebrow and punch the shite out of you. Then you pay next week.

Rafa was a smack dealer who was also an addict. He borrowed from me every week for over a year. I never had a problem with him until Peter lent him money. One payday, Rafa gave me half of what he owed me, saying he would pay the rest tomorrow. That was fine by me because he had a good credit rating. That night in the cell, Peter angered me by telling me he'd lent Rafa some money. He said he had watched Rafa pay me but Rafa had refused to pay him. I got into Peter's face and bollocked him for poaching my client. Peter was surprised and taken aback by my reaction to his infraction of the rules. We had become good pals and never argued over anything other than his stinking arse. He said that Rafa gave him a sob story last week and this was the second week he'd dodged payment, so tomorrow he would punch Rafa's lights out. I told him to hang fire until I got my money, then he could kick fuck out of him.

Rafa must have smelled a rat because the next day he was missing. I asked a screw about him and I was told he was locked in his cell with *gripa*, the flu. He was not very well. He wouldn't be very well when Peter got hold of him, that was for sure. I told Peter where Rafa was hiding and he became quite demonstrative, smacking his fist, gobbing off about Rafa, saying how sore his feet would be after kicking him around the yard. Presumably, he was gobbing off the day before, too, because you can't fart in here without everybody knowing about it and Rafa's absence was suspiciously coincidental. Today's remonstrance would soon reach Rafa's cell.

After feeding time, we headed back to our cells to get locked up for the afternoon. As we passed Rafa's, Peter couldn't resist opening the peephole to loudly abuse him, stupidly warning him of his intentions. Peter explained to me how he was going to damage Rafa when we got unlocked at five o'clock. I again reminded him about my money, because I now envisioned Rafa spending time in the infirmary. Peter is a big lad.

The screw unlocked the cell door and Peter quickly marched along the gallery to Rafa's cell, quickly entering with me right behind him. Rafa scrambled off his bed, verbally attacking him, poking his finger in Peter's face, shouting and cursing aggressively. Peter visibly wilted, and stepped back, defeated. Elated and cocky, with arms akimbo, Rafa turned to me, saying he was not paying me either. I resigned myself to the fact that I would have to wait for my money as I heard the crunch and squeak of cartilage as my fist smashed its way into his gizzard. One blow was sufficient to cause lasting injury to his larynx, thyroid and trachea.

We put him to bed, leaving the cell door wide open so the screw would check him before locking him in. There would be no response from Rafa today. The gurney arrived 20 minutes later to take him to the *enfermería*. Fortunately, Rafa was high on smack at the moment of impact and genuinely knew nothing of my right fist kissing his Adam's apple. Initially, he was being treated for a heroin overdose until they discovered his real problem.

Peter never again poached my clients and funnily enough I heard no more about the Swedish police. Some time later, Rafa returned to the wing and paid me the instant he saw me. Peter Ackerman had been on a three-stretch for the few kilos of hashish found in his apartment. Three weeks later, he was transferred to Salamanca prison.

Alone again. Such luxury to have my privacy back and no further need to suffer the ludicrous tales about Swedish sex bombs, robberies and murder which I good humouredly listened to, whilst choking on the incredible gaseous outbursts from the world's most putrid arsehole. At last, I could close my cell window without the fear of choking to death. Whenever Peter Ackerman farted, everybody in the vicinity quickly walked away from him. It was as though an invisible wall of shit had been built around him, as though you could touch or feel it. The reek was unmistakable.

I got busy with the bleach before the cockroaches discovered Ackerman's absence. I threw out his debris and rearranged the photos of Susan and my mother. I put my jottings and writing materials on the table with my other familiar bits and pieces, which I no longer needed to stow away to appease a cellmate. I don't actually have a table in my cell. I do my writing on a concrete shelf fitted beneath the cell window. It is moments like this when loneliness is savoured and welcome. Wallowing in my own loneliness is easier to cope with than sharing a cellmate's feelings of deprivation as well.

That night, I sat in my *seiza* meditation posture, sitting on my heels in a kneeling position for the first time since Ackerman had shared my cell. *Seiza* is the traditional way of sitting in samurai society; it is also a position of balance and stability used worldwide as a meditation posture. Maintaining this position, I spent several wonderful hours performing breathing exercises and *zazen* (Zen meditation); it was like having a hundred baths in one night.

Zen philosophy indicates that enlightenment comes about by allowing your mind to meld with the universal mind, creating a state of timelessness and thereby a oneness with universal *chi*. These practices are difficult for the Western mind to understand but fortunately for me I spent some time with excellent Eastern masters so I reap the rewards of ancient teachings to strengthen me on my journey through the nether regions of this cruel Spanish prison. One particular mind-cleansing exercise I use often was taught to me by Master Tang in Fanling, New Territories, Hong Kong, during 1974. Other powerful mind exercises were taught to me by Master Nidt, a Buddhist monk whom I met in Thailand in 1965. He lived in a temple south of Leong Nok Tha on the road to Amnat Charoen: a most skilful martial artist.

Cleanliness is one of the keys to survival in these Spanish shitholes, but cleanliness of the mind is also most important to survive the constant temptation and teasing of the heroin traders who are persistent irritants waiting to strike when you are at your lowest. I learned these exercises for the mind years ago and on this night I thoroughly enjoyed my revision of these obscure ancient methods of dissipating stress, after which I slept like a babe, with heartfelt pictures of Susan sending me along the road to dreamland. I imagine Master Nidt and Master Tang will have passed on now, because they were not young men when I knew them. So tonight I will pray for them in respect and gratitude for their priceless lessons of life that have helped me so much to survive my journey through the netherworld.

TWENTY-ONE

The massive sliding bolt on my cell door slammed back with a loud clang as the screw opened my cell. Standing next to the screw was a monster. He was over 6 ft tall with a big head of black greasy hair hanging down to his lantern jaw. His bright sloping eyes, which were visible through the hair hanging over his anthropoid features, were fixing me with a threatening glare. I was off my chair, blocking my cell door in a flash. I was arguing with the screw about not having a smoker in my cell when Genghis shuffled into me, wrapping his hairy arms around me, trapping my arms in a powerful bear hug.

He lifted me to throw me aside, so I head-butted his nose and cheekbone, then took a mouthful of his bottom lip, which I was trying to bite off. I drove my knee into his testicles three times before he let go of me. His blood tasted metallic in my mouth as his screams deafened me. I got my left arm around his neck, forcing him to kiss me harder as my right fist pounded his guts. I grabbed his dick and bollocks and started to yank them away from his crotch. I sensed a sudden weakness in him, so I quickly released my teeth and his wedding tackle as I slid around, furthering my left arm into a *jime-waza* chokehold, then quickly choked him out.

The screw had run for help. When the reinforcements arrived, they were knackered. The gallery where I live is two floors up from their office. They'd galloped up, waving their big sticks and gasping for breath. Don David, an immature pansy dressed in a screw's uniform, gestured with his truncheon to get away from Genghis. As I stepped backwards, three screws waded in with flailing truncheons to the torso and testicles. Then they turned him face down and gave his kidneys and buttocks the good news. Red-faced and panting, they locked me in my cell. Ten minutes later, I heard the recovery team from the infirmary doing their job.

A screw came to see me that night, telling me to forget the incident. Genghis had fallen down the stairs. The message was clear: keep my gob shut and I can live alone in my cell. Genghis was the sadistic murderer of two little girls. The playmates were raped and battered, then hidden in a well. I shudder whenever I think about this beast sharing my cell. Mixing nonces in with other prisoners is a sick practice which is normal in this twisted administration. Genghis is now where he should be: manacled to a bed in isolation.

I named him Genghis because he reminded me of a bloke I knew in the army in Thailand in 1966 by the name of Caan, Corporal Caan, who was sometimes known as Billy, Tin, Piss or Genghis. He was a friend of a friend. The friend was Sailor Crowford, a tall good-looking bloke, full of fun.

Thoughts of sarongs and firm young breasts on beautiful Siamese girls come back to me very often as I languish in this Spanish filth trap. I laugh to myself as I remember the tricks some of my pals got up to with their lovely girlfriends. There were bad times as well but I prefer to laugh at the funny times.

One night, we were in the Sawadi bar in the tiny village of Leong Nok Tha in north-eastern Thailand, not far from the Mekong River near the border town of Mukdahan, another muckpile in the arsehole of nowhere. Sailor's *dhobi* girl brought us another half bottle of White Cock whisky, Thailand's answer to Justerini & Brooks. The difference being J&B doesn't take the enamel off your teeth.

The *dhobi* girl is the young Siamese lady who does your laundry. She waits every evening to receive your pillowcase full of shirts, shorts, skids and socks. She would pass the bundle to a younger sister or brother who would disappear into the jungle with the laundry. The *dhobi* girl would then walk behind you until you found the bar of your choice where she became your servant, fetching whatever drinks you asked her to order for you. When sated and you needed to empty your sac, she would oblige, or if you wanted a change she would be your pimp. Sailor's girl was a beautiful Siamese slut by the name of Newt, who'd been recently chased out of Ubon, where she was spreading pox like a flu epidemic among the Yanks who probably infected her when she first discovered how to fill the purse between her legs. Like all the girls in her tribe she wore only a sarong. No bra, no knickers, just a colourful silk wrapping covering the bits you had to pay to see. She was absolutely stunning, especially after a bottle of White Cock.

Newt had her own little shack on the outskirts of Leong Nok Tha, as did most of the *dhobi* girls, to entertain her soldier friends. Sailor was a practical joker and quite mercenary. He had drilled small peepholes in the side of Newt's shack and had organised an *exhibish*. He charged a crowd of his pals ten bhat each to watch Genghis shag Newt one night. It was hilarious, because Genghis was put off his stride just as he started his vinegar strokes. Genghis knew nothing about his audience till the cheering started. Nor did Newt. So Sailor had to find a new *dhobi* girl and avoid Genghis for a year or so.

Sadly, Newt was put to death, shot through the head by her own countrymen for passing military information to the communists across the Mekong River just a few miles away from Leong Nok Tha. The only thing Newt passed to anybody was the pox. The memory pisses me off so I come back to my cell.

The silence in my cell is sometimes oppressive, adding to the stress of the periods of loneliness. But I am still enjoying my privacy in the lee of Ackerman's departure. I spend my time reading and writing. I am indebted to Wilbur Smith and James Clavell for taking my mind beyond these dank walls, also to Len Deighton for taking me back to Berlin.

Such wonderful tales from the craftsmen of the book world. I read their stories over again just to escape. There are many other writers who have helped me to do my bird; too numerous to mention here. But special thanks go to Susan for her weekly supply of books.

I read stories about Northern Ireland which are purportedly true, but I find myself favouring recollections of my own escapades in that green land: treasured memories of lovely girls and good men. And some not so good memories: flashbacks of senseless violence carried out in the name of religion, which was a lie, an excuse for violence. Religion was merely a handy vehicle to ride on. Many men on both sides of the divide had never set foot inside a church apart from attending funerals. So to my mind, religion is just another gun or truncheon used to vent bellicose bigotry.

TWENTY-TWO

The great and holy religious festival of Easter 1971 had arrived. My Easter bonnet was made from best British steel, adorned with a beautiful webbing chinstrap and a wee bit of cam-net to complete my interesting collage of military headgear. All ready for the Belfast Easter parade, off I tripped to join the other contestants in this jolly Irish competition of seeing whose bonnet could withstand the most bottles, sticks and stones being crashed upon it.

The formal attire that I was wearing for this Easter parade was more suited to a scene out of *Dad's Army*. I suppose we were similar to the Home Guard, standing here in our own country waiting to repel not Jerry, but our own countrymen. British citizens, gone mad.

The eyes of the world were on us this day. The media were here in strength to cramp our style. Our response to injury and abuse had to be tempered because of influential liars from the press. I have never bought a newspaper since Easter 1971 because I discovered that shite is printed daily to feed the gullible public everywhere. It is my opinion that the press is to blame for everything that is shite in the world. I can live without newspapers; so can the rainforests.

A snarling, malevolent mob – no, horde – of drunken Micks

came swaggering into the street. My grip tightened on my 30-inch long baton in my right hand. My left hand was resting on the butt of the Very pistol holstered on my hip, loaded with a rubber bullet – a baton round, the black dick-like object which was as useful as a rubber crowbar.

The noise was alarming as they drew nearer. Shouts and screams were drowned out by more shouts and screams: absolute bedlam. I was later to read in a national newspaper how peaceful and orderly they were. There were a hundred of us; my squadron, all standing parade-ground still, as though we were about to be inspected by a visiting general. Behind us, voices were growling, 'Steady in the ranks. Eyes front, you lot. Steady-y-y . . .'

Taff, standing to my left, grunted, 'This cunt will give us an "eyes right" any minute now so we can't see 'em coming. Maybe he thinks they'll fuck off if we don't look at 'em.'

'Quiet in the ranks,' said the sergeant-major.

'Are we in Rorke's fucking Drift or Rorke's fucking Street?' said Taff, raising his macrillon shield to protect his Welsh face as the leading Micks drew near.

British soldiers were quite naive in the early days of conflict in Ulster. Nobody really believed our own countrymen would attack us. Young men from England, Ireland, Scotland and Wales wearing the uniform of the British Army, here to protect fellow countrymen from each other. Our lives would change this Easter; violence in the name of the Lord would ensure that.

Our lives would change in the next few minutes as stones and bottles were hurled into us from the head of the column of drunken gobshites. Nutters from further back were pushing forward to get a better shot with their missiles. Bricks and bottles rained down on us as we stood there waiting for an order to move.

'You fucking Mick bastard.' A bottle shattered across Ginger McAbe's chin, so he took part of the perpetrator's face off with his baton. Ginger broke ranks to achieve this result so several Micks attacked him. Orders shmorders, who gave a fuck now? We waded in with batons flailing. Crunch, crunch, crunch, as heads cracked like Easter eggs.

The adrenalin screamed through me as I clumped head after head. All around me was the happy sound of hard wood hitting hard heads. The fitness and youth of the Brit squaddie showed the Micks how it should be done. Micks were pushing forward from behind as their mates were trying to retreat. The sound of rubber bullets being fired seemed to do the trick. In the chaos of combat, the Micks thought small arms had come into play, so the fear of getting shot helped to disperse them so they could go home to sort out the Easter eggs for the kids.

The squadron was blooded that day; it was probably the Micks' baptism of fire, too. There were many riots and confrontations, deaths and injuries to contend with during the holy Easter festival of 1971.

Instead of resting between riots, many of us practised our baton swing, perfecting the face-shattering strike and the gut-wrenching thrust to the solar plexus. Thrust and swing, thrust and swing. Blokes were practising and laughing as they recalled the heads they'd busted earlier. Didja see me whack that fucker's teeth out? Didja see this, didja see that . . . and so on. Young men exhilarated by victory and especially because they came out of the mêlée unscathed.

During the first few years of that decade, some were not so lucky in Ulster. I see the faces of dead comrades, which fade out as I come back to the reality of my cell. I feel like the lid is coming down on my coffin and I'm not dead yet. Gut-wrenched, I pray to God to put me back with Susan, promising never again will I do anything wrong in this life.

TWENTY-THREE

In July 2001, my lawyer, the famous Gabriel Pineda de las Infantas Beato, came to see me to tell me that he would get bail for me quite soon. He informed me that a Moroccan chap would be paying my bail on the proviso that I'd do a RIB job for him. Gabriel told me that Abselam Endoueli had taken care of his fee and had given him a blank cheque to cover my bail. That same week, Gabriel the lawyer was tragically killed with his brother in a traffic accident. Some people say it wasn't an accident, but what the hell, he's dead and gone. So is my bail; it died with him on the *carretera*.

I heard nothing more from Abselam Endoueli until just before Christmas 2002 when Mo Ouassini told me there was a job waiting for me with Abselam when I got out. There are a thousand jobs waiting for me when I get out.

After Gabriel's death, I was called to the *comunicación* block. It was there I met for the first time Juan Garcia Ballester, my new lawyer, bought and paid for by my good friend Dutch. Ballester told me that Dutch had paid for everything, including his fee and several million pesetas on deposit to cover the cost of *fianza* (bail). My spirits soared as Ballester told me he would get me out on bail in two weeks' time. Face-to-face, he guaranteed it. I should have known better than to believe a Spaniard. Lawyers, judges, policemen, all of them; I wouldn't trust a Spanish priest to tell me the time. Ballester fed me on shite for weeks. Then one day I was called to the screws' office to sign a receipt for notification of my trial date, September 2002.

The lying bastard came to see me, telling me I would now get bail because the police had lost some papers and would not be able to convict me without them. Again, my spirits soared. It must be prison mentality that makes men clutch at straws and allow themselves to be led down the yellow spick road. Why do I allow these liars to lead me on? I know in my heart he is a professional, legal, Spanish deceit merchant, serving his apprenticeship to become a Spanish judge.

The day of the trial finally came and I was handcuffed to another inmate who possibly had tuberculosis or dengue. He looked like shit and could hardly stand as we were locked into the devil's charabanc for the journey to court, the Audiencia in Malaga. I was put in a dungeon beneath the Audiencia to await my call to trial. At 1.30 p.m., the guards came for me to put me back on the bus for the return journey to Alhaurin de la Torre. There was no trial for me: Ballester had one-day influenza so he didn't come to court.

He came to see me the following week to tell me that there would be a new date set for my trial. Also, he would procure my freedom because the police had not found the lost papers and because my witness, the interpreter Raja Bechar Bechar, would be in court to prove my statement was made *por compulsion* – under duress.

When I was arrested, the police told me to admit to the Algarrobo beach job immediately or Susan would be put in jail with me. This is normal procedure in Spain. The police will resort to any dirty trick to get a conviction, no matter how cruel or disgraceful it is. And, of course, you are only an *extranjero*, a *giri*, a foreign git. They know an Englishman will agree to anything to keep his wife out of prison; unlike their countrymen, who grass their wives, brothers, sisters, mothers, fathers, children, priest . . .

The yellow bastards used firearms to arrest me. We were on the way to Fuengirola at the time. Susan was driving. She noticed a Ford Mondeo following us, so I told her to drive into the next lay-by to let it pass. The car followed us into the lay-by and four men in civilian clothes scrambled out of their car and surrounded us, with handguns pointed at each of our heads: two at my head and two at Susan's head.

I had a flashback of shitting dogs in Belfast, because they were all nervous. My hatred increased dramatically as I looked at two shaking pistols aimed at my Susan's head. Susan sat motionless with both hands on the steering wheel, looking ahead, refusing to look at the two shitting dogs pointing handguns at her head.

I whispered, 'Don't move, sweetheart,' as I exited the car to face Lee Van Cleef and Clint Eastwood on my side of the car. I shouted across the roof of the car at the two shaking spicks to point their weapons away from Susan. All four then focused on me: four nervous cowards aiming at my head. I quietly told them to point their weapons at each other because they were making me feel as nervous as they were. '*Tranquilo, hombres. Ustedes muy nerviosos.*' I couldn't understand why they were being so aggressive until one of them said, 'Jaime Padrun says you are a very dangerous man, Chancer.' Padrun is a Swiss bloke who also skippered for Rouge. He knew about the Algarrobo beach job. Clearly, he'd been trying to wriggle out of his own crimes by grassing about mine.

I pulled down my shorts, exposing my wedding tackle and said, 'This is the only weapon I have.' I pointed my bare arse at the Moroccan type, knowing he would hate the insult. The others laughed, exposing their racism to their fellow officer.

The English-speaking spick said, 'We arrested Jaime Padrun yesterday and he's singing like a bird.'

'You mean singing like a Spanish bird, eh? He's married to a Spanish whore so he'll sing like one. What's he saying that could have anything to do with me?'

'Oh, plenty, Chancer. Eleven and a half tonnes' worth of information about you, *giri*. Plus one tonne on Algarrobo beach. That's twelve and a half tonnes of problems for you and her. You are in the shit and so is she,' he said, pointing at Susan. 'You agree to all we say or she gets locked up in the *mujeres modulo* in Malaga prison today.'

'You scumsucking maggots have got nothing, so get fucked.'

'We have Jaime Padrun and Rouge in prison and their words are all we need.'

I knew I was in a tight corner so I said no more. I was handcuffed and put in the Ford Mondeo while the two other spicks got in with Susan for the ride back to my home, Casa Budo.

Had I not agreed to plead guilty to whatever they said, Susan would be here in this rathole now. So at the first hearing in Coín on the day after I was arrested in 2001, I told the interpreter, Raja Bechar Bechar, about how the police used my wife to get a guilty statement from me.

When the proceedings began on that day, Raja stood up and asked the senior officer if my statement had been taken after the police had agreed not to arrest Susan. The officer brazenly answered, '*Si*.' So she made notes and told me she would help me later when I got organised.

A young woman was at the hearing who told me she was my state lawyer. She didn't even give me her name. When the hearing was over, she cleared off without a goodbye, kiss my arse or anything. Apparently, the police had appointed her as my lawyer. They had threatened me with Susan's freedom if I'd contacted the lawyer I'd wanted, Gabriel, before the hearing. The police were pressing me for information about other players, and Susan's freedom was an ongoing threat, so when she came to see me in Coín jail I had to tell her about what the dirty bastards were up to.

The horrible realisation she had to flee hit her like a sledgehammer. I will never forget nor forgive those scumsucking bastards for causing so much heartache to Susan. I couldn't appoint a lawyer until she was safe. So we agreed she would leave our lovely home and flee to England.

I'd had to appear in court for a magistrate hearing on 25 May 2001, so Susan had come to see me for the last time because she knew I would go to prison from there. She had come to terms with leaving our home, and the pets had all been taken care of. This possibly ranks as the worst day of my life.

The judge was a fat, greasy slob of a woman who refused bail with a perfunctory wave of her pudgy hand. I half expected her to fall asleep, snoring and farting as she slouched in her chair. Her full name and title was Doña Soledad Velazquez Moreno, Juez del Juzgado de Primera Instancia e Instrucción de Coín: a big fat name for a big fat lump.

We said our heartbreaking farewells and the police separated us. I was taken to Alhaurin de la Torre, handcuffed in the back of a Guardia-Civil police car. The two sadistic bastards who took me left me inside the car in the broiling sun while they sat in the shade to have their break. I called to them to open a window but they refused, laughing at my discomfort. Had I been a nonce or child killer, they'd have taken me for a drink with them.

Eventually, I was processed into Malaga prison and here I am listening to Ballester telling me more lies about my trial. At last, the trial date was fixed for 11 November 2002. The eleventh hour of the eleventh day of the eleventh month – Armistice Day.

It soon came and again I was handcuffed to a Spanish lunatic for the journey to the Audiencia. Again, I was shoved into a stinking bus to be locked inside a square-metre cubicle and off we rattled to the Juzgado de lo Penal Numero 5 de Malaga.

Again, I was pushed into a dungeon beneath the courthouse. In the heavy silence of this dank rathole, my thoughts took me back to sea. I couldn't escape physically so I dreamt my way out.

TWENTY-FOUR

Another shite November: my birth month. I'm a Sagittarian: half man, half beast. I often wonder if my halves are the wrong way round. Sagittarius, the archer, is the sign of the optimist: eager for new experiences, lusting for adventure and travel. I got my fill on my birthday two years before this trial. I was aboard the *Harlekin*, a 48-foot cutter, getting the crap knocked out of me in a force ten storm.

The adventure started in September 2000 when I received a telephone call from Kennedy, who was in Mallorca with Carlino Gelli, a mafioso from Palermo, Sicily. Rumoured to be a 'made man', Carlino had a calm, unruffled personality. But the eyes said it all. This man was ruthless and homicidal, regardless which mask he chose to wear.

I first met him in Marbella; he needed a skipper, he was assessing me. I personally didn't give a shit because I had work coming out of my ears. He offered me a cigarette from an elegant gold case with a diamond motif. I politely refused. He then offered me beer, hashish and Charlie respectively. I again refused.

'What da fuck do you like, Chancer?'

'Good wine and good money.'

'Aw fuck, dat's easy. Hey you, waiter. Bring a bottle of your best wine.'

'Red, please,' I called after the waiter.

Carlino eyed me over the rim of his expensive designer bins. 'Can you handle a big cruising yacht?'

'Does a one-legged duck swim in circles? I can handle the fucking *Cutty Sark* if the money is right.'

'What da fuck's a Cutty Shark? What da fuck has dis to do with sharks?' He had an amused grin on his face and my knowing grin told him that I also knew about sharks, especially wop sharks.

'Oh, the *Cutty Sark* is a really big tea-clipper, a really big yacht. We could load some shit on that thing but she's too old now.' I couldn't go into a spiel about the *Cutty Sark* so I let it drop and asked about his plans.

'First, I want you to take me sailing,' he said.

That was two months ago. Now he was in my ear again. Kennedy asked if I was interested, then gave me a rendezvous in Mallorca.

That night, I took my lovely Susan out for a farewell dinner. We wore casual clothes, so just to be different we went out on the big Honda. I had to ride slowly because of Susan's hair. We didn't wear our crash-hats; nobody wears them around here anyway. It was a lovely evening and the townsfolk were out congregating in the town square, chattering and showing off before the sun went down. The beautiful noise of the big Honda sucked envious glances from the young bucks, their bullfighting dreams momentarily disturbed by the black and chrome beast roaring through their tiny world, envious at the sight of the beautiful English girl clinging to her Sagittarian mate riding the Japanese beast through their midst. I downloaded the horses to a lower gear and purposely blasted away from them, leaving a momentary vacuum of silence in the square.

We rode to the No. 9, an English restaurant situated in one of the narrow alleyways behind Coín church. The thundering exhaust sounded incredibly loud as we approached. I parked the motorbike next to the front door as Klaus, the queer kraut waiter, came out to see what all the noise was about.

'Aah, Chancer. I should have known it was you. A crazy Englishman, bringing his lovely wife to dinner on a motorbike. *Guten Abend*, Frau Chance! Exhilarating, eh?' The simpering tosser took us to a nearby table from where I could keep an eye on my bike.

We ate a couple of juicy steaks washed down with a bottle of Rioja. We held hands to share a few tender moments and then went for a roaring scratch around the mountain roads before going home. Great care is essential whilst night-riding in Andalucia. Drunken horsemen dressed all in black, sitting atop black horses, tend to wander into the middle of the road. Their only illumination is the glow of the cigarette dangling from the drunken gob. Luckily, we didn't plough into any horses this night. I have had many narrow escapes on these mountain roads, so with my precious cargo holding me tight, I took extra special care.

Our three big dogs welcomed us home at midnight. The joyful expressions on their faces were a great source of delight. Such beautiful loyal creatures, their memory will live with me for ever. Susan and I sat with them for a few minutes under the stars, a happy bunch of souls.

The next morning, Susan drove me to Malaga airport to board the flight to Palma, Mallorca. We kissed and hugged our goodbyes in front of an audience of a thousand tourists on the airport concourse. Fuck them, they didn't exist. There wasn't a direct flight to Mallorca, so I flew first to Barcelona, then on to Palma. I was travelling light so I had no baggage worries. The flight was uneventful and boring.

The rendezvous was at the yacht in Canpastilla marina, so when I cleared the airport I took a cab, which dropped me near the marina entrance. I paid the thief his fare, then walked away from the marina to a nearby bar. Nobody was on my tail, so after a cool drink I went in. Strolling around the moorings, I soon found the *Harlekin*. She was moored near the *gasolinera*.

She looked beautiful, with polished stainless-steel fittings from bowsprit to galleon-style stern. Her shining Oxford-blue paintwork was reflecting wavelet patterns, creating a dappled effect along the waterline with the afternoon sun glittering like shards of broken mirrors. She was cutter-rigged with a roller-furling mainsail, an electronic-roller reefing genoa and a manual-roller staysail. The light breeze gently fluttered the German flag on her stern, making me feel more comfortable with her because krauts normally keep things properly maintained. Love at first sight: a becoming, handsome craft, 48 ft of graceful excitement.

I could see Kennedy's blackness in amongst the four olive-skinned wops boozing and laughing in the cockpit. Kennedy clocked me as I approached. He jumped up, waving and shouting, dazzling me with his great white teeth, reminiscent of my gran's old black piano. I knew he had a nose full of Charlie.

I walked up the gangplank and took off my shoes. I was doing this and admiring this lovely yacht when an impatient loud voice cried, 'Get over 'ere, bro. We got some great red wine especially for you.' Kennedy's Caribbean patter echoed across the water. I had a mental image of Bob Marley banging out reggae, with Kennedy wearing a top hat, sporting a bone through his nose like a voodoo witch doctor.

'Just a minute, I'm taking my shoes off.'

Carlino gave me his benign smile, letting me know it was him who'd bought the wine. I knew there would be more than one case of the finest wine on the island waiting for me. Kennedy and Carlino made a big deal about welcoming me aboard. The other three blokes sat there, half smiling, waiting to be introduced. I looked at them each in turn, their smiles fading. 'If any of you three are spicks, I'm putting my shoes back on to kick fuck out of Kennedy.'

'Hey, bro, dem's Italianos, not fuckin' spicks. *Tranquilo, amigo*. Relax and meet da boys. Dis 'ere is Mario, Carlino's brudder.'

I took his offered hand in a firm grip.

'I am skipper of a fishing boat in Sicily, a trawler,' said Mario. 'But that was long ago before I started the cocaine-fishing business.' Everybody roared with laughter except me. I gave Kennedy my sulphuric-acid stare. The laughter ceased instantly. 'Where the fuck are we working? You black cunt. You let me think we were working the Mediterranean. What the fuck's going on?'

'We are workin' de Med, bro. Calm down. Mario is only talkin' 'bout general t'ings. Dis job is local, man, we's carryin' puff.'

I relaxed and shook the hands of Dino and Frankie, two elegant button men, completely out of tune with the surroundings. These killers were Carlino's troubleshooters, used to clear all debts and awkward business deals. Each had a Beretta under his left armpit and a stiletto strapped to his calf. Each knew I had them sussed in those first moments.

'Today, we party,' said Carlino. 'Tomorrow, we sail. Chancer, you are skipper tomorrow. I want to see how you sail my investment.'

'Well then, you lot get pissed while I check everything out.' I wanted to see what shape everything was in, to check all the relevant bits and pieces before sailing. I didn't want to check anything with a possible thick head tomorrow. Kennedy came with me. He had been on board for a week so he knew his way around and had checked everything anyway. He had quite a shopping list, but nothing to prevent us from sailing tomorrow.

I got stuck into the wine and quickly entered the spirit of things, swinging the lamp with tales from Malaysia and Belfast, while they snorted illegal substances. They had lines of Charlie like tiny white furrows all across the saloon table. Kennedy offered to cook some fish, but Carlino was having none of that. He surprised us by saying he had booked a table in a Japanese restaurant in Palma. So they all took a noseful of Charlie and off we went to Palma.

The place was very nice but Jap scran is shite. I would rather have had Kennedy's fish. Nevertheless, everybody was happy and eager to get back on board where the little white furrows awaited them.

I try not to be a romantic, I lean more to being a realist, so right now this was how the world wagged. So bollocks, I'd fill my boots. The wine was excellent, so I got well pissed and hit the sack. However, I now knew that Kennedy had a problem with Charlie. He started as merely a social user, but now he was an addict. Fuck it! I sang myself to sleep with, 'There will be troubles ahead.'

When I awoke the next morning, they were all still partying, so I had my doubts about taking her out to sea. I need not have worried because the light breeze had strengthened to a force four, which was fine for sailing but enough to give the revellers an excuse to keep partying.

During the night, Frankie had been sent out to get some girls, so now there was girlish giggling all around me. One of the girls was Japanese. She was draped all over Carlino. 'So that's why we went to the restaurant last night, you have a penchant for Japanese things,' I said.

'No, I've never screwed a Jap, so I'm going to put things right just now. I think she'll like my salami.'

Kennedy called me down to the galley for breakfast. 'That little Jap is hot stuff,' he said. 'I gave her a length an hour ago, so hopefully it's healed up before Carlino pokes her. He'll go apeshit if he finds out I've wet her nest before him.'

'You fucking idiot. Why didn't you shag one of the others?'

'I did. I've shagged all t'ree now.'

'Oh, fucking hell. Did you wash your dirty fucking hands before touching my food? I don't want any gonococcal pus contaminating my sausages. You fucking slut.'

Kennedy laughed, his grinning black face accentuating his gleaming white teeth. 'All t'ree o' dem bitches wantin' my black gun up 'em. So dey all gorrit, man. Fuck dem wops wid der little guns. I gave dem bitches some real cannon.' He was laughing into the frying pan. 'Sunny side up, bro?'

I didn't take the *Harlekin* out that day because Carlino had better things to do in Barcelona. So at 6 p.m. we started to clear away all the debris. At nine o'clock, we were enjoying ourselves in one of the kraut restaurants near the marina. Kennedy was hyperactive so I guessed he had a stash of Charlie onboard.

The *Harlekin* ended up staying in Canpastilla for another week. Then we took her to Andratx, one of Mallorca's picturesque ports. The journey was uneventful but quite enjoyable, with a 20-knot wind keeping us on our toes. We moored in Club de Vela marina, in Puerto de Andratx, a lovely place to stay.

Andratx is predominantly kraut, so is kept quite clean and orderly. Because of kraut influence, the services are good and there is an air of regularity about the place. Because of kraut preponderance, the prices are high. Fuck the krauts.

Carlino came to visit, bringing Joe Gorolla with him. We immediately put to sea for an afternoon shakeout in a 20-knot wind. It was an opportunity for Joe to show his mettle, which he did. I put him to the helm, telling him to call me if he had a problem.

Carlino and Kennedy were struggling to chop a line of Charlie on the saloon table. I needed to put Kennedy in the picture, but not while Carlino was on board. He told us that Joe was permanent and would live on board until all contracts were finished. Three of us would be sufficient to handle the *Harlekin* and her cargoes. Extra hands meant less money per person, but Carlino was paying Joe. His money was none of my business. That was fine by me. But Joe had to realise that he took his orders from me, or over the side he'd go. There are no trade union rules on this job. Rule no. 1 reads: what the skipper says, goes. Rule no. 2: if in doubt, rule no. 1 applies. Carlino assured me that Joe knew the score. I look back on things now and I can honestly say that if I ever go back to sea, which I won't, I would take Joe before anybody else. He hasn't got the experience and expertise of Kennedy, but he is a far superior mechanic and has much more bottle.

We spent the next few weeks perfecting everything from stem to stern. We sailed every day except Saturdays and Sundays until the order came to be ready to move any day now. The job was about to start.

We had enough rations on board to last at least three weeks at sea. Everything had been prepared for the cargo. Rubber matting had been bought to limit the damage to the beautiful interior. The stowing of three tonnes of Morocco's finest herb had been well planned. All the relevant sea charts were to hand, the RV coordinates had been studied and the weather forecast was good. We waited for the green light.

On 22 November 2000, we received a coded message which was our green light. We did our last-minute shopping for fresh meat and vegetables and filled the water and fuel tanks. The *Harlekin* slipped her moorings at midnight; we were on our way.

The sailing plan was to head due south to a point 40 miles from the Algerian coast, then take a south-westerly heading, keeping us approximately 40 miles from the North African coast until we reached a point north of the Islas Chafarinas where we headed for the RV point with a fishing boat 20 miles off the Moroccan coast near Nador. The RV was actually 20 miles due north of Qariat Arkmane, a tiny village near the eastern edge of Sebkha bou Areq.

This was where three tonnes of top-grade hashish would change hands. Transferring this amount of hashish by hand from one vessel to another at sea is not so easy, especially if the sea is lively. Hopefully, the sea would be like a millpond.

That first night out from Mallorca was unforgettable. All the stars in the universe had come out to light our way south. The winds were fair so we used the mainsail and genoa to move us south at about seven knots. We were in no hurry; we had plenty of time to reach our rendezvous.

Without the Perkins diesel engine running, the only noise was the swish of the sea and the wind singing through the rigging. The *Harlekin* was on automatic pilot, heading towards the first waypoint over 100 miles to the south. The lights of the Balearics soon disappeared behind me, leaving me alone to enjoy the universe's cabaret with all the real stars dancing just for me.

Kennedy and Joe were below. Joe was to relieve me at 0400hrs. I had all this natural beauty to myself and I was wishing that Susan could experience this powerful feeling of being at one with nature under the sails of the *Harlekin*.

'Lucy in the sky with diamonds,' I sang as I gazed at the millions of glittering diamonds dancing for me in the sky. I wondered if John Lennon was looking down at me from one of those diamonds. So just in case he was, I gave him a wave. 'Hiya, John. Yoko's doing well and Liverpool won last week.'

I didn't see another living thing until four o'clock when Joe came up into the cockpit with a cup of tea and a salmon and cucumber sandwich for my breakfast. A heart of gold has Joe, but a salmon and cucumber sandwich at four o'clock in the morning is a bit too much for my guts. He knew I liked salmon so bless his little Dutch bollocks.

I threw it overboard when he went to check for'ard. Besides, Joe's fingernails were packed with grime because he was always tinkering with nuts and bolts, cleaning pumps and oiling things that were already in tip-top condition. The *Harlekin* provided Joe with lots of quality tinkering time.

I went below and slept like an old crocodile. I awoke four hours later, about eight o'clock in the morning. Kennedy had started the Perkins diesel so we were sailing with power and sail. The weather was fine just now but the darkness of the horizon looked ominous. If this was what I thought it was, then it wasn't forecast.

We hurriedly prepared for bad weather and heavy seas, but we weren't quite prepared for what came at us. The gods of the sea were pissed at something; I hope it wasn't my salmon buttie. The weather got rapidly worse. At first, the wind was erratic, but it quickly built up to 30 knots coming from directly aft so we trimmed with the mainsail almost square. The sea was heaping up to a 15-foot swell and foam was streaking everywhere and seemed to be getting worse by the minute. Over the next 6 hours, the wind increased and was gusting to 50 knots and the sea became white with foam and monstrous waves with long, overhanging crests. Visibility was zilch. I couldn't see more than 100 feet all around and the noise was deafening.

I took the helm at midday to spend four unforgettable hours in that maelstrom of a sea. I have never seen a freak wave, but something hit us on the port beam with such force that I somersaulted over the wheel, crashed into the canopy and dropped to the deck, impacting my kidneys. Fortunately, Joe witnessed this and came to my aid. I couldn't move; the pain was internal and paralysing. Black humour always helps in these situations. 'Why the fuck did you do a circus trick at the end of your watch?' shouted Joe. 'I'm impressed but there's no fanny here to see it.'

'Fuck you, Joe. Get on the helm, I'm going below.' I didn't realise how badly I was hurt. At that moment, my prostate gland was growing to twice its normal size, but I didn't know that yet. I must have been very tired because I slept for a few hours. I awoke in great pain and fought my way to the heads because I needed to piss. But I couldn't piss. The pain was incredible.

I explained to Joe and Kennedy that I was in too much pain to do my watch. Joe knew I was badly hurt but Kennedy thought I was swinging the lead. Coke addicts think like that, it's part of the paranoia symptoms they suffer. But I didn't care a shit about his opinions. In my book he was now a quarter-wit.

I sat in the toilet for hours until I eventually managed a trickle. I was now convinced I had a stone in my urethra blocking the waterworks. I was straining, pulling and stretching my poor old

John Thomas wishing for a stone to fly out of the Jap's eye. I thought, if I aimed it at Kennedy it would kill him: Kennedy killed by supersonic kidney stone.

The little drop of pee that came out smelled really bad, so I became alarmed as I realised it was something serious and I was feeling worse by the minute. Joe visited me in the heads to ask if it would be wise to put into Oran, Algeria. I was quite disorientated, but told him I would decide when we got nearer to Oran. Joe helped me to my bunk, telling me not to worry and get some sleep. I didn't know the time but I knew Joe was very tired.

I awoke some hours later with sunlight shining through the porthole onto my face. Joe arrived and helped me to the heads. I heaved and strained to piss but only managed a stinking drop. Then came the diarrhoea and biliousness. It seemed every orifice was opened and pouring at the same time. Liquid poured from my nostrils, mouth and arse, with just a dribble from my nob. I cleaned myself up and Joe helped me up top.

The sun was shining and the fresh breeze blew away my cobwebs. My instincts prompted me to look aloft. I was shocked to see a foot-long rip in the mainsail parallel with the top spreader. I told Joe and Kennedy to drop the sail and repair it by stitching a canvas hatch-cover to the sail. Kennedy argued, saying he could stitch it without ruining a hatch-cover. I wasn't myself at the time and that moment of weakness was to cost me later when the wind speed increased to blow away Kennedy's expert stitching. I was truly very ill when this calamity occurred, but I managed to scream at him, 'You useless black cunt, all this fucking around because of your precious hatch-cover.'

We had a hell of a job repairing the sail. The wind was gusting harder and the swell was building rapidly. I knew the lull in the weather was over as a ripple of unease washed over my soul, hardening my resolve as I looked at the approaching storm. Spray from wavetops drilled into my face as I lay across the boom, holding the lashing that was retaining the sail folded over the boom, as Joe and Kennedy fought to stitch the hatch-cover to the torn sail.

My life jacket restricted my movements as I struggled to keep my weight on the boom. I felt as though my insides were drowning as the raging wind tried to prise me off. A faint smile of steely defiance curled my lips as Joe punched the sky in victory. His war cry was carried away unheard on the savage wind.

Joe helped me from my precarious perch as I clambered below. I refused the offered drink because I didn't want any liquid in my infected bladder. I was desperately ill and I knew worse was to come as Joe helped me to my bunk. It felt as though I was walking on a trampoline giving somebody a piggyback ride. I was helpless as the storm raged around me. I became delirious but at the height of the storm I concentrated on Susan: my reference point, my mental secure area, the safe haven in my roller-coasting life. I vaguely remember somebody securing me in my bunk as I struggled with my dreams.

I awoke the instant I hit the floor as the *Harlekin* tossed me from my bunk. The burning pain in my bladder drove me to the heads where I at last succeeded in having a decent piss. I think the *Harlekin* shook the piss out of me. Inexplicably, I felt strong and able to join the fight with the angry sea. So I determinedly fought my way to the cockpit where I could be of some use. Kennedy was at the helm and Joe was lashed to the handrail, lying on his back. Kennedy gave me the thumbs-up sign and indicated for me to join Joe and lash myself next to him.

As I struggled to join Joe, I looked back at the compass and noticed we were heading north. I didn't think too much about that as I tied myself down so we could shout at each other. Joe had to get right next to my ear to tell me what a cunt I was for leaving my bunk. I lay on my back, head to head with Joe, looking at the black sky as wave after wave crashed over us. I looked across at Kennedy, who was shitting bricks as he struggled with the mighty sea. Kennedy's eyes were like white ping-pong balls stuck on a black ten-pin bowling ball.

I was trying to take it all in, then I noticed we had no navigation lights, only the spreader lights were on. The cockpit window had gone and the tender was missing. I looked at where the tender used to live and all I could see were torn straps and cordage hanging from the davits. My instincts prompted me to look for'ard but I could only see stair rods of foam driving into my face. I pulled my hood into a funnel over my eyes in an attempt to see through the barrage of sea water. Visibility was shite but some strange force kept me squinting into the murk.

I sensed something was to our front but I could see nothing. The waves were like pyramids rising from the deep all around me, hiding the threat, which seemed almost palpable, straight ahead of us. There was something there: I knew it.

I screamed at Joe, telling him to untie himself and take his torch for'ard. The puzzled frown on Joe's face changed to terror as he saw what came looming out of the dark. A monstrous container ship was bearing down on us. Joe's big muscular frame galvanised into action, moving for'ard, making large circles with his powerful torch. An amphibious Buckingham Palace was about to crush us beneath the waves as Joe frantically waved his torch at the advancing monster. Her bow and superstructure seemed to be towering above us as she ploughed through the angry sea.

I calmly freed myself from the handrail, waiting for my past life to start flashing before my eyes. Instead, this great black steel juggernaut flashed past, inches away from the starboard beam. The gods of the sea pushed us out of harm's way. Death was very near as I lay down again to look at the sky. The *Harlekin* was dancing like the whirling dervishes of Islam. I lay there feeling invincible as the world crashed all around me. The fear had left me and I cared about nothing.

The figure of Joe came looming over me. He crouched down, putting his face close to mine so he could be heard. I closed my eyes and pretended to snore loudly. Joe went apeshit, screaming about how near to death we all were and here was I snoring my fucking head off. I laughed in Joe's face, then sat up looking and pointing at Kennedy who was clinging petrified to the helm. I was in stitches laughing at Kennedy as Joe collapsed into fits of laughter with me. To this day, Kennedy will never understand why we were laughing.

Joe wiped the smile off my face by telling me we were heading north because during my delirium we had reached the RV and been told to fuck off because the job was postponed due to the storm. The realisation that all this effort came to jack shit was soul destroying. Who says smuggling is easy?

At 0500hrs on 27 November, the storm abated. The sea was

like a millpond as we entered Agua Dulce marina near Almería on the Spanish coast. The job was a washout so we were all pissed off. We made plans to contact each other during the next week as we prepared to leave the *Harlekin*.

I called in a local rigger to sort out the torn sail and fix several other bits and pieces. The joys of owning a yacht include the repair work and maintenance of your pride and joy. Men like us have no such pleasures. Vessels are merely a tool for smuggling. There are no love affairs with the tools of our trade; but I will never forget the *Harlekin*.

Joe organised a taxi to take him to Almería airport because he was going home to Rotterdam. Kennedy and I got a taxi to Malaga where Susan met me and took me to hospital in Marbella, where the outpatients' department diagnosed an infection of the urinary tract. They lie, even in fucking hospital.

I immediately went to see a consultant urologist at Clinica Europa in Marbella. The Italian doctor told me I had severe bruising to my kidneys and my prostate gland was swollen to twice its normal size. My poor arse felt as though a badger had been in there rummaging around. The consultant had his hand up there, grabbing bits and pieces I didn't know existed until that day. It took several weeks before things got better, but nothing mattered, I was in Susan's care.

'Remember, remember, the fifth of November.' We used to sing that song when I was a kid. It was to commemorate Guy Fawkes, that well-intentioned bloke who tried to kill all those politicians in the Houses of Parliament. I was born in November and I nearly died in November and now here I am in a dungeon underneath a Malaga courthouse and it's November again.

TWENTY-FIVE

Juan Garcia Ballester came down to the dungeon to discuss my case. He immediately told me the secret police had chased away my witness, Raja Bechar Bechar. They told her that she is an *extranjera* and she would be jeopardising her work permit by helping me. 'She has left the courthouse,' said Ballester.

He then went on to explain that if I pleaded guilty I would get a sentence of less than three years. If I fought the case, I would get a five-stretch. He advised me not to fight the case because the judge had made up his mind already. 'You haven't got a chance with these people,' he said. 'Also, the secret police want to see you before you go into court.'

The guards came to take me up into the courthouse. Before I got to court no. 5, I was taken into a small room where Ballester was waiting. He told me the secret police were coming to see me now, then he walked out, leaving me alone. Two seconds later, six men in civilian clothes came in, very jolly, and greeted me like a long-lost friend. Very strange behaviour: I knew something was up.

The senior officer stood behind me so I couldn't see the slimy bastard. He knew I hated his fucking guts. The other five stood in an arc to my front, grinning like the Joker in *Batman*. Antonio, the poncy moustached scumsucker who spoke poor English, told

235

me that if I helped them with their case against Rouge and Jean Jacques Padrun (Jaime), I could walk out of here. If I told them what they wanted to know, agreed to whatever they wanted to throw at Rouge and Jaime, corroborated their lies, then I was a free man. They offered me accommodation in Alicante as part of the witness protection scheme, and after the trial I could live anywhere in Spain with a clean sheet.

I told them that I'm English, not Spanish, so my principles aren't fucked to high heaven like yours are, so fuck off. They left the room and Ballester returned, saying that maybe I should have taken their offer, revealing the fact that he knew all about it. I realised I was farting against thunder with this bunch of maggots, so I decided to plead guilty and see how much less than a three-stretch I would get.

In I went and stood in front of an evil-looking old coot called Rafael Diaz Roca, my judge. He looked as though he'd just polished off a case of sherry. His eyes stuck out like racing dogs' bollocks and there was snot on his moustache. It was plain to see that Ballester had given them the welcome news about my capitulation because the prosecutor was the image of Oliver Hardy with chubby cheeks and a squinting grin. They knew they had the rest of the day off. The prosecutor recommended a sentence of three and a half years instead of the five years he'd put on his *petición fiscal*, so I had a result from that conniving turd.

The judge then waved me away, and the guards immediately dragged me out to put me below in the dungeon where I waited in vain for Ballester. A few minutes later, I was handcuffed to another lunatic and shoved into the back of a police van for the ride back to Malaga prison.

I was locked in my cell until 4.30 p.m., then I dashed down to the screws' office to ask permission to call my lawyer. Roberto the screw told me to hurry because nobody was supposed to use the phone until 5.30 p.m. I called Ballester, who was quite excited and gobbing off about how lenient the judge would be with me and I would be free soon. He was certain I would get two years or less. I felt great. If I got two years I would be out quite soon because I'd already done 18 months on remand in this rathole.

Like a fool, I called Susan to tell her about the glad tidings I'd just got from Ballester. I was walking on air for a week, then my sentence arrived. A sheet of paper was given to me in the screws' office informing me of a three years and two months sentence.

My spirits plummeted to an all-time low. These lousy bastards know how to do your head in and my hatred of all things Spanish was so intense I prayed for a nuclear attack now: immediately. Please, whoever is in charge up there, wipe this scab off the planet's arse.

I remembered something about the laws of appeal, so I asked around to verify what I thought to be true. I quickly discovered my way out. According to Spanish law (E/art. 504 L.E.CR), any prisoner appealing against a sentence must be released if the appeal is not heard before half of the sentence is served. My sentence of 38 months minus the 18 months I had already served meant I had only 1 month to serve to reach halfway. I reckoned that the halfway mark would be Christmas Eve 2002, one month away.

I telephoned Ballester and told him to appeal now. To make sure he did what I ordered, I sent a friend to visit him to underline my instructions. I called my friend the next day and he told me the appeal was in. Hoo-fucking-ray!

Ballester came to see me and told me he had a problem with the judge and the prosecutor. They refused to sign the appeal papers and were refuting them, saying this was a ploy to gain freedom, a conspiracy initiated when Ballester absented himself from the first trial. I asked who he thought was actually breaking the law right now. Somebody was breaking the law by not dealing with article 504. If I was in here at Christmas, then my detainment would be illegal. The judge and prosecutor were breaking their own laws simply because they were making this a personal issue.

I told Ballester to inform the British consul and explain how Laurel and Hardy had taken this personally and to point out that as of Christmas Eve my detainment would be illegal. When I got back on the wing, I called my friend in Fuengirola and asked him to contact the British consul and explain my predicament, emphasising illegal detainment.

It is Christmas Eve and everybody knows I am being illegally detained. Even the screws don't understand why I am still here.

I've been feeling numb all day. My mind is in a whirl. Each time the Tannoy sounds, I expect to hear my name called for *libertad*. The prison day ends and I am locked up for the night.

This kind of stress is horrible. It feels as though a blowtorch is burning across my shoulders whilst, at the same time, ice is forming beneath the skin. I try to analyse these harrowing sensations to come to terms with spending another Christmas in this rathole.

Hark! My heart stops as I hear footsteps along the gallery. I'm holding my breath as the heavy bolt slams back and my cell door opens. A grinning screw, arms akimbo, says, '*Feliz Navidad* – Merry Christmas, Chancer.'

The screw walks away, leaving my cell door open and my heart pounding, then in comes Don Fernando, an English-speaking screw. 'Sign here for your *libertad*, you'll be in the pub just after ten o'clock.'

I ask him to open my Moroccan friend Larbi's door so I can give him my TV. An English bloke by the name of Mick has just arrived on the wing, so he gets all my books and the kit I leave behind. The screw lets me use the phone, so I call my pal Peter Smith to pick me up at the prison gates at 10 p.m. when I will be processed out. Peter collects me in his car and within the hour I am dining on smoked Scottish salmon and champagne. Before getting into Peter's car, I telephone Susan and my mother bursting with happiness and excitement to wish them a very merry Christmas.